LIVING ON THE EDGE

NEIL SELINGER

FriesenPress

One Printers Way
Altona, MB R0G 0B0
Canada

www.friesenpress.com

Copyright © 2021 by Neil Selinger
First Edition — 2021

All rights reserved.

No part of this publication may be reproduced in any form, or by any means, electronic or mechanical, including photocopying, recording, or any information browsing, storage, or retrieval system, without permission in writing from FriesenPress.

ISBN
978-1-03-912739-5 (Hardcover)
978-1-03-912738-8 (Paperback)
978-1-03-912740-1 (eBook)

1. BIOGRAPHY & AUTOBIOGRAPHY, PERSONAL MEMOIRS

Distributed to the trade by The Ingram Book Company

TABLE OF CONTENTS

Preface		3
Chapter 1	Australia, stops in Malaysia, Indonesia, Taiwan	
	December 1998 - January 1999	9
Chapter 2	Caribbean Cruise	
	December 2000	16
Chapter 3	Thailand	
	December 2001 – March 2002	18
Chapter 4	Sweden	
	May 2002, a three week visit	29
Chapter 5	Central America	
	November 2002 - April 2003	32
Chapter 6	Spain with side trips to Morocco, Portugal	
	10 weeks, June to August 2003	47
Chapter 7	South America The Pacific Coast	
	Seven Months, November 2003 - May 2004	55
Chapter 8	Czech Republic with side trips to Switzerland and Greece	
	Three Months, summer of 2004	75
Chapter 9	South America - Argentina, Brazil, Bolivia	
	Six months, December 2004 - May 2005	83
Chapter 10	Africa, Seven amazing months in eight amazing countries.	
	December 2005 - June 2006	96
Chapter 11	Canada and United States	
	Various trips in various years	119

Chapter 12	Canary Islands - Tenerife
	September 06 for a couple of months 129

Chapter 13	Mexico
	December 2006 - January 2007 131

Chapter 14	Panama
	January & February, 2007 146

Chapter 15	Cuba
	A 40 day visit, December 07 & January 08 155

Chapter 16	India
	A stop in Singapore, six months in 2008 158

Chapter 17	Turkey
	A two month quick trip 2012 170

Chapter 18	The Balkans
	2012 183

Chapter 19	Hungary
	2012 190

Chapter 20	China
	A two week tour 2014 196

Chapter 21	Germany
	A two month adventure 2018 199

Chapter 22	South Korea
	April - June 2019 212

Looking Back 221

Living on the Edge

To My Kids

I dedicate this book to my children. . .
so they may better understand my life.

www.neilselinger.ca contains a series of photos, arranged sequentially with the events in the book. This website will also serve as a space for readers to post comments and questions about the book, as well as a section for blogging.

Preface

It is Victoria Day, May of 2020. I sit in isolation on Vancouver Island, safe from the ravages of the Covid-19 Pandemic. I wisely returned from Mexico in February before travel became a problem. I suspended plans to spend three months in Japan this spring as travel is restricted due to the virus.

I'll spend my very liberal time writing about my many years of travel since 1998. I often think about the numerous wonderful moments and beautiful places, but mostly about the beautiful people. I also think about the many scary moments…when you live on the edge, you sometimes fall off.

My style of travel has been to be away from home for three to seven months. As no two people can be travelling together 24/7 and survive each other, I leave home alone and travel with people I meet along the way. I've been single all these years. I much prefer spending my time away from tourist areas, as well as away from tourists. I want to be where the local people are, and live with them in their homes when appropriate.

I've stayed in hostels, backpacker accommodations and pensions when I could, along with other international travelers of the same mindset. They are truly amazing people with tales of adventure from around the world. Although I leave home alone, most often I don't travel alone. A great benefit is getting to know people, then being invited to visit them in their countries—something that has happened about a dozen times. Imagine visiting a country and having a local person pick you up at the airport, staying at their home, seeing how they live, and avoiding the tourist places. That's what happens when you have a local friend who guides you around.

You may be wondering, "Doesn't it cost a lot to travel like this?" Well, it depends how you travel. I found the cost to be less than it would have been to stay at home in Canada. The trick is to avoid tourist areas. Travelling in the USA and Europe can be very expensive, but Asia, South and Central America, and Eastern Europe can be very inexpensive. I've spent as much as $500 and as little as three dollars for a night in a first-class hotel. Hostels, besides costing much less, are cleaner with much better security, and best of all, I was able to meet the most interesting people.

I also continued to work the stock market while travelling. Being away from home for such a long period requires a diversion, or travel would become like a job. It was also financially rewarding.

My intention is to "die without a dime." I've never seen a Brinks truck follow a hearse to the cemetery. I've tried to teach my kids to look after themselves financially, and it seems to be natural for them to do so. They both have more money than I have. I question the idea of leaving money to children. If they need the money, they won't take care of money they inherit, and if they did take care of themselves financially, they won't need that inheritance. My kids were jokingly bugging me one day about how much money I was going to leave them. I told them, "The day I die, I'm writing a cheque to a hooker, and it's going to bounce." They laughed.

People say how lucky I am to have been travelling all over the world for so long. There was no luck was involved; I made it all happen. That's a choice most people have; if it's your priority, you can make anything happen.

I've written as accurately as my memory allows. If you think you recognize a person, know that the names have all been changed to protect the innocent—or the guilty, as the case may be. I hope you enjoy reading this as much as I have enjoyed writing it, and especially living it.

Safety should be a big concern …

Travelling alone can be dangerous. Although people are exceptionally nice everywhere, it only takes one person to make your life miserable. I've been robbed a few times and suffered numerous attempts. Pick-pockets are amazingly talented. Taxis, bars, crowds, buses, airport baggage handlers, all can be problems. Groups that assemble in countries with political issues offer individuals a feeling of security to do whatever they want. Because I'm tall and don't have black hair or black, brown, or olive skin, I stand out in most countries. And, while I speak a bit of a lot of languages, I always have an accent. I'm often alone, and away from the safety of my own home. Some of the difficulties have been my own fault for being unable to stay focused day and night for multiple months at a time.

I've often thought that if someone on a bus did bad things and left me in a ditch somewhere, no one would know for a long time. And, if they were to start looking, where would they look? I've stayed in touch with my kids by sending frequent emails from ever-present cyber cafes, and leaving a trail with my credit cards. It's much easier in today's world to keep in touch and be tracked with computers and cell phones.

The good news is that most of the world is safe and you are not likely to be physically harmed. Perpetrators only want your money, camera, shoes, clothing or other valuables. I personally consider the USA to be the most dangerous country to travel in. There they tend to rob you in groups. If you happen to see a face, you're likely to be shot or knifed because you can identify them. In other countries, they only want your goods and, at times, they are even kind and give some back to help you on your way. My only really scary incident was having a five-foot machete aimed at my head.

In most cases, trouble is a result of individuals not knowing and not thinking, or believing they are invincible. They may have the idea that they can do anything they do at home. People think their embassy will protect them, or that they are better than the poor people around them. Often they make targets of themselves by flashing cash or jewelry, being loud and obnoxious, drinking too much and in unsafe places, and using unregistered taxis to save money.

Stay under the radar, become invisible, and you'll likely not have problems. Obviously, staying at a resort, going on tours in groups, and having a guide are the best ways to be safe. Unfortunately, that's not my style, so I expect to encounter problems even though I don't drink unless it is perfectly safe to do so, and try to be invisible. So far, I haven't had a hair on my head damaged.

Patagonia in southern Chile, January of 2004.

How Travel Became Everything - - - -

It's a Tuesday in October, long ago. I'm off to the airport in Edmonton, credit and debit cards, passport, visa, and air ticket in hand, for an amazing journey to far away. My style of travel would be unusual for most people. There's no planning. As I see it, if there are no expectations, there will be no disappointments. I like the adventure of surprise. When I arrive at a destination, I collect my bag, get local money from an ATM, use the kiosks in the airport to arrange for a place to stay, and find a safe taxi to get there. However, I've found if my arrival is late at night, it is safer to book ahead.

My travel pack contains a tooth brush, a couple of meds in case needed, and one or two changes of clothing. Often, where I travel, it's cheaper to buy clothes than to have them laundered.

My "first nights" have almost always been difficult, leaving me wondering why I am doing this. Come morning, it's a new day and the adventure begins. Since time is not of the essence, it's important to me to explore the neighbourhood, understand the currency and language, and sample the local cuisine. If I was fortunate enough to be visiting a friend, most of this was unnecessary.

Within days, a sense of calm and peace would come over me. All the little things at home are removed from my mind. The burden of bills, complaints about the government, the horror of my team losing again, the price of gas--are all gone. This clarity of thought gave me some understanding of how fortunate I was, and I saw how wonderful people really are if treated respectfully with a happy face. Although the scenery is beautiful everywhere, people hold most of my interest. My focus has always been on the culture of the local people, their language, food, dress, education, politics, celebrations, work, and family.

To this day, where I spend time is quite selective. Tourist places and tourists are out of bounds as much as possible. I try to live with the local people, eat their food, even live with them in their homes. It's not easy for people in a foreign land to trust you enough to become their friend and it's very satisfying when it happens. I've spent the night under a thatched roof, in a home with dirt floor, in a home with no furniture, as well as in some upscale places. As I said before, respect, a happy face, with no attitude of being there to "help" them, makes them receptive. I am reminded of the old saying, "smile and the world smiles with you."

A lot of my destinations haven't been at the North American "First World" level. So many people live a simple life, with family being their priority. They don't have much money, if any, but they don't feel poor. They put food on the table, provide clothing and shelter, and love their families. Often, the less they have, the happier they are. They're happy for every little thing they have, while we tend to be unhappy for every little thing we don't have. Most people believe these people are "poor" because they don't have a big house for two people with a big lot, and two cars in the garage. They may be living as they have been for 1,000 years, and they are happy!!

The scenarios I speak of in this book are entirely my interpretation of any event as I experienced it, what I heard, how I felt about it at that time, and what I learned from the behaviour I witnessed. Usually there are a lot of factors resulting from being 'in the moment' that influence my observations and my thinking.

I understand that someone standing beside me may see an entirely different picture and come to totally different conclusions. I like to discuss their points of view with them; that's how we learn. I have very few opinions, rather, I have points of view. Opinions belong to a closed mind. A different observation is open to discussion, and is helpful to the understanding of a different culture.

The book is a compilation of memories and moments in my travels, arranged mostly in chronological order. The first trip happened with my kids, after my divorce while I was still working. Subsequent financial successes allowed me to work part time and travel for a couple of years, then take full retirement.

I took no notes and have no travel journals, until recent trips. Prior to my visit to Africa in 2006, my stories come from memories, aided by thousands of photos. It has been an amazing journey in my mind, as so many moments from the past flooded in, connecting so many events and faces, smells and tastes, sounds and sights. Of course the many photos were a tremendous help. They are naturally saved on disc in order of time and location, some of them with a time stamp. Some reminders came from the internet, an inexhaustible source of information.

I have a chronological record of my travels with dates and costs of each trip, which helped to organize the sequence of events. I thought that I would run short of money sooner or later, so a history of expenses could help me decide how to live in my later years.

Love, Peace & Bacon Grease

I love food. If I had to list my favourite 500 dishes, I would agonize over which ones to leave out.

The opportunity to partake in delightful culinary experiences around the world has been a large part of my joy of travel. The usual fare offered to tourists is the equivalent of "fast food" in North America. In tourist areas food is almost always "Americanized" to be more palatable for tourists. I prefer the real unadulterated food that natives of a country eat.

Needless to say, food played a significant part in the delights of my adventures.

Australia, stops in Malaysia, Indonesia, Taiwan

DECEMBER 1998 - JANUARY 1999

Malaysia

I had two months of vacation from my employment. My son and I flew to Los Angeles, at the start of a trip that would eventually take us to Australia. It was an exciting time for us. Randy was working in Alberta after a three year stint at a college in Texas, which was a lot more international experience than I had. I had never been out of Canada, except for a couple of car trips to California and to Mexico for an afternoon. We marvelled at the grandiose LAX, got to the hotel, and set alarms so we wouldn't miss our flight in the morning.

We boarded a long flight on Air Malaysia with stewardesses in brightly coloured dresses. When we finally arrived at the airport at Kuala Lumpur late at night, we walked outside and were amazed at the warmth and the hot breeze blowing on the palm trees. Why wasn't it cool, like in Alberta? We sat outside, revelling in the warmth.

We checked on our continuing flight to Jakarta, Indonesia, and discovered the date was incorrect. We had an extra 24 hours in Kuala Lumpur. We were going to stay at the airport hotel, but couldn't check in until three am. Fortunately, the lounge was open until three am.

We talked with the lounge manager who offered to take us into the city, quite a drive from the airport. We arranged for the room *and* off we went to the city of Kuala Lumpur. The manager had hired a car and asked the driver, Haha, to show us around for the day. We stopped along the way and went into the jungle in search of a wild banana plant. I've never tasted anything so good. We saw a lot of sights and wondered why it was still so hot. In the early evening, Haha drove us back to the airport and our hotel for a much-needed rest.

Indonesia

After a good sleep we were off to Indonesia where my brother was living at the time. He met us at the airport, and we stayed in Jakarta for a few days. Randy sat by the pool instead of going to bed, sucking in the warm tropical air that neither of us was used to. We tripped off to the countryside to see the tea plantations and golfed at a 54-hole course with 18 more holes under construction. I'd never had a caddy before, and it was fun to watch the kids dive into the water hazards to retrieve golf balls. We went to a night club, the likes of which I'd never seen before.

We stopped at an ATM to get some local currency in Jakarta. The CDN dollar was worth just under 9,000 rupiah at that time. I remember having trouble with all those zeros when I requested 100,000 rupiah. I got about $11 CDN worth of their currency.

Our trip so far had been amazing. Although I took no notes, these memories are tattooed on my mind. Everything I saw or heard or felt was brand-new, and likely set the tone for the rest of my life.

At the airport in Jakarta, on our way back to Kuala Lumpur, a nice young woman sat beside Randy, rubbing his arm. Indonesian men don't have hair on their arms.

On to KL and our transfer to Sydney for an exciting month-long visit to Australia.

Australia

Australia was different. The people were supposed to be very laid-back but I've never seen anyone more aggressive at having a good time. They love drinking beer, gambling, playing, betting, watching rugby, cricket, and horseracing, and especially laughing and enjoying life. The fauna of course was fantastic, with a lot of incredible animals. We saw lots of kangaroos, koalas, wombats, tame parrots and others. We were sad to see so many road-kill wombats.

The city of Sydney, with a population of five million, was 50 percent gay. The Olympic Games parade in Sydney a couple years later was comprised of 50 percent gay floats. It was interesting for us to go into a gay bar and be greeted by friendly people. Near as I can figure, because they were not a minority, they didn't need to prove anything or account for themselves. We enjoyed socializing with them. It seemed to happen all over the country. There was a lot of friendliness when people found out we were Canadians, and they sometimes stood in line to talk to us. They use strange references such as Aussies, Kiwis, truckees (truckers), and weapees (weapons). That's the one that blows me away. The enemy has big guns and tanks, the Aussies have "weapees."

My daughter, Megan, arrived to join us for about two weeks in Sydney. We spent some days at a hostel in Bondi Beach, a topless little beach, with wild and crazy people, and a lot of drugs and booze. Randy and I stayed in a dorm for many men, while Megan stayed in the ladies' dorm. She didn't get much sleep because of a fear of bats flying around in the room. There certainly were a lot of them outside.

I rented a car, which meant driving on the wrong (left) side of the road. That was scary, as we picked up the car downtown in rush hour. Megan closed her eyes and screamed at me. I couldn't hear her very well, what with all the horns honking at us. The biggest driving challenge was at the roundabouts, as I was uncertain who had the right-of-way. Street lights were scarce and roundabouts were everywhere. One town only allowed parking with vehicles backed in.

An interesting note is that sports, like cricket and lawn bowling, have clubs, with members able to drink and eat at a buffet in a big clubhouse. One had to be properly dressed and invited in. We had no trouble, but I recall one tourist almost getting into a fight because they wouldn't let him in with shorts and t-shirt and flip-flops. The food was delicious, and the people friendly and interesting to talk to. We sought out these places often as we travelled.

We headed south from Sydney to Melbourne along 90 Mile Beach. You'll never guess how it got that name; 90 miles of white coral sand, always cool, a beautiful beach with nobody on it.

In Melbourne we met with a young fella, Rod, who had been our neighbour in Alberta. He took us to a beautiful park, a farmer's market, and other interesting parts of the city. His lovely wife made a living by designing ladies' hats for events that were expensive and a must-have. The Melbies have a beautiful and interesting city.

We drove on to the Twelve Apostles, Adelaide, then on to the Snowy Mountains on the inland highway. A friend from the Athabasca days lived in Alburi-Wodonga. We stayed at her home over Christmas and had the traditional Aussie Christmas dinner, delicious cold seafood. Horse races were the focus of Boxing Day. Everyone had coolers with copious amounts of beer, bits of food, and money for betting. Besides the government windows, there were many private bookies set up for betting. The bars were rockin' all evening.

Strange animals in Australia are expected, but when one lands on your shoulder it can be scary. I noticed a giant Praying Mantis on the edge of a roof in Alburi. When I moved closer to get a good look, it took a sudden drop to my shoulder. This animal of at least three inches was peering into my eyes and looking hungry.

We headed to the Sydney airport as Megan had to return to Canada to her job. While my daughter winged her way back to Edmonton, my son and I hung around Sydney for a while then headed north toward Brizzie (Brisbane). We wanted to stay by the Opera House for New Year's Eve to watch the fireworks off the big bridge. It was the trial run of fireworks costing a half million dollars for the Olympic Games coming in September of 2000. Rooms there were wanting a king's ransom, so we moved on.

We had no plan, just stopping at each and every interesting place along the Gold Coast. Traffic was terrible. The main highway ran through school zones, but everywhere was a great beach. It seemed everywhere we stopped, there was a drowning that day or within a day. The riptides are very scary. Lifeguards were everywhere with boards and sea machines, yet good swimmers were drowning. I got caught about three feet off of a ledge, near the shore but couldn't touch bottom. I couldn't get back and had to call for help. My amazing kid got behind and gave me a push back. It scared the hell out of me. That night I killed a cockroach with my shoe, first one I ever saw. I felt better then. I guess I led a sheltered life.

On New Year's Eve we were in a hotel somewhere. We headed downstairs to the bar. A young lady in a Forces uniform smiled and said hello. She recognized the accent and invited us to their table. A most beautiful girl with black eyes and long black hair snuggled up to me and I felt like the luckiest guy in the world. She told me she was meeting a friend. When this girl showed up, she ran over to her, gave her a big kiss on the lips, waved goodbye to me, and left. I said, "Wait a minute." But it was too late.

At a bar along the way we had some trouble. Some big Aussie sucker-punched Randy and split his lip open, all because the bar was closing and wouldn't sell beer to him. I broke a bone in my hand, not sure how. The police came. They gave us a ride to a hospital to stich up Randy and look at my hand. The nurses were wonderful, as they always are. We had them call the police to get us back to the hotel. We sat in a caged back seat of a small truck while they made conversation with us. They asked what our address at home was. When I answered "Box 222, Athabasca, Canada," the reply was, "You don't live in a box!!!"

The next day we carried on up the coast, both very sore. I think we were around Surfers Paradise. Randy couldn't even smile, much less laugh, and I couldn't use my right hand. I remember sitting in a room feeling sorry for ourselves while a family in the next room were singing, "Old McDonald had a farm." They went through all the animals until they couldn't think of another. They paused for a while, until the father yelled out, "Chook!" That's the Aussie way of saying chicken. We both broke out laughing, with Randy in pain trying to hold his mouth together, as the family carried on singing.

We met an interesting fella in Brizzie who said he was a hunter heading north to hunt crocodiles. It seemed crazy. Like what do they do, set out decoys? He had some great stories about hunting and growing up at a cattle station, which is an Aussie ranch.

We passed what appeared to be orchards, which turned out to be macadamia trees. A grocery store had a huge bin of some kind of nuts. We got a bag of them. We needed rocks to break the shell, and to our surprise, they were those delicious macadamia nuts.

We went inland and headed south toward Sydney, as our flight back to Kuala Lumpur would be leaving soon. Randy got impatient with me, wanting more action, I think. The next day he apologized. One disagreement was pretty darn good for a young guy travelling with his old-fart father 24/7 for two months.

We stopped at a small town called Kurri Kurri, a name from an aboriginal word meaning 'the first.' Kurri was repeated to emphasize the "very first." It was the first location where aboriginal people were attacked and slaughtered. When we went to a bar that used to be a train station to ask where we might find a place to stay, the bartender said we could stay upstairs. That was convenient, wasn't it?

We shared the upstairs with the guy who cleaned the bar after closing and got it ready for the next day. He was a retired high school history teacher. His name was Hennessy, related to the family that makes whiskey or cognac. He took us to the Lawn Bowling Club for dinner. His story of how he arrived in Australia was interesting. His grandfather, or great grandfather, lived in England. An officer in the Forces happened by and requested a place to spend the night. They sent their daughter to his bed to keep him occupied while they stole his money. They were charged with theft of two pounds, two pence, found guilty, and sentenced to live in Australia. Their family has been in Kurri Kurri ever since. He was appalled at how the aboriginals had been treated.

From Sydney we flew to Kuala Lumpur which was a one day stopover on the way to Taiwan. We saw some of the countryside and met a young group of local musicians that had a band. Randy was happy.

Taiwan

From the Taipei airport we took a taxi to a hotel in the city. The taxi driver was crazy, using all seven lanes of the highway plus the shoulder to pass everybody at 140 km/h while using his cell phone. We made it.

As one would expect in Taiwan, the hotel room was full of gadgets. The mattress was made of slate, and I doubled over the sheet to make it softer. There were motorbikes by the thousands parked outside. I thought there must be a dealership nearby, but it turned out there were over a million bikes registered in Taipei.

Breakfast was included, if you like soup with little fishes in it. We left the hotel, looked around, and then realized we didn't recognize the place we were staying at. Fortunately I took a card from the hotel, as I thought that might happen as every place looks the same and I can't read the Mandarin signs. We showed someone the card and he pointed to the place right behind us.

One of the sights we saw was Snake Alley, where people gathered to witness the wonders of blood from snakes and turtles. They told tales of 70-year-old men who drank such blood and went on to father another 18 children. They killed the snakes and turtles as requested and collected the blood, while men eagerly waited to drink it and become virile again.

We had dinner at a restaurant where one person spoke English and one menu was in English. They informed us that dog was no longer on the menu. I had a marvelous meal, Randy didn't eat.

We toured a place where a different race of people lived. They were said to be Indigenous, from the Philippines centuries earlier. They put on a show in English. When they asked for volunteers, Randy and I both agreed to go. After all, no one knows us there. The show included a wedding ceremony, with the brides riding on chairs on our backs. So we got married apparently. Meanwhile, they were making plates with a photo of the married couple in the centre. It was amazing, I still have mine.

After a week in Taiwan, Malaysia Air flew us back to Canada and home. We'd had two full months of amazing experiences.

It was the trip of a lifetime for me and set the stage for many years of incredible travel adventures. We had several culture shocks, realizing that every place presented something much different than the others. It was wonderful for me to spend that much time with the kids, although it was a shame Megan could only be with us for about 10 days while Randy was with me for the full two months. I was able to go on a Caribbean cruise with Megan at a later time.

It's hard to believe that so much came back to me after all this time. I had no notes and no pictures. I had been thinking, "What would there be to take pictures of???" So, I had no camera. Maybe I was wrong.

Caribbean Cruise

DECEMBER 2000

Since I was still working at the time, as was Megan, this was a short trip, only 10 days. . . . . . It was her turn, as she was with us for such a short time in Australia.

We were going on a cruise out of Florida. We were scheduled to fly from Edmonton to Toronto to Montreal to Ft Lauderdale, while our luggage went from Edmonton to Toronto to Miami. We had only the clothes we wore and our carry-ons until they delivered our luggage to the ship about four days into the cruise. When we didn't make the connection from Montreal, they eventually put us up in a hotel. We were only asleep for a couple of hours when a fire alarm sent us to the street. Our flight was at six a.m., so after another hour of sleep, we were off to the airport—and a lineup of 300 people—to check in.

It was the usual cruise stuff, eat, sleep and gain weight, all while surrounded by thousands of tourists. A couple on board were jumping for joy, thrilled to be celebrating their 35th cruise on that ship in the same room. They felt they should be invited to have dinner with the captain, very impressive. I know I've always wanted to do that.

On the special night of dining, we were seated beside a 70-year-old doctor from Toronto. He seemed extremely relieved when Megan was introduced as my daughter. He then politely conversed with questions about Alberta, such as, "Do you have a prime minister or a premier," and other relevant questions.

I felt sorry for one fella, whose wife obviously controlled the purse. He asked her if he could have a drink. She said, "No!! You had your drink already today."

The ship mostly sailed at night and made island stops with tours most days. We were able to go on our own a couple of times, avoiding the groups of people and the hawkers selling trinkets at every stop. The Islands I remember were St Martin and St Thomas, plus one other. We took taxis for quiet tours to nice beaches with trees.

Megan bought a ring with a blue stone, tanzanite, that later disintegrated. We found out subsequently that that particular mineral falls apart when it freezes. Guess what happens during Canadian winters?

The food was wonderful, the service was terrific, and entertainment on board—including Amateur Hour with guests performing, the casino, and swimming pool games—was interesting. It was my first cruise and I swore it would be my last. Although it was enjoyable, it's just not my thing. It was certainly a new experience for Megan as well, and I believe she had a good time. She claims her takeaway from the cruise was: Don't go on a cruise with your old father!!

Thailand

DECEMBER 2001 – MARCH 2002

By now my confidence was building. I was full of knowledge about different cultures, I knew what to expect and I didn't anticipate problems. Who was I kidding??

I arrived at Bangkok airport Dec 1, 2001. I withdrew bahts, the local currency, from an ATM, then headed to a kiosk that advertised hotels. I picked one that was downtown and central to the action. Little did I know that action was everywhere! In little more than three months' time, I would see and do things unimaginable prior to that trip and meet the kinds of people I didn't know existed. I had no idea what to expect and was in for many surprises.

I took an inexpensive tour, "inexpensive" because they take you to stores where you are expected to shop. I purchased three shirts and two pairs of dress pants, all custom-made. The quality of the material and workmanship were outstanding and the price was great. Not too smart though, as I had to carry the clothes with me for the duration of the holiday. The rest of that tour was like a dream. I took a long-boat ride to the "three levers" (three rivers) with floating markets, street-side kiosks, unfamiliar restaurants, and a jewelry shop with the most beautiful yellow sapphires, Thai gems.

I settled into a nice hotel and began exploring that evening. Some places had big windows with bleacher seating and scantily clad young women on show. There was always some guy there encouraging men to have a look. Okay, I'm not stupid, after a couple of days I had that figured out. Thailand is known as The Land of Smiles, and it's easy to see why. The women are pretty, and people always seem happy.

The rooftop beer garden and restaurant at my hotel provided a great place to rest and reflect on what the heck was happening. A pretty woman named Tisa sang and played the guitar. She was talented and attractive, and came to sit at my table. We became friends. She was born in Florida, brought to Thailand when very young, and raised like an orphan. She had a PhD and spoke English perfectly. A lover of animals, Tisa took in street dogs to her home. She was socially not in tune, but was happy, leading a simple life. Her claim was that she had never been kissed.

One evening Tisa took me to a local home with a music studio. They played and sang music popular in North America, which was not at all popular in Thailand. The owner, who was obviously very well-to-do, had a large room full of audio equipment, and liked to sing and invite friends who were also talented. Tisa was one of them. They took turns playing for me, the only audience. They served me delicious plates of food really appreciating that I was listening to them, but not as much as I was enjoying it. When Tisa drove me back to the hotel, I gave her a thank you kiss. She said she drove around the block three times before she recovered. She made a CD for me with her songs, which I still have.

Meanwhile, back at the hotel, another event was unfolding. People at a table in the rooftop beer garden spoke to me, you know, "where ya from?" They were interesting, people of colour, well-spoken, from Africa somewhere. The woman and her brother were supposedly seeking their lost uncle, and another couple was with them. Eventually, to make a short story long, they decided I would be a good candidate for money laundering in Canada. They took me to their room, brought out plates for making US $100 bills, and proceeded to make money. The plates were stolen from Idi Amin, the President of Uganda. They gave me one bill and told me to cash it at a bank, claiming there would be no problems. I hid it my luggage for a day until I got to a bank, but the housekeeper got to it before I did.

The other lady arranged to come to my room to explain how this money thing was going to work. She was rather gorgeous, very sexy, and obviously intending to persuade me to participate in their scheme in a manner that would be hard to refuse. I ran. She tried again the next day. I was a bit frightened, and rightly so. To this day I imagine what the turn of events could have been. I did not accept the offer to participate, with a promise of no knowledge of this business on my part. They accepted that, it was done and over, and the story has been my secret until now. I still wonder, how would I spend all that money from a jail cell??

As an aside, after telling one of the ladies about the yellow sapphires, she took me shopping the next day. We found a beautiful ring, priced at US$1800. She said okay, whipped out 15 $100 bills, gave them to the vendor, and took the ring.

ABOUT THE THAI PEOPLE

The dominant religion in Thailand is Buddhism, serving nearly 95 percent of the population. Buddha statues of all sizes, many with a lot of gold leaf are everywhere. Small statuettes are on street corners. Buddhist followers appear to be happy and at peace with themselves. Their temples are much revered, colourful and beautiful, and where there are temples, there are parks with a lot of tropical flowers.

One park had a temple on a hill, with about 300 steps up to it. An older lady with a bad leg struggled to make the climb, but got to the top and back down. When we asked her what had happened to her leg, she explained that she caught a ride on a motorcycle in Moscow the previous Christmas and they hit a patch of ice.

I found the Thai language difficult to learn. The inflection of the voice can give the same word several different meanings. I learned enough to understand when they were talking about me, using the tone of voice to tell their intentions, but when I tried to speak it, I had problems. When I told a woman she was pretty, she gave me a dirty look, and I later found I told her she had ugly private parts. I did more listening than talking after that. Since tourism is their main industry, most of the people speak English. I knew when I heard the word 'farang' (meaning foreigner and pronounced 'falong'), they were talking about me.

Not unlike other Asian cultures, the Thai culture seemed to be male dominant. I saw and heard about women being beaten. The law states that it is the man's responsibility to keep order and control of his family and if he has to beat his wife and kids, that's what he has to do. The police do not get involved in domestic quarrels.

When an expat, North American or European, meets a Thai woman, she is happy, smiling, and respectful to him, just being her normal self. In return, he treats her well. She likely isn't used to this and the end result can be a long-term relationship. While these relationships often work, there are considerations. Because she's from a different culture, if you stay in her country, you are not only with her, but you get to support the entire family. If you take her home to your country, she will be lonely and miss the things she's used to in her native country. She is likely Buddhist, not common in her new country.

LADYBOYS & LADIES

Ladyboys deserve a special place in any story of Thailand. Why there are so many is due in large part to the matter of employment. Many young people have university degrees, but few jobs are available. As a result, many women work in the sex trade simply as a means of survival. Because the sex trade works much better for females, the incidence of sex changes are surprisingly high, with thousands of doctors specializing in these operations. Thailand has long been the number one sex trade country in the world, giving up the title just recently to Brazil. This is my perspective on the issue, but my impressions come from a lot of firsthand information. Of course, you may disagree.

Bars are often set up in groups, with several small bars—all separately owned—attached to each other. Ladies talk to prospective bar clients, bringing them into their particular spot to drink beer. The weather is hot, the ladies attractive, the beer is cold. The ladies play games, like pick-up-sticks (don't want you to get the wrong idea), to keep the clients there to support the bar they work at. I was never propositioned, but if I would ask, they were available.

I made friends with a lady at one of the bars, then got to know another worker there who was a ladyboy. He explained everything he had gone through for the sex change, and how it turned out. He spoke of the high degree of sensitivity in his private areas. He had his Adam's apple shaved, which gives away the fact that a male has had the change It cost a lot for each operation, and I don't know how he could afford it. He suggested that I should have sex with him so he'd know if he could handle others. He was an interesting person, but I just couldn't go there.

It is really difficult to know which ones have had the change. It was a month or more before I got the word about the ladyboys. There was a club that had quite tall ladies, good looking. I thought they must be from some particular tribe. Then someone pointed out the reality. I was embarrassed. Silly me!! Eventually someone told me to look at their feet. Ladies have beautiful tiny feet; men have scraggly ugly feet.

CULINARY

A restaurant on a bicycle, with a big tray of arranged insects, is not unusual. A bar across the shoulders of an elderly lady, with a hot burning pot hanging from one end and a pot with cooking ingredients on the other end, is common. A tiny hole-in-the-wall restaurant can have 200 items on the menu—with salt, with pepper, with salt and pepper, no salt or pepper—there's four right there. When you add four options to each meat and vegetable, you have 212 menu items. The best restaurants are where the locals eat, most of them cooking and serving on the sidewalk.

The food can be very spicy but always delicious. Chicken, shrimp, pork, rice and fried noodles, with coconut soup and papaya salad, are a big part of Thai cuisine. Of all the fresh herbs they use, I could never get used to lemongrass.

The morning markets with fresh fruits, many I had never seen before, were a great delight. I recall bringing fresh juicy mangos to my room. I ate them in the bathtub, because the juices were running. It was so hot and I needed three showers a day anyway.

The food stocks come from rice fields, orchards, vegetable gardens, and everybody's back yard. Since it's hot all year round, rubber trees in the winter, strangely, have no leaves. Poppies are grown in the north, and although the country has an opium problem, it's not as great as neighbouring Myanmar. The highly respected King and Queen of Thailand asked the people to curb the use of opium. Since they love their royalty, opium usage declined, except for the area east of Chiang Mai, where it has been a big part of life for many generations.

Phuket

From Bangkok I flew to Phuket City on the big island in the south. A small bridge connects Phuket to the mainland. Patong Beach is the most popular beach, a short ride from the city. The area was filled with British, Aussie and Canadian tourists, and life is a lot quieter than in Bangkok.

The hotel where I stayed looked down on the sea. This area was the hardest hit by the tsunami a couple of years later, when 5,400 people died on that coast, among them 2,000 foreigners.

Daytime has lots of sunbathers on the beach. It is a favourite area for scuba diving, and tuna fishing boat tours. At night, the beach is plagued by mosquitos carrying the Japanese encephalitis illness which can be fatal or seriously disabling. I was protected by injections of the vaccine.

I went to a large outdoor restaurant that featured live entertainment, singing and dancing. Performers interacted with the crowd by going to tables and dancing for them. One poor man had to bear the wrath of his wife when a young lady, who had the misfortune of one of her bazooms falling out, continued to dance unaware of the situation. I felt that laser-like look from far away.

A bar managed by a couple of my buddies from BC, Buck from Vancouver and Rob from Prince George, was the base of operations for me and many other Canadians, Brits and Aussies. So many things happened there, like Canada vs England pool tournaments, cards (mostly Dutch Hearts), or bowling excursions, all with copious amounts of beer.

I stumbled on a hall full of people, with dozens of talented female singers. The rules were, if you liked a girl's singing, you bought a malai, a Thai floral garland. You walked up to the stage and placed it around her neck. When she finished singing, she'd be your companion, and follow you around. It was entertaining, interesting, and a nice way to spend an evening. I got to know one of them, and she invited me to visit her family in her village. What an opportunity I thought, until I was advised to not go. When you get there, the mother needs new teeth, the father needs an operation, they have no food to eat, and there's a long list of other needs you are shamed into providing. I didn't go. She was very nice, but really strung out on drugs at times.

One of the clients at Buck's Pub was a young Brit who happened home with a lady of the night. On the way, he stopped at an ATM. At his place, she slipped him something to put him to sleep, took his ATM card, knew his PIN, removed the daily max, then again after midnight took the daily max, a total of about 12,000 pounds. When he reported it to the police, he was advised that they look after their own people.

In another incident, a BMW convertible, owned by an expat, was parked legally near a college. Seven young students on a motorbike went out of control, hitting the car, with injuries to some of them. Recognizing that the car owner should have lots of money, they successfully sued the car owner. So the story goes ….

Another story: a Brit lady put on her shoes and felt a stinging sensation. She thought no more about it, but soon started feeling light headed, and eventually passed out. She died soon after. There had been a deadly poisonous spider in one of her shoes. Ever since then, even today, I shake out my shoes before putting them on. It paid off one morning in Malawi, Africa, but's that's another story for later in the book.

One day, the Bangkok English newspaper featured a front page story about a man in Calgary, Canada, going to real estate open-house showings. While there, he would go into a bedroom and steal a pair of panties. He got caught and a search of his home found more than 100 panties. Must have been a slow news day. Buckie, knowing that I was from Alberta at the time, named me 'Panty Snatcher,' a name he calls me to this day.

One of the tours on a longboat was to James Bond Island with amazing limestone tower karsts, well worth seeing. The name was from the location being used in the movie, *Man with the Golden Gun*. From there we went on a canoe trip into a cave that was open only when the tide was low. We were trapped on this lake in the dark for a little while until the tide went out.

On a tour of the local temples and other spots of interest on the Island of Phuket, I met a Swedish lady who I would visit in her home country at a later time.

It was too comfortable and too much fun and too much beer being at Buck's bar. Eventually, I had to force myself to leave Phuket, or I would have been there for the rest of the vacation.

I left Patong by bus across the bridge out of Phuket, where I took a long boat ride to the far end of Khao Lak. The thick impenetrable jungle was said to have tigers. The resort has floating rooms on the lake. I noticed a four-inch spider with a web in a corner in the bathroom. The racket of howler monkeys fills the air all night. The resort workers were eager to please the guests. One took me on a romantic rowboat ride under a full moon. She happened to be very short, and one of the boys there told her that she wasn't short, her shirt was too long. Laughter ensued amongst the workers, who were much fun to be around.

There were two guests of particular interest who were taking a long break from work, camping around China, Thailand and neighbouring countries for the past year. They just didn't seem to fit in. As we rode out on the boat together, they admitted fibbing to everyone about their backgrounds. She had been a vice president of a large firm producing movies and he had been a practicing lawyer when they met in Australia. Neither were satisfied with their careers and both quit their jobs to travel. A year or two later, I heard from them. They were in England, both teaching kindergarten, the happiest they had ever been. They are married now, with children and education degrees, and still teaching.

I returned to Bangkok for a short stay, then an hour's flight to Chiang Mai on Thai Air. Thai Air had never had an accident or incident, and so claimed to be the safest airline in the world.

Chiang Mai and places North

The hotel was nice and comfortable, central to downtown Chiang Mai. The scenery from the room window was awesome. Loaded vehicles arrived to an empty street in the early morning. Vendors set up kiosks with large displays of whatever they were selling: clothing, jewelry, cookware, anything you can imagine. They completely filled the street on both sides. When I walked the corridor of vendors, I saw next to nobody there shopping. How they survived I can't imagine. Late in the evening, everything was packed into their vehicles and the street was left vacant. And yet they were smiling, happy, and not stressed at all. This was their life.

It rained. And I mean it RAINED. I had to hold my head down to create an air space, with my mouth open just to get some air. A ditch around the centre of the city, about 200 feet wide and 30 feet deep, caught the runoff. It was empty before the rain and full after.

I had heard about a hotel called the President which sounded interesting, so I got a *tuk-tuk* ride there and checked in. It was magnificent, and I was one of about three people staying there. Something had happened so that they were being boycotted. They had a great seafood restaurant, with entertainment that was some of the best I'd seen in Thailand.

By the way, a *tuk-tuk* is a tricycle with a motorcycle engine and a fancy seat for two behind the driver. They get into a lot of accidents, so when hit (*tuk*), they bounce into the car in front of them (*tuk*), and so the double hit becomes *tuk-tuk*. That's the story.

From there I walked to a bar that was equally barren. When they saw the tourist come in, I was treated like royalty. A small band was playing and singing to nobody when I arrived. The lady singing had a great voice. She sat at my booth and sang to me a lot. I returned to that bar a couple of times. She wanted me to return in a year's time, during which time she was to learn to speak English. Sometimes the temptations are powerful.

Another bar I went to was a bad experience. When I entered, I was taken to a table. A lady came over and asked if she could join me. She asked if I would buy her a drink. She had what looked like orange juice, and probably was. When I went to leave, the bill was okay for my beer, but her drink was about 30 dollars. They had the exit blocked and a couple of tough looking dudes with weapons. I paid the price and learned. The same thing happened again years later in Turkey.

Heading east out of Chiang Mai, there were a lot of rice fields and a lot of poppies. Along the road, leafless yellow India trees with the most striking yellow flowers were eye catching. We stopped in one area where the long-neck people of the Padaung tribe live. They stretch their necks at a very young age by placing rings on their necks to hold their heads higher and push their shoulders down. The Padaung are not considered Thai residents, having migrated from Burma ages ago.

A small island on the Mekong River at the intersection of Thailand, Myanmar, and Laos Is known as the Golden Triangle. It has long been noted for the opium trade. Tours to this area are very much tourist traps, with some begging. I can't remember any other time I saw begging in Thailand.

My flight back to Bangkok departed from the Chiang Mai airport, the only open-air terminal I've ever seen.

Pattaya

My hair needed a trim so I went to a nearby salon (or a 'saloon' as their signs read). They started with a back massage, then the shampoo, then a scalp massage as the hair was being dried. The actual haircut followed, all scissors, good work. Another shampoo followed. Then, out came the blade to shave my face, with a fragrant aftershave oil rubbed in along with a shoulder massage. It cost about eight dollars, exorbitant, but after all they were an award-winning parlour. When someone asked what it cost, he laughed when he heard the amount and told me I'd been taken for a ride. Actually, I gave them a big tip beyond the eight dollars. As an added attraction, there were several tiny girls about three years old, with amazing costumes and makeup to make them look like little dolls. It was interesting, but I didn't see the point of it.

I went to Koh Samui, an island not too far from Bangkok. I spent a couple of days on the waterfront, listening to the waves crash on the shore all night, and loved it. It was quiet and restful.

I met a very short lady who was such a pleasure to talk to. She was half Thai, half Chinese, well educated, well spoken, and worked in a clothing store. She ate those little hot red peppers one after another, then fan her mouth with her hand. I simply touched one of the peppers and it burned me!

My visa, only good for three months, was running out. My options were to leave the country, then return, or go to a government office and get an extension. She said there was no need to leave the country. My short friend drove me to a visa place, walked in the door and made her presence known. Everybody stopped working and looked at her. A dozen other clients waiting their turn looked also. She spoke in Thai loud enough for everyone to hear, then motioned for me to go to one of the agents. He took my passport and 10 minutes later my visa was updated, with everyone helping out and ignoring everyone else. We left, it was done, good for another three months. I have never seen anyone command such a presence!!

My next stop was Pattaya, a city with a population of about 100,000 and lots of large hotels. I had heard so much about it as a hot spot for expats, especially Americans and Canadians. Also known as Sin City, it is famous for its sex trade. It was interesting, but I knew the hazards, and knew of people going home with diseases not yet known to medicine.

Returning to Bangkok once again, my little lady friend gave me a ride to the airport. We said goodbye and have remained in touch.

It was really the trip of a lifetime, following the trip of a lifetime to Australia. Memories of those beautiful Thai people, the very large Buddha statues in the temples and the small ones on the streets, and parks with all the flowers, still live with me. I recall riding an elephant down a hill when it decided to run. Incredibly, what I have written and 10 times as many things are very vivid in my mind even this long after being there. \I learned about so much that I didn't know existed. Again, I knew that I would want to go for more delightful experiences and fantasies in the future. And I did.

Home to Alberta, back to work for a while.

Sweden

MAY 2002, A THREE WEEK VISIT

I was invited to Sweden to spend some time with a lady I met in Thailand. We had been in touch since we met in Phuket.

Sonja met me at the Stockholm airport. Our first stops were to private yards that had big rocks with Viking writing on them, centuries old. I was surprised to hear everyone greet each other by saying, "Hey," so familiar because that's what the kids were saying at home. I had no idea that "Hej" is Swedish for hello.

Sweden is very expensive, taxes are crazy. A meal that would cost under 10 dollars in Canada cost more than 30 dollars. In addition to the meal cost, there was city tax, county tax, national tax, and equivalent GST. A beer that cost around three dollars at home cost more than 10.

While on a walk, I asked what a building in a weedy field was used for. It looked rundown and badly needed painting. It turned out to be a school. Apparently the government doesn't have enough money to paint schools or trim weeds in the school yard. With all their taxes, they're still not able to keep up with the costs of their social system and, at that time, were falling further behind with the national debt. "So the story goes," is one opinion.

The Vasa Museum in the city centre of Stockholm houses a 17th century gunship, the Vasa, salvaged after 333 years on the seabed. The Vasa was made of oak, and the absence of shipworms in the Baltic Sea kept it in excellent condition when it was recovered in 1961. The plan was to recondition the 1200 brightly painted sculptures on the ship to the original ornate colours. The ship itself has been restored and is displayed in one of the most visited museums anywhere.

The Vasa was the pearl of the Swedish fleet. In 1628, the ship left the harbour on her maiden voyage. A gust of wind caused it to keel over and sink in the deep water. Of the 150 people on board, 30 went down with the ship. The rest were in reach of help, since the ship sank close to shore. The theory is that the centre of gravity was too high, and the gun ports which were left open allowed water to flood in.

One of the churches we visited was an ancient cathedral, about 800 years old. It was the first big old European church I'd seen, so I was very impressed. Important people were buried inside, with massive stones covering their graves. I wondered how they moved those huge stones and fitted them so precisely.

Sonja showed me something very interesting. If you hold divining rods at a position in front of the church entrance, they react to line up with the altar. This worked at other churches as well.

The same happened at Viking grave sites. The size of the mound depends on the importance of the person buried there. There were many very large mounds, and the larger the mound, the stronger the reaction of the divining rod.

The Swedish countryside has rolling hills, trees, green farmland, and well-maintained farms. I saw my first Smart Car and a gas station with no attendant where you paid using a credit card at the pump. There were none in Canada at that time that I was aware of.

A highlight of the trip was a ferry ride to the Aland Islands, between Sweden and Finland. The Islands belong to Finland, but are totally autonomous. They had an interesting lifestyle with friendly people. The ferry ride had a great seafood dinner, entertainment with a band, and dancing. It seems everybody on the boat was an accomplished dancer, except me. And they were all dressed up. It was a bit embarrassing, but I think no one knew me.

A couple of Sonja's friends owned a sailboat. They had an old beater for a car, just good enough to get around. The word was, for a lot of people a sailboat is much more important than a car. Early one morning we met at the dock and spent a delightful day sailing around the archipelagos. We went through a lock, between the North Sea and the Baltic Se which is actually a lake with fresh water.

We stopped for lunch at a food stand on a little island. We forded channels where one can still see the damage from wartime shelling centuries ago. It was a memorable day.

A story that keeps coming to mind: I was told there is one day a year in Sweden when everyone can have sex with anyone they choose. Doesn't that paint a picture! Sounds pretty crazy to me. I have no idea if it's true.

Back to Canada. I had a business and a contract for work at a paper mill.

Central America

NOVEMBER 2002 - APRIL 2003

By this time I was fully retired, although I was still an active trader on the stock market. Trading gave me a purpose in life so I wouldn't feel like a bum. Travelling was comfortable, so much so that I needed some kind of diversion, or travel would start to feel like a job. It was very part time, rewarding emotionally and good financially. Five months in Central America was just what I needed.

The governments In Central America all had signs of fraud. Maybe they're no worse than in North America, and we just know how to hide it better. Every country except Costa Rica had serious scars from American-aided aggression, direct or sponsored. Most countries are poor, and the great loss of young male warriors has added to the poverty. While they may be poor, I never saw anyone without food. They know how to look after themselves and their families. Again, I found the poorer they are, the happier they are.

Costa Rica

November - Dec 2002, six weeks

Costa Rica was not my favourite country. Many decades ago, they were being called the Switzerland of Central America. They must have thought,

"Okay, we're now where we want to be, we don't have to do anything more." Their superior attitude still exists. They are the only country in Central America that hasn't been at war.

Their favourite hobby was to make jokes about the Nicas, Nicaraguans. The Nicas are poor, dubbed the poorest nation in the Western Hemisphere, taking the title from Haiti when the price of tobacco dropped. Nevertheless, they are the nicest people.

Many expats from the US and Canada have moved to Costa Rica, built houses, and made a life of blissful retirement. The first order in building a house is to build a 10-foot wall with razor wire on top, with a steel gate that locks. Once the land is secure, you can bring in the materials to build the home. If you're lucky, the security guard you hire won't steal everything. I've seen it and heard about it a few times.

A big scam was in progress while I was there. An investment company, run by the 'Villabos Brothers,' (that's a guess) was offering a return of investment of 35 percent annually. Many expats invested large sums of money. It didn't make sense to me, as the inflation rate was running rampant on CR money, the colon. I was in the square of the capital city San Jose one morning and saw a large gathering of sad-looking expats. They had just received the word that one of the brothers ran off with all the money and everything was lost. The resulting investigation by the government cleared the other brother, and it was determined that nothing could be done about it, case closed. It was widely considered a cover-up, with government people being part of it.

One sad story was that of a younger fellow who put his mother's entire retirement assets into this fund to show her how good he was at investing. Many people could no longer afford to live there and had to put their property up for sale, only to see prices plummeting. I felt for them, but that's one of the hazards of owning property in a foreign country. Personally, I wouldn't own foreign property, not when I can rent or lease and avoid all the stressful and messy pitfalls.

One day at the beach, my shoes were stolen. Okay, they were old and stinky, and I bought a new pair. Next day I buried my new shoes while no one was watching. When I got back, they were gone. The third day, I hid another new pair in a tree, high up where they could not be seen, and I thought no one could have been watching. Upon my return, the tree was empty. From then on, I walked to the beach barefoot through weeds and gravel. I also had my wallet stolen from my pocket.

A part of San Jose is noted to be totally unsafe and tourists are told to stay away. People I know got a room overnight waiting for a forwarding flight. That night they lost everything. Someone gained entrance to the room with a card from the night clerk and sprayed some kind of gas into the room to knock them out. They awoke to find their computers, phones, wallets, passports and luggage all gone. I trust the story is accurate, as one of the persons involved told me about it.

I almost fell into a large unmarked excavation in the sidewalk, about four feet deep. Later, while I was watching the sidewalk to avoid further dangers, an overhanging air conditioner took a big gouge out of my scalp. People are shorter there. Lesson learned.

An English newspaper story on the government budget said cutbacks were needed, so they cut the education budget by 40 percent. A big mistake in my opinion, but there was little concern.

Some years later, while travelling through on a bus, I saw vast areas of what used to be forest planted with palm trees. They were being grown to produce palm oil, and stinky palm oil processing plants were proliferating. The word was that the government had sold off more than 90 percent of its forests to foreign companies for the production of palm oil.

THE GOOD THINGS

Of course, there are many nice people in Costa Rica. Because their flora and fauna are the best, half of all nature documentaries are made in Costa Rica. As the land mass narrows, the concentration of migrating birds increases and the temperate climate is perfect for tropical animals. I found many of the species in Costa Rica that had been decimated along the Amazon in Brazil. There are beautiful parks and great beaches, rain forests, and cloud forests. The Arenal Volcano is a beautiful National Park. Turtles are amazing to watch as they come ashore to lay their eggs on different beaches on the east and west coasts at different times of the year. There are fruit trees like the carambola, and big iguanas which the locals hunt and eat.

There are many safe places to be in Costa Rica. The resorts are mostly owned and/or run by Americans and Europeans, so are very safe. Scores of tours are available, again very safe. Unfortunately for me, that's not how I travel.

At a Costa Rican restaurant in Jaco, I met a most charming lady from the Czech Republic named Marie. I did some travelling with her and her lady companion to some of the parks. They were good guides, more familiar with the countryside than I. Later I would visit her in her home country.

At a rented condo in Jaco, I was close to a great beach with beautiful sunsets. I met a couple from Europe there. Interestingly, her father was Chinese and her mother was German, and his mother was Swedish and his father was Italian. They were living in Portugal. It was indeed a pleasure to spend time with them drinking beer, playing cards, eating out, and enjoying the beach.

I moved on through the cloud forest to the east coast by bus. Limon seemed a scary place, so I went south into Panama, to the province of Bocas del Toro.

Panama

January 2003

BOCAS DEL TORO & CHIRIQUÍ

Bocas del Toro Province is located on the north-east corner of Panama, on the Caribbean side, on the Atlantic. The customs office is located at the end of a long hanging bridge. With beautiful beaches and small islands, and lots of beer and weed, it's a paradise for surfers. It was a short visit, only a few days.

The bus across country took me over a beautiful landscape of mountains to the city of David in the province of Chiriquí. Their annual carnival was on at the time. I stayed at a nice hotel, where I was approached by a lady who wanted to get even with her husband for cheating on her.

Many times I've seen that. In the Latino culture, it is not uncommon for married men to have a mistress. While not always accepted, it seems little can be done about it. Most couples don't live this way, but it seems to be more common there than in North America.

After a few days in David, I was on the bus again, heading north to Nicaragua with a brief stay in southern Costa Rica. It was a small town with a great beach on the Pacific coast. I hung out with a couple of real estate people from San Diego. The hotel, a resort operated by Americans, had great outdoor entertainment.

I recall walking up a road to a restaurant on a hill. All was well until I left the restaurant to return to the hotel. When evening falls, daylight to darkness takes only a couple of minutes. Light was suddenly dark and I was on the road alone, no streetlights, with imaginary seedy characters following me. Paranoid me scurried down the hill in a sweat, arriving just in time to be saved from nothing. Another lesson to take better care of myself.

Nicaragua

2003

Of all Central America, I found Nicaragua to be the most amazing. People were poor and friendly. I took beginner Spanish lessons in a government academy, where I met a few English-speaking people. On one occasion, I was involved in a most memorable rescue of a family at sea and I lost my camera and passport while on a ferry. A volcanic blast had blown a mountain to pieces a few thousand years ago, and the lake is large enough to have fresh water sharks. Most mountains had erupted at some time and earthquakes have left property damaged. The effects of Hurricane Mitch in 1998 could still be seen. There was a lot of chatter about the president getting wealthy on the hurricane relief funds from around the world that never reached the needy. President Aleman was sentenced to 20 years for corruption later in 2003, so it likely was true. The country was still on the long road to recovery from the revolution.

I took a bus to northern Costa Rica, then a boat on a river into Nicaragua. From the Nica customs, I arrived in the little city of Granada, on the shores of Lake Nicaragua. The taxi to the hotel cost 10 times what it should. The driver knew that I didn't understand the currency, and was quite intimidating. It wasn't much, but nonetheless, another lesson learned. The hotel was expensive but nice. Expensive means about 1,000 *córdobas*, or CDN$10 at that time. Now the conversion is four cents to a Cordoba. I got some one centavo paper money. One Cordoba equals 100 centavos, so the one centavo paper bill, which is now worth .0004 cents, makes an excellent bookmark. They had just stopped printing the paper one centavo. Foreign currencies can be confusing.

At the open restaurant at that hotel, an elderly woman would come by twice a day with her hand out, saying, "I'm hungry." I returned to that restaurant four years later, and guess what—she was still there, she was still hungry, but she had gained about 20 pounds.

Close to the hotel was a government building with the purpose of promoting tourism. They were advertising classes to learn Spanish. My Spanish was very weak at that time, so I joined the class. Their idea of learning was total immersion into the language, from which I learned zero. Others seemed to be learning, but I got nothing from it. The instructors were nice and the students were a nice group, Americans and one Englishman. All were well educated, concerned about the people, and great to socialize with. As part of the program, we had dance lessons where we learned to do the salsa and merengue.

At dinner, we students usually gathered at a local outdoor restaurant, oft times with entertainment. Local kids liked to hang around us, knowing they would get handouts. One youngster, about 12 or so, would buy glue to sniff if anyone gave him money. Another little girl, about nine years old, a real sweetheart, was selling gum and cigarettes from a tray held by a strap around her neck. She hung around us a lot. We went to a few baseball games, and we'd find her there. Teams there have provided a few players to the big leagues.

I saw her again four years later and she was not such a sweetheart anymore. She recognized me on the street and we talked about the good old times. She was about 13 then and was with an older teenager, who turned out to be her sister. She whispered in my ear, her sister for $20. She wasn't selling gum anymore.

The town square had many small food stations, with women cooking meals in ceramic pots. The pots were made locally. Charcoal burned in the bottom chamber with the food being cooked in the upper chamber. It was always delicious. I wanted to buy one of those pots, but the chance of getting it home in one piece was near zero.

There was a church nearby, where I went to relax, think, and get away from the locals selling beads. I'd usually find a dog laying on a pew, quiet for him also.

There was obvious damage from the Civil War to both people and property. We were in a home that had bullet holes in the siding. They explained that during the shelling they were hiding under the table, which turned out to be the table we were sitting at. I later went to see a fort, which was also a prison for the enemy. There was an opening by the stairway that went down about four or five floors onto concrete, where the prisoners were thrown. If they survived, and not many did, they had a chance to get out after the war, if they didn't starve. I saw a similar thing in Spain years later, an opening where prisoners were dropped about 100 feet; same result, if they lived they could leave when the war ended.

The story I got from American tourists was that the rebels were armed by the American government, with a fear of 'Communist' governments. Just enough arms were provided to make the sides equal. The Civil War in Nicaragua would cost the lives of more than 60,000 young men and left 600,000 homeless, with a ruined economy. Families were torn apart by sons choosing opposing sides. I talked to a lot of American volunteers working there because of the shame of what their country had done to the Nicas.

One day a small girl came to me begging, wanting money for school. Her mother was there, looking quite forlorn, explaining that she didn't have a dress uniform for school. I thought, "Yeah, yeah, maybe for drugs or glue." So I said, "Okay, let's go, I'll buy one for you." To my surprise, she took me to a store. I expected to buy her a uniform, but it was cloth she wanted, to sew one for the child. I bought enough cloth to make two uniforms, with some needles, thread, and buttons, and then went off to another store for paper and pencils. You need to be careful how much you give them as the other kids will become jealous. School was free, but you couldn't attend school if you didn't have a uniform! The look of joy on both their faces was a moment to remember. It was as if their lives had been changed. Maybe they had. Certainly it made me happy.

Our Spanish language group went on field trips, to visit and volunteer our time and provide materials to help the local people. One trip was to a schoolhouse in a small village, a building that was bought by an American and donated to the town. However, that's all there was, a building. We took packs of paper, pencils, chalk, erasers, and books to write in. That was nice, but there was no blackboard, no desks. We hiked a mile up a mountain because of a story of a kid who could not go to school. The family had a cow, and made a living from the milk. The poor kid had to go down the mountain every day to fetch a couple of pails of water for the cow. There was no time to go to school.

I made a trip to Managua, the capital city. An area of the city, including several multi-story apartments and a big church, were abandoned due to damage from a recent earthquake. Towns along the way were set up for one kind of artisan, a town for ceramics, a town for hammocks, a town for copperware, a town for jewelry.

A visit to a coffee plantation was a shocking experience for me. Remember Juan Valdez on the mountain with coffee beans and his donkey? They advertised that his beans were the best because they were hand-picked. I discovered that all coffee beans are hand-picked. They don't all ripen at the same time so they all need to be picked by hand.

Another part of the program was to live in a local home, just what I wanted. The home was about 70,000 square feet, including a large courtyard with surrounding open fronted buildings and a garage. The property was surrounded by a wall 12 feet high and four feet thick with razor wire on top. The entrance was a really heavy large gate with a smaller door built into it. It was all built centuries ago.

The father of the family, who was a professor of economics at the university there, spoke some English. He was a pleasure to talk to, providing a great deal of insight into his country and its people. His very pleasant wife made breakfast each morning for her husband, their teenager, and me. I was be awakened by the sound of a hawker's horse clopping on the cobblestone street as he delivered milk.

THE LAKE

Lake Nicaragua is about 110 miles long and 44 miles wide, and averages 50 feet in depth. It's thought it once was a saltwater bay, which explains the presence of freshwater sharks. At one they were thinking of building of a canal there rather than in Panama. There are many islands in the lake, big and small, as a result of a volcano.

The Mombacho Volcano erupted 20,000 ago, throwing large pieces of the mountain into the lake, forming 365 islands. The depression in the mountain appears to be a mile wide and half as deep, so one can imagine how much material flew out. Some of the islands are a good size, and the lake is big enough to have pretty rough waters.

Four of us from our student group hired a guide to arrange a trip to an island on the other side of Lake Nicaragua. We packed our lunches for a day trip to see the ancient hieroglyphics. Although the sea was quite rough that day, it wasn't a problem for our boat.

One of our group spotted what he thought was a small boat with people in it. We watched and when we both hit high on the waves, we could see some people were in trouble. Two men and two children were struggling to keep afloat in a dugout boat full of water. They had thrown the engine off to help keep the boat afloat. The father was on one end with his three-year-old son on his shoulders, and the grandfather was on the other end with the six-year-old hanging on. Every wave would swamp the father and be up to the neck of the three-year-old.

When we pulled alongside, we found that getting lined up for rescue was difficult. Their little boat was being tossed about relentlessly. The right moment came when their boat was thrown up and our boat dropped. I reached out and grabbed the boy, successfully pulling him into our boat. I wasn't about to lose him and he hung on. The rest was easy. With plenty of room on our boat, they boarded. With their boat secured to ours, we went on to the island we were headed for in the first place.

They had been out fishing since early in the morning when the wind came up unexpectedly, filling their boat with water. They knew that three of them could swim the couple of miles to shore, but the little guy would likely not make it. That's why they stayed with the boat. Once on shore, we gave them our sandwiches. They were happy for food while they dried off. Their home was one of the islands, on the other side of the lake to the east, and we needed to get them there as their women would be worried.

Upon arrival at their island, the women waiting saw a strange boat approach and thought the worst—that we were bringing bad news. The sea was really rough there also. Their faces exploded with joy when they saw their husbands and the kids. The little one walked up to his mom who picked him and held him tightly. The older child was cool, showing little expression. Those Nica kids are really tough!

We followed them on to shore, as their boat was still attached to ours. Everyone stood around and smiled, looking relieved and happy to be alive. The father then invited us to join them for some mangos from their tree. The California woman in our group suggested that it would be good to give them some cash to help pay for the motor they had to dump in the lake. She and I each had 50 American dollars, which we slipped into the father's hand. He put it in his pocket. Later, when I saw him look at the money and count it, he started crying, but only for a moment. It was all a very emotional time. The money we gave him paid off the mortgage on the motor, and provided a down payment on a new one.

When the father found out why we were there, he said, "Follow me!" We walked about a quarter mile and he showed us where there were several hieroglyphic rocks.

It was soon time to leave Granada. Sharon, the California girl, and I headed north to explore more of Nicaragua.

THE REST OF NICARAGUA

Sharon and I visited small communities along the road to the north of Granada. At our first stop, we awoke to a funeral. Two bricklayers walking home on the highway were hit by a tourist vehicle. They were killed, the driver of the car was arrested, and is likely still locked up to this day. Next day funerals are the norm in hot climates with no refrigeration. The whole town was there for the funeral.

There are support clubs for mothers who lost sons in the war. In that town the club had more than 300 members, with many losing more than one son.

We split along the way, as I wanted to go to Guatemala. Shortly after, still in Nicaragua, the case containing my passport went missing. It was my fault, as I was on a ferry, and left it on a table when I got off. A minute later I returned to find it long gone. I lost focus for a minute, and that's all it takes. My camera was also in the case, so I lost the photos from Panama, Costa Rica, and Nicaragua, and then no pictures in El Salvador, Guatemala, Honduras, or into Mexico.

The loss of the passport had to be reported to the police. Not a one spoke English, and my Spanish was not good. I emailed Sharon, and she was right there to help. Her Spanish was pretty good.

I carried on to the Canadian Consulate in Managua, the Nica capital city. The consulate had a French speaking lady, the rest spoke Spanish. I guess Canada is French, no? I got through all that, and the info was sent off to the Canadian Embassy in San Jose, Costa Rica. In three days, I got a call to pick up my new passport in Managua.

Returning from the trip to Managua, the bus I was on suddenly stopped. The back door of a truck in front of us had unlatched and opened. It spilled part of its load, pink toilet paper. Everyone on the bus jumped out, including the driver, and each returned with an armful of pink toilet paper. They were all laughing hysterically. They hit the jackpot!

I was on a bus out of Nicaragua with a new passport in hand. Oh, but there's a problem. The Nica customs agent saw my passport had no record of entry to the country. How could I be leaving if I never arrived? I showed him the police report stating that it was a new passport. He was not impressed, said he had to make a few phone calls. With each phone call, he asked for money in US funds. I knew they did this so I asked for his boss. He was the boss. After a few calls and more than an hour later, I finally told him I was out of money. He stamped the passport and let me go. I stepped out of his office, and saw that the bus stayed there and waited for me. I couldn't believe it, everyone on the bus was concerned, and nobody was mad at me.

I had no idea it was so dangerous to be in the two Honduran cities I was in. Fortunately, the situation was obvious. Keeping a low profile was essential, as seedy characters were everywhere. One night in the city of Tegucigalpa, and I was on the next chicken bus outa there. A lot of dodgy-looking characters made me very nervous about being there in the daytime, and more so at night. I recall going through a historic area on the bus, some pyramids I believe. Other than some young guy tourist crawling around the floor looking for chickens, it was uneventful. Incidentally, there was a chicken and some duckling chicks on board. The chicken bus ride ended when we reached the main highway, then another bus to San Salvador.

Another border to cross, into El Salvador. Customs officers were generally nice and thorough, and with a fee every border, in and out of countries. It was small then, but next time through Central America, every border had a large fee attached, in and out.

The bus stopped in San Salvador for the night. After having a beer with a beekeeper I had met in David, I looked for a room for the night. Some fella convinced me to look with him for a place to stay, and we found a couple close to the bus depot. He insisted on the cheaper of the two, at an outrageous cost of about two dollars for the night. The shower had the electrical panel within easy reach of the water. It was not covered. The water was heated with an electric element a foot from the showerhead, again bare wires. Still alive and tired, I headed for bed. I almost stepped on a roach, but fortunately it was very fast. A spilled ashtray lay on the floor, so apparently no cleaning. Sometimes you get what you pay for, or you still get that and pay much more.

El Salvador also had a civil war. Half of the 80,000 casualties were civilians, with 70,000 others with serious injuries. About 80 percent were child soldiers, under the age of 18. Once again, the US was involved, in fear of a Communist regime taking over. This time the US sided with the government, providing arms to take down the guerrillas who were demonstrating for change. All these wars followed the McCarthyism in US. I had wanted to head to the beaches on the coast from San Salvador, but was warned about gangs and the hate for anyone that was white or American. I'm not sure it was that bad, but there are other beaches. I knew people who spent time volunteering in El Salvador without problems, but I got a lot of stares while walking in the street markets.

AS A NOTE ...

Four years later, in 2007, I was passing through Granada. I wondered what had happened to the family we had rescued from the stormy lake. I went to the office of the guide we had four years earlier. He was still there! He said he had seen the family since, but not for a while. We made plans to go out to their island for a visit the next morning by boat out of Granada.

On arrival, we saw the family come out of the house. The little guy was now seven years old. When he saw me he ran up and grabbed my leg. Incredibly, he remembered me. He let go when we left. They were all gracious and very happy to see us. They were still using the dugout boat, had found the motor and recovered it, although it was not usable. The father was in

Managua at the hospital with their daughter who was sick with cancer. We had tea and chatted awhile, a nice visit.

On that trip in 2007, I had met this big black guy, who resembled Shaquille O'Neal. We travelled together for about 10 days. He was happy and interesting, with a lot of travelling and some good stories to tell. I recall walking down the middle of a street and finding a drug party that I would never have gone to on my own. By the way, neither of us participated, but we were offered a beer.

Guatemala

The next morning we were on our way to Guatemala. I ran into a 75-year-old fella I knew from Granada. He too was going to Guatemala. I wondered if it was safe for someone that age to be travelling. Well look at me now!

I stayed in Antigua for a couple of weeks. It is a UNESCO world heritage site, and easy to see why. Being such a popular place, there were lots of tourists, and I met a few of them. A young lady from BC and I made a day trip to a village across a lake. At the end of the day, we were ready to return. The boat was inexpensive to go across, but those crooks wanted a fortune to return. They girl said no, she would not pay that amount to return. The option was to sleep there for the night, then pay that amount to return the next day. She was very stubborn, and I ended up paying for the two of us. She didn't have a lot of money, like many travelers.

A lot of native Mayan people were selling their beads and other goodies to the tourists in the big plaza, or town square. I laughed, as one poor schmuck was carrying several bags: obviously he bought from every vendor there. They know a mark when they see one, so another kid approached him with a goodie to sell. I guess he had enough. Setting down his many plastic bags, he lost it and lit into the poor kid.

A Mayan lady was selling some hand-made goods for cheap at the end of the day. They need cash to feed their families. Some jerk was trying to bargain her down to next to nothing. She was near tears. I bought all of her stuff at the going price. He swore at me and left. Then I paid her, and gave the stuff back to her. It cost me a couple of dollars. She had made little ceramic ornaments which are hand-painted. It is delicate and time-consuming work, and

I felt sorry for her being taken advantage of. BTW, I'm not a hero, I just have a conscience, and it felt really good to do that.

A local artist painted a scene of a street with houses and mountains in the background, while I waited. I still have the painting. It wouldn't mean much to anyone else, but a lot to me.

Guatemala is a rough country, known for its thousands of unsolved murders. I was advised to stay clear of Guatemala City, and likely it has very dangerous areas. There is a story of a bus that was stopped by bandits who took everything from everyone, made them strip to their underwear, and left the bus stranded without keys.

The country had been devastated by civil war, not unlike El Salvador and Nicaragua. The story from several American volunteers is about a banana plantation owned by an American, supplying inexpensive bananas to the US. The President of Guatemala tried to improve the state of poverty by giving every family a piece of property. The American government had intervened, removing the elected president because he was "soft on Communism," and would break up the banana plantation. An estimated 200,000 Guatemalans were killed, the genocide being directed to the poor, and the Mayan people in particular. Most of the executions were carried out by government forces.

The volunteers from the US were sympathetic to the Mayan people, again, ashamed for what their government had done to the people. They said that losing the supply of cheap bananas was fundamental in the American intervention.

I'm just telling it from what I hear and see.

HEADING HOME

On the return to Nicaragua, I visited Managua this time. I ran into a Nica couple who had left Managua and went to live in Toronto when the civil war began. He was an architect, and she taught school. After the war they returned to their country to live.

Sharon had come back to Managua to catch a flight home to the US. She wished to relax for a week and scout around the city. We had an amazing time with the architect and his wife. He arranged for us to have the honeymoon suite, as a surprise to us, at a nice place across from the airport. We were pampered with fresh fruit and hors d'oeuvres.

A wedding reception was held at that hotel for a young Nica couple. We were able to watch from the pool. The reception was all about the groom. He was being hugged cuddled and congratulated without stop. A lot of drinking was going on. The bride on the other hand, was sitting at an outside table with her bridesmaid while being totally ignored.

I was back on the bus to San Jose in Costa Rica for my flight home. At the border from Nicaragua, all our belongings were opened and searched. After crossing into Costa Rica, we were stopped by the CR police a few miles down the road. We all got out, opened our luggage which they went through, leaving most of it spread out on the highway, and then let us go. That being pathetic enough, 10 minutes later we got stopped again with the same procedure. Apparently, they don't like the Nicas entering their country.

I was happy to be on an airplane leaving. It was a wonderful five months in Central America. I met so many nice people, different cultures, delicious foods, while being left to reflect in wonderment how fortunate I was to have what I have and be living in Canada. I had been completely unaware of the political difficulties in Central America. I find it disturbing that this kind of bullying is going on in the world. I cannot begin to imagine the tragedies those people have endured. I was beginning to come out of my sheltered world of naivety.

I saw a lot of posters with a picture of a man running for political office, all by the name, 'Alcalde.' I thought they must be a rich powerful family, until I discovered the word alcalde is Spanish for 'mayor.'

Spain with side trips to Morocco, Portugal

10 WEEKS, JUNE TO AUGUST 2003

With not much rest since the five months in Central America, I was off to Spain to meet my red-haired Swedish friend Sonja. She was familiar somewhat with Italy and Spain, where she dealt with fabric companies at her job. She spoke perfect English.

Spain was a little less than hospitable to tourists, making it difficult to get around at times. They had an organization that was dedicated to getting tourists out of the country. There were four bomb threats at bars where foreigners gathered while I was visiting. I was at a couple of those bars, and they were only threats, scare tactics.

I believe I understand their position. So many people, mostly from Britain and Germany, had built winter homes in all the choice places. That drove up the cost of housing, materials, groceries, restaurants, and everything that made the life of a local person enjoyable. Most people had to have two or three jobs just to feed the family. It's unfortunate that they were rebelling, as tourism is their greatest source of income.

Some of the things they did to me were unpleasant but not dangerous. Taxi drivers were making jokes about me, until a bus ride became the alternative. I walked a mile to where I was told the bus would be, only to be directed back to the first spot. I missed the bus. A taxi driver pointed me in the wrong direction, I got lost, and had to return in another taxi. I could understand enough words to tell when things weren't right, but could do little about it. I was served hot beer and a bacon sandwich that was pure lard. Some refused to understand simple words I was saying in Spanish.

Although annoying, they were a small part of the people. Most were very gracious and polite, good to be with. The beaches at Costa del Sol were great. The trains were comfortable, enjoyable rides. The countryside was mostly agricultural, lots of olive groves. The cities were filled with history. Restaurants served great food, with lots of outdoor tables. I was not used to eating outside, you know, Canadian weather. I really enjoyed it. Most of all, I loved the tapas being served at the bars. My favourite was under glass in a bar counter, as every downward gaze found several delicious little dishes. Of course, you have to have one, or three, and eventually you have had a big dinner.

I can eat anything, have a cast iron stomach. But not so much in Spain. The touchy part came at about a month in, when my stomach started rebelling at the oil intake. Spaniards want to pour olive oil generously on all their food. I had to be careful what I ate. I loved the touch when herbs in pots were brought to the table, although I didn't really know how to use them.

It's difficult to adjust to the Spanish schedule for meals. They get up late, have a lunch around noon, close up shop around two to three p.m. to have their siesta time. The country opens up again for dinner starting around nine or ten p.m., running to about three in the morning. I was devastated when hours went by while all the restaurants and pubs were closed for the afternoon and a good part of the evening. Tourists were left hanging around, wondering what happened.

Spain had become a part of the EEC, the Euro replacing the peseta as the accepted currency the year before, in 2002. Goods and services were becoming expensive.

Along the way, we spent a couple of weeks in Morocco, and I travelled some in Portugal. I wanted to go into Gibraltar for a day, but was told it is just a rock.

Spain

June 2003

I arrived at Malaga Airport by the beaches of Costa del Sol. After a few days, Sonja arrived.

Malaga is a modern port city with historical sections, including a beautiful ancient cathedral. The inner city was surrounded by a wall with a big castle on the hill inside, where Ferdinand and Isabella lived. The wall protected the city from invasions centuries past. A bullfight was scheduled the next day at their big modern arena. I wanted to go, but tickets were about 200 dollars. It was sold out, believe it or not, even with an enormous seating area.

I was in the wrong place, my fault, and got hit by a car while in Costa del Sol. I was pretty bruised up. They took me to a hospital for x-rays, nothing was broken. The medical staff was very obliging and refused to take any form of payment. I hobbled for a few days. While waiting for a bus, a kid on a bench saw me struggle to walk, got up and had me sit. Very kind of him, but the other two boys sat while Sonja remained standing.

The train to Seville was comfortable. Many stork nests were on top of the power poles beside the tracks. The landscape is flat with olive groves as far as the eye can see. Time was spent conversing with a young boy travelling with his father. He was learning English in school; I was learning Spanish on the train.

Seville is a beautiful city, famous for its barber. I had the pleasure of attending 'The Barber of Seville' at the opera house in Budapest, Hungary. The cathedral in Seville is where Cristóbal Colon (known to us as Christopher Columbus) is buried. There is an ongoing controversy, as Santa Domingo in the Dominican Republic believes that he did not return to Spain after his fourth voyage. While we are speaking the truth, Christopher actually arrived in North America 500 years late. The Vikings and Leif Erickson had a settlement in Newfoundland around the year 1000 AD.

The Seville Cathedral is said to be the third largest in the world. Building started in the year 1430, completed in 1500. The beautiful stained-glass windows, the statues, and the rich alters are a sight to behold. The sheer size of the structure makes one wonder how this could be constructed without modern tools and technology.

Other features of the beautiful and historic city are the baroque-style architecture, the murals, museums, parks, and bridges. It was the best experience I had in Spain. While being many miles inland, the only navigable river in Spain, Rio Guadalquivir, runs through Seville, making it a port city. Five modern bridges were built for the 1992 Expo, adding to the many older ones. Seville is now linked to Madrid by high-speed rail. An oddity to me were the postal service vehicles, bright yellow scooters used for mail delivery. Tourists were everywhere, not surprising, as it is a beautiful city.

We left Spain for a tour of Morocco.

Morocco

July 2003

We hopped on a ferry to Morocco. It was a tour visiting different parts of the country, attending cultural events. The ferry left Algeciras on the southern tip of Spain to Ceuta in Morocco. The tour patrons on the bus were mostly from Spain, with a Norwegian diplomat to Saudi Arabia, and the Canadian and the Swede with red hair. The diplomat turned out to be a most interesting fellow, with many stories of Arabian customs and his association with the officials.

The hotels we stayed at were all top-notch and the meals were excellent. Moroccan cuisine was totally different from the oily Spanish food, and I loved it. Their markets always had great mounds of spices for sale. I took home a large package of Moroccan curry, which I loved and have not been able to get again.

Morocco is an Arabic Muslim country, very poor, with the vast majority making a living in agriculture. Harvesting of grain is done the old-fashioned way, like we did a 100 years ago. Tractors, combines, and wagons pulled by burros were a common sight on the highways. The roadsides are lined with eucalyptus trees to provide shade for the walking traffic and wagons. The trees certainly enhance the scenery, but they suck up all the surrounding soil moisture. The desert landscape becomes greener as one travels from the seaside into the Atlas Mountains.

The cities of white buildings have some streets so narrow it is difficult to pass another person. The colourful street markets, called medinas, sell carpets, jewelry, leather items, spices, and teapots. Ornate mosques are common of course, as the population is Muslim.

Very few people need glasses, but very few people have healthy teeth, if any, due to their sweet diet. Men wear a heavy clog type of shoe, some a bright yellow. Alcohol is available, but only tourists are allowed to drink in public. We were warned about the dangers to young women, as a couple of the tour ladies were in their twenties.

I had spent time with the Muslim culture in Jakarta, but this was my first real connection with the people and their way of life. I was not disappointed.

THE CITIES OF MOROCCO

It was a pleasant ride in an air-conditioned bus from the ferry, across the semi-desert, and into the city of Fez. We had a great guide, an Arab who spoke in English and Spanish. Fortunately, the bus was cool, as the temperature outside was above 40 degrees C and the sun was unrelenting. The land was mostly agricultural, less as we gained altitude, but more greenery. We toured the city, in particular a leather processing place. There were many huge vats, filled with urine to condition the hides. It stunk as I recall. Our hotel was very comfortable and had a bar with good beer. Dinner was delicious, but I can't remember what we ate. Hey, I'm trying to remember from 17 years ago.

The next morning we headed into higher ground, into the Atlas Mountains. There were more trees, including pomegranate, date palms, and fig trees. Nothing tastes better than fresh fruit off the tree.

We arrived in Marrakesh later in the day. We toured the Cemetery of Kings, then on to our hotel. That evening we were treated to a horse show. The horses were well trained, an enjoyable performance. Surprisingly, there were hundreds of tourists there. The weather was cooler. The show was colourful, men dressed in white, women in red. The next day was spent at the medina, with thousands of people milling about. Food booths were aplenty and we grazed through a lot of them.

Henna was being painted on hands at several places. Henna is made from a plant and is painted on like a tattoo, lasting a couple of weeks. It is an Indian wedding tradition, called Mehndi. Originally it came from an Arab part of Asia. I was told that one of the ingredients is cow dung.

Onward to the coast, to the city of Casablanca, a more modern city of nearly three million people. It has busy tourist resorts and attractions. One large pool along the shore has sea water in it, but is protected from the waves by a wall.

One of the mosques, the second biggest Muslim mosque in the world, was available for viewing by outsiders. The fee to get in was nearly $100, so I declined. I regret not seeing it now, forever wondering what was in there. Besides, I can't find the money I saved.

I was able to see another mosque, abandoned half-built in the 12th century. It would have been the biggest mosque in the world. There were many giant pillars, with a central square building about 15 stories high. The story was, it was not set pointing due east, so a roof was never constructed, abandoned forever. You can't imagine the size of that place.

You may recall, the movie *Casablanca* was filmed there, with Humphrey Bogart and Ingrid Bergman. I was there in that bar, sitting at the piano that Sam played. That's as close to being famous as I have ever been. As the story goes, Ingrid Bergman was the pride and joy of Sweden for her part in the movie until the news came out that she was having an affair, while her husband was at home in Sweden.

Tangier was the last stop before returning to Spain. This city is the summer site of the Moroccan royal residence. The history goes deep into BC times, because of its location on the Strait of Gibraltar.

We left on a ferry to return to Spain. It had been an interesting and entertaining trip, quite memorable.

After returning to Spain, my friend Sonja left for home in Sweden. She was an enjoyable companion. I carried on to Portugal.

Portugal

I did not find Portugal to be the most scintillating travel experience. It was nice, but not exciting. On the western side of the country, the beaches had nice sand with wavy and cool water. Sand dunes with vegetation gave it a unique appearance.

Algarve had warmer water, but so many expat homes. The beaches were crowded and commercial. Everybody wanted to rent you an umbrella with sand space. It brings to mind '90 Mile Beach' in Australia, where you could have a mile of privacy for free.

Lisbon is an interesting city. I rode the hop-on hop-off bus for two days and saw most of the sights in the city. I love those buses. Museums were great. A bridge there was identical to the Golden Gate Bridge, in fact the same engineer built both bridges.

From Lisbon, I headed north to Porto, then that exciting ride to Salamanca in Spain.

BACK TO SPAIN

I left Portugal by bus enroute to Salamanca. Normally buses have been exceptionally comfortable, a very nice way to travel. But not this time. My seat was on the upper level, the air conditioning was out, there was no washroom on board, and the two girls across from my seat were killing me. They had armpit hair long enough to braid, and every time an arm was raised, a wave of stench blew over me. Finally, we stopped somewhere. I ran out of the bus to find a washroom, but upon my return the bus had moved. There were about 50 buses to choose from as I scurried along trying to recognize something. I caught sight of the driver as he was pulling out without me. When I jumped in front of the bus, he stopped and let me back in.

Salamanca is an ancient inland city, famous for its university which is one of the oldest and best in Europe. Established in the 13th century, it hosted such people as Christopher Columbus and Ignatius Loyola. The city boasts incredible gems of ancient architecture such as two fused cathedrals, the new one built in 1509; the University; the Plaza Mayor, which sparkles at night with activity; the town hall which was originally used as a bullfighting arena; and an elegant bridge constructed in the year 89.

The language in Madrid was very different. One can equate it to the "Queen's English." As the story goes, one of the royal sons had a lisp. The people had to speak as he did, in fear of insulting the royal family. And thus, Castilian Spanish became the only "proper" Spanish in the country. Meanwhile, the language to the northwest, in Salamanca, was very different. Later in Toledo, just south of Madrid, they spoke very differently from either of the other two. I basically understood all three versions, but all three insisted that they didn't understand a word of the other two versions of Spanish. All three areas spoke some English.

Toledo is an amazing ancient city, a UNESCO heritage site. The city is filled with religious buildings, museums, and fortresses. I was in awe of an old bridge over the Tagus River, built in the 13th century, when I was told that was the new bridge. The old bridge, upstream, was rebuilt by the Moors in the year 866. Once again, I was in a city that was very memorable.

Back at the airport in Malaga, I caught the scheduled flight returning home to Alberta. The flight was an adventure. We were an hour late leaving Malaga, stranded on the apron waiting for an opening to take off. Of course the plane was an hour late arriving at Heathrow. After a long bus ride, I walked forever until I saw an Air Canada counter. They assured me that I could get to my plane if I hurried. I finally arrived at the centre of the terminal, where I found the route to my gate. It showed the ETA to my plane was 45 minutes walking. I scurried like crazy. When I arrived, sure enough, they were waiting for me.

I arrived in Vancouver, but my luggage did not. They called Air Canada in Heathrow, and it was there. They promised to put it on the next flight. I needed to get my boarding pass for the connecting flight to Edmonton. The attendants were on a work slowdown, and would not give me a pass until it was too late, after standing in line for an hour with three people ahead of me. I caught a flight a couple hours later.

At the parking lot in Edmonton, I discovered that the vehicle keys were in my lost bag. A nearby dealership cut a key for me. Finally I am on my way. Just out of the parking lot, a light came on and the vehicle died, so into the dealership for a new alternator. My luggage arrived two weeks later.

There had been a lot happening in those two months. The ancient cities in Spain were wonderful to see. The two weeks in Morocco were the best. The trip home was a reality check.

South America The Pacific Coast

Peru, Chile, Ecuador, Galapagos Islands, Colombia, Bolivia

Seven Months, November 2003 - May 2004

THE LANDS OF SOUTH AMERICA

The Latino culture is to be admired for their value of family and caring for each other. I was made to feel welcome and was invited to join them quite often. It's a joy to see four generations of women holding hands, walking down the street. When was the last time you saw a 14-year-old boy walking with his eight-year-old sister, talking and laughing! New Year's Eve is a family event, like a barbeque with a bottle of wine. Of course a family event can mean 40 people.

An interesting fact about the southern hemisphere is that there is a hole in the ozone layer. It meant wearing sunscreen at all times. Sheep had to have eye drops once a year, or they could go blind.

Many restaurants have a display case, representing the menu with real dishes. One of everything on the menu is made and put in the display, for you to choose to order.

Spanish is the language used throughout most South America, as in Mexico and Central America. However, the language changes from one country to another, and was an obstacle to learning for me. There are different levels of Indigenous wording mixed in.

Mexican Spanish is different, containing words found in no other Latin country. The Spaniards were out of Mexico 150 years earlier than their neighbours to the south, so there is more native influence in their words. For example, a *zocalo*, a town centre square, in every other country is plaza, or *plaza de armas*. In Chile, so many colloquial words and phrases are used, other Latin countries cannot understand. They made a very successful movie in Chile that had to have subtitles to be understood by Latinos other than Chileans. Argentina, especially around the city of Buenos Aires, has an infusion of Italian in their language.

The purest of all Latino languages is spoken in Colombia, and is good in Ecuador. It didn't matter very much, as everybody talks too fast. I did learn better when I lived with families that spoke only Spanish.

Peru

ABOUT THE COUNTRY OF PERU

An interesting fact about Lima is the population of Asian people. History tells a story of Chinese and Japanese coolies, or slaves, brought in by Spanish and Portuguese traders. Slavery was terminated in 1854. One hundred thousand Chinese and Japanese immigrants came as contract laborers in the years 1850 to 1875 to work in the sugar plantations and the guano mines. As a result, not only Lima, but Peru, has an Asian population of about five percent. As a result of a concentration of residents of Oriental descent in Lima, you can find a restaurant, known as a chifa, on every street corner. Their food is different and delicious, a mix of Chinese, Japanese, and Peruvian cuisine.

Peru is considered one of the top foodie destinations in the world. The chefs are well trained and educated. Amazing foods are grown there, such as camu-camu fruit, cassava, and over 3,000 types of potatoes. Cuy is a traditional dish of roasted guinea pig, eaten on special occasions. Many times I have eaten cuy. Quinoa is grown in the Andes, a staple food for more than

5,000 years. It was eaten before going into battle because it was so healthy for the warriors, making them strong.

Peru to me has been the most diverse in peoples, food, climate, and geography, with the sea and the Andes. I spent a long time there, and returned because I loved everything about it.

Peru has 90 different microclimates, allowing for an abundance of wildlife and plant species. The giant Andean condor is native to the Andes mountain range in Peru. They can weigh 12 kilos, and stand 1.2 metres high, with a wingspan of up to four metres. The tallest flowering plant, the Puya Raimondii stands five metres high, taking 80 to 150 years to bloom. When it does, it can have over 30,000 white blooms. It grows in the high Andes. Manu National Park holds a biodiversity record after recording more than 1,000 species of birds, 1,200 species of butterfly and 287 species of reptiles. The largest sand dune is located just east of Nazca. Lake Titicaca is the highest navigable lake in the world. The Cotahuasi Canyon has a depth of 3,232 metres, deepest in the world. Isn't Google wonderful? I did see many of these, but needed a nudge to my memory.

Peru had recently become a democracy. Democracy can be said as "Demo-Crazy," so I've been told. And I believe it. While downtown, most days had a parade of some kind blocking the street. They were nonviolent, yet intimidating. Something was wrong with everything, from cost of living to gay parades to Indigenous discontent to anti-government sentiment.

As well, there was always something to celebrate. The many Indigenous groups each have a dance of their own with colourful distinctive costumes, in a competitive atmosphere. The local families dress up and gather in parks for lunch and barbeques. Each month has a major festival. Music concerts are very popular, as every Latino believes they can sing and dance. They can all dance, and some are talented singers.

Religious activities are very important, as 97 percent of the people are Catholic. Semana Santa, or Holy Week, is South America's Easter extravaganza. Carnival is the week leading up to Lent. Navidad, or Christmas is a big family celebration.

Inti Raymi is the most important festival in Cusco's events calendar, is held on winter solstice in June. It celebrates the sun king Inti Raymi, and Pachamama, the Earth mother, and the solstice. It has been an Inca ritual for more than 600 years.

There were many museums to visit. A very big mausoleum had centuries-old bones stacked in circular patterns. Cemeteries are always interesting. Some build a better home for after-life than they live in while alive. Families are usually placed together in layered tombs. There are plenty of archeological sites, recovering ancient buildings buried in the sand.

MY LIFE IN PERU

My South American experience begins in Lima. It is a lot different than Central America, except the weather is similar, warm and inviting with lots of sunshine.

At an airport ATM in Lima, I took out enough Peruvian Sol to get me through a few days. At a kiosk promoting hotels and hostels I found a good safe place to stay, a Sheraton Hotel. I did not feel very secure yet, being in strange surroundings. I arranged a taxi, a registered one on advice. In Peru, anyone could run a taxi just by putting a cardboard sign in the window. They are half price, but were known to be dangerous.

The ride was on a ten-lane street to the Sheraton. I was excited to be there. I went down to a lounge and had the specialty drink, the spirit of the country, a Pisco Sour.

The next morning I scouted the neighbourhood, all commercial. The front desk had a notice for a free shuttle ride to a shopping mall on the water's edge. Excellent!

A lady from Toronto was on the shuttle, dressed quite nicely, in fact a bit over-dressed. We hung out together while shopping at all the stores in the mall, and having a pleasant relaxing time. She offered to buy me dinner at a restaurant on the water.

A long pier led to a seafood restaurant. It was exceptional, pricey but delicious food. She told me all about herself, an interesting person. She was a real estate agent in a market going crazy, making hordes of money, living an expensive lifestyle. As we were leaving, she told me she gave her son a million-dollar home on a golf course. The idea was that he should get used to living this lifestyle because he would be rich all his life. As she said that, a big sea gull flew over and dropped a deposit on her $3,000 leather jacket. I did not laugh, but helped her clean the goop off. After all, she did buy me dinner, and it wasn't cheap.

The next morning as I lay awake, the bed started shaking pretty hard. It threw me out of bed. A couple of guys playing tennis on a rooftop below asked if I felt that; it was an earthquake. They have thousands of tremors in South and Central America almost every day. Everywhere you go, you will find signs of earthquake damage, and many mountains have blown their top at some time in the past.

The local money was gone, so I used the ATM at the hotel. It ate my card! This is one of two times I have had trouble with an ATM in 20 plus years of travel. The front desk referred me to the bank down the street that serviced the machine. At the bank, I was escorted immediately to a lady at a desk, where I showed her my passport and she gave me my card with an apology. I felt guilty for being looked after so quickly while dozens of locals watched and waited their turn.

After a few days at the Sheraton, I wanted a bit of a rest. I met a nice couple who had a house for rent in a small town south of Lima. They drove me there, and set me up with groceries and showed me around. I was to stay for a couple of weeks.

On Sunday, I decided to go to church. Many times in my travels I would spend time in a church, just to relax in the peace and quiet, to ponder the happenings.

There was a cathedral nearby. There was a ceremony going on, a Catholic First Communion. The cathedral was packed. The bishop was calling up each kid and asking him or her questions, and they would answer into the microphone.

Being very warm, the doors were wide open. A dog walked in, strolled to the front and started barking at the bishop. Several well-intentioned gentlemen tried to chase the dog out. What a performance! The dog just continued barking, making a game of it. Eventually they succeeded, but the dog returned through another door and continued barking at the bishop. It got pretty warm in there with all the doors closed.

With all the good food available, I chose to have some seafood soup. Apparently it's very common to become ill from it, without refrigeration it goes bad very quickly. I was quite uncomfortable, enough that I called my rent people to rescue me. On return to Lima, we stopped at a medical clinic. It took about 20 minutes and $20 to see a stomach specialist doctor, get prescription meds, and be on my way.

I moved into another hotel, Delfines in Miraflores, the safest area of Lima. It was luxurious but expensive, a step up from the Sheraton. Couple days later, another clinic visit was needed as I wasn't feeling quite right. The specialist there said, "Of course, the bad bacteria have been killed, but the good bacteria as well. Here's some good bacteria." A day later I felt great.

Miraflores is a beautiful area, nice parks, high-end restaurants, good retail business area. It was nice, but time to move on to something more interesting.

Chile

I decided to head south, on a bus to Chile. There is a huge copper mine near the Peru/Chile border that can be seen from outer space. Huge trucks similar to the ones used at the McMurray oil sands drive in circles to climb out of the big pit, hauling thousands of tons of ore to the surface every day. My first thought was what they did when it rained, but it doesn't rain there.

In Iquique, a coastal city in Chile, I caught a bus south to Santiago, the capital city. It was a 24-hour bus ride. There were stops for meals and for stretching. We were in comfortable sleeper seats in a very modern bus with attendant services for water and snacks. I met the lovely Paula on the trip. She was headed to Costa del Este in Uruguay with her colleagues as an award for service at her employment. It was embarrassing, as she made sure I was introduced to every one of her work-mates. I was on display.

Santiago subway service was the quietest ride ever, as the trains run with rubber on the wheels. This meant quick stops and starts, while allowing for a smooth and quiet ride. At that time they carried about 800,000 passengers a day.

I spotted a huge building near the hotel. It was a church, not Catholic, where I ran into a minister who was from Montreal. He invited me to come to their five o'clock daily service, but don't be late. I looked around at the seating, and thought it must hold about 10,000 people. Anyway, I showed up early and was lucky to find a seat. The 1,000 seat balcony was full, and sparse seats were left on the main floor. It was like a movie, with people flailing their arms and declaring things to the Lord because they are sinners. Several photographers were taking Polaroid pictures of couples for donations. I'd never seen the like of it.

Great music and art displays were on the streets downtown. Huge markets featured everything fresh with great variety, seafood, fruits, and veggies. The restaurants were classy, usually with a display of meals to be served.

The next morning I headed to the coast, to Valparaiso, a pretty little city with lots of hills. I had a painting done of one of the strange elevators that goes to a hilltop. I met Jami at the hostel. He is a Finn who came there because his uncle, who is married to a Chilean, brought him there. He had never been on an airplane before, so was a bit intimidated.

We went to the beautiful little town called Vina del Mar, where Jami went every day to drink coffee. Strong, dark, heavy, black coffee. He asked me to teach him how to travel. And that's when his fun began. It was fun for me too, as he was a prince of young fella. He was to go to Santiago and catch a flight to Patagonia, where we would meet.

PATAGONIA

Patagonia is on the southern tip of South America, in Chile and Argentina. We were in Punta Arenas, Chile. The big employer there was a Methanex plant. The Humboldt Current from the Antarctic is very cold, and so is Patagonia. They have about two weeks of summer, during which the locals keep on their winter boots and coats. The wind is strong and forever from the west, causing trees to bend over permanently. The countryside has nesting penguins, red skunks, emus, sea birds, vicunas, and beautiful flowers.

Beavers were brought in from Canada to control erosion in the hills, but the beaver soon went out of control. The waterways were dammed up in several places causing much flooding.

In Punta Arenas, I was admiring their beautiful flag when a very pretty lady walked by with her tiny twin girls. She flashed a big friendly smile and said, "Hello, hola!" We talked for a while. As she left, she gave me a kiss on the cheek, which is normal. Then I felt some tugging on my leg; it was one of the twins. I got down on my knees while the little one gave me a kiss on the cheek. A tug from the other side was the second twin wanting to do the same. We said goodbye and I spent the rest of the day recovering. If they like you, the first meeting is usually a handshake, and after that a kiss on the cheek

Jami arrived from Valparaiso. There was a big glow on his face, the start of a real adventure on his own. We went on tours, visited the penguins, went to see blue icebergs, watched the cormorants do their fishing, and checked out the restaurants and bars. Jami even got into the dating scene. He was in heaven.

The penguins were interesting to watch, returning from their fishing trip and walking back to their nests to feed the young. We stood beside them and watched. We booked a trip to Penguin Island where there are many thousands, but the trip was cancelled due to heavy seas. That area has a lot of storms.

The only downer was in a bar where everyone was very friendly to us, except one jerk who was making jokes about us in Spanish. When I told him that I understood what he was saying, he decided to stop, and everyone else laughed. Besides, I was bigger than he was. Jami was the star though, with his almost creamy-white Finnish hair, the girls spent a lot of time staring at him. There are not too many blonde Latinos.

We visited the Torres del Paine National Park, just north is the Los Glaciares National Park. There is a big cold lake there fed from the mountains, with a glacier and steely blue icebergs floating around, with high jagged mountains in the background.

BACK TO MAINLAND CHILE

Summer in Patagonia is over, time to go back north where it is warm, out of the effects of the Antarctic waters and the icy Humboldt current.

We left on a boat to Isla de Chiloe. The sea is always really rough around the horn, so much that the big boat was getting tossed around and so was my stomach. The island Chiloe was like Vancouver Island was 60 years ago. We stayed at a hostel in Chonchi. It is a great tourist spot, and guests at the hostel were from all over the globe. We all mingled and enjoyed the time there. Some pretty good singers performed at karaoke, especially one Dutch girl. They had a pig roasting underground, and we had it for dinner. The Island is located across from the Lakeland area on the mainland, where there are many wineries. It reminded me of the wineries and vineyards in the Okanagan in BC.

We returned to Santiago, where we met people from Montreal and Vancouver at our hostel. We bummed around the city together. When heading out for dinner and a beer, the student from Montreal decided to not go. When asked why not, it came out that his line of credit was cut off, and he had only enough money to get home. Despite the warnings from the other guys, I gave him some money. If I were ever in that situation, I would hope for someone to do the same for me. "You'll never see that money again," they said. When I arrived home in Canada some months later, there was a letter in the mail with a cheque inside. The letter said, "Thank you and call if you are ever in Montreal."

He went home to Montreal, while Jami decided to go with the Vancouver guy to Argentina. I headed north to Iquique.

Jami had graduated with honours, and since then, he has been travelling every opportunity he can. We are still in touch. His last trips that I know of were in the USA chasing tornadoes and in Chernobyl, chasing radiation I guess.

I arrived in Iquique in time for Christmas. I tried to contact Paula but she was not checking her email. I checked into a hotel by the sea.

I took a walk by the water while I was feeling sorry for myself, alone on Christmas day. I came upon a family in a tin shack in the rocks by the beach. They had opened their presents that had been wrapped in discarded paper. The mother played with their six-year-old child, while the father was barbequing meat on a wood fire in a banged-up grocery cart, while drinking soda pop. I wanted so much to go down there and give them money, but I knew that would only satisfy me, and be insulting to them.

I haven't felt sorry for myself since. The next day my friend Paula answered my email, and we met for lunch. She showed me around for a week or so, a lovely lady. One of the places we went to was a big duty-free warehouse, which sold inexpensive good quality items.

BACK TO PERU

I stayed in Tacna, Peru, just across the border from Chile. There I met Martina and her daughter. They were laying by the pool, and on vacation from their home in Lima. We would meet again later.

There is a large impression of a man on the side of a hill near San Pedro that has been dated pre-Inca. Rain has not fallen there, ever, so it would never be washed away. It can be seen from many miles away. San Pedro is near the Chile/Peru border.

The famous Nazca Lines are south of Lima. From a plane, the figures of animals became more distinct. The lines run straight for miles. They are visible from orbiting satellites, but not so easy to see from the ground. It's no wonder people think they were made by aliens. From an airplane, I was able to make out the hummingbird, the monkey, and others. It would have been much better from another mile higher, but it was a good flight. It is truly a mystery how they were able to be so exacting. Unfortunately, they did not show well on my photos from the plane.

I returned to Lima, in time to collect my friend Gerty from BC at the airport. We were off to the hills for a carnival in Northern Peru. We arrived in Cajamarca to the 'paint wars', where they hurl paint at cars and people. It's pretty much harmless, as the paint washed off easily, and they were having a blast.

Next day's carnival was a parade of costumes and colours, floats with beauty queens, something they prepare for all year. Indigenous people were a big part of the parade. A drunk in drag exposing himself in the parade was busy dodging the police. That whole scene wasn't funny, but brought some degree of humour with the disgusting charade. Pick-pockets were in full force. I had my language converter taken out of my shirt pocket. A woman passing me head on got her hand in my pocket, but removed it when I gave her all I had with a fist on her arm. She didn't even flinch, just walked on. Aside from that, it was good.

We left for Ecuador for a flight to the Galapagos Islands. We were in a taxi in Trujillo, with a traffic jam at an intersection. It seems all the taxis entered and wanted to turn, but nobody could move. They all just sat there and honked their horns. After some time, we hopped out of our cab and walked down the street to another taxi.

There were a few excavations of ancient buildings and many artifacts in museums. The original sea-going vessels had replicas on display. One or two persons sit at the back of the boats made of reeds, while the front extended ahead and rounded upward, strange-looking things.

Ecuador

GALAPAGOS ISLANDS

We crossed the frontier Into Ecuador, to Guayaquil for a flight to the Galapagos Islands. Tickets to the Islands had been purchased for flights and

10 days on a boat, with tours around the islands. They were expensive, but we got "last-minute" tickets to fill the boat for much less. My extrovert friend Gerty scoffed and told me I couldn't get a decent price, so she bartered for her own ticket. To this day she doesn't know that she paid $400 more than I did.

The Islands are very closely guarded, the number of people going there is restricted, a careful watch for unauthorized boats coming in, and tourist activities closely controlled by the government of Ecuador.

The boat was comfortable, sleeping about 10 guests plus the crew. It towed a small catamaran which we used to get ashore. One day a sea lion jumped aboard it as we were travelling. He wanted to ride along, and was not shy about it. We went to some of the islands, great scenery, but nothing compared to the amazing fauna.

One bad scene was the goats, brought there to help with something, maybe to keep the grass down. It worked for a while until they multiplied to a quarter million. The army was brought in to reduce the herd, but they caused more damage than the goats, so they were made to leave.

We saw the giant 800-pound turtles that walked through barb wire fences. The Islands have their own penguins. We had towels laying on a beach while we were sunbathing, one empty towel in the middle while the rest of us played soccer. A sea lion came on shore, waddled to the towel and squirmed around on it until comfortable. It closed its eyes and went to sleep, with people on either side.

This happens because the animals have no enemies, so they fear nothing. It was incredible behaviour, so amazing to see lizards looking into your eyes, then curl up against you. Birds fly to you and sit on your shoulder. Blue-footed and red-footed boobies (birds) walk on your feet if you are in their path. Some animals that normally drink fresh water have adapted to salt water. Frigate birds inflate their bright red sacs under their head to the size of a football to attract females.

We were snorkeling in waters with tropical fish, and hammerhead sharks. One fella got caught in a current, pulling him out of sight to the other side of the small island we were at. He and his wife work half a year on an oyster boat they own in Nova Scotia, often scuba diving to harvest oysters just for sport. He knew how to swim, so no problem. It's a good thing it wasn't me.

We were returning to the boat offshore in the catamaran, when we spotted a pod of dolphins feeding well in front of us. While we tried to catch them, another pod was jumping out of the water around us. We travelled full speed ahead, with dozens of dolphins jumping for about 10 minutes. It was a highlight of the trip.

I can't say enough about the Galapagos Islands. It is a must do for any bucket list.

RETURN TO THE MAINLAND, ECUADOR

The return flight was to Quito, capital of Ecuador. The city is built on the equator, at an altitude of 9,350 feet, so is comfortably cool. Most of the people from the trip got rooms at the same hotel. One of them, a young lady from Saskatchewan who had just spent some years teaching in China, left the next day on a bus.

She returned a day or so later, under the influence of drugs, with no money, luggage, passport, or camera and only the clothes she was wearing. She had been injected with a drug in her leg by a passenger beside her on the bus. All she remembered was a little pinch from the needle and being awakened by the police at the end of the bus trip. All her belongings had been taken. She spent the night in jail, as the police believed she had been taking drugs herself. She remembered where she had stayed the one night in Quito, so had the police call to verify. Fortunately we were all still there. They put her on a bus returning to Quito, where we rescued her. It took about three days more before the effects of the drug wore off. Being travel-savvy, she was able to look after business quickly, and was on her way.

An interesting visit was to a monument, named "Middle of the World," that had been surveyed a few years prior to be exactly on the equator and a degree of longitude. It was surveyed again, and found to be off. When the new site was set up, they dug to find the point where the ancient people had designated hundreds of years before. So sayeth the local legends. Ancient buildings indicated exactly when the solstice days were by aligning sun beams through an opening. It is fascinating to see the artifacts showing their knowledge from so long ago.

We caught a flight from Quito to Lima, then by bus to Cusco.

MOUNTAINS OF PERU

From the sea, across the desert, ever upward to high peaks, travelling becomes a chore. The burning sand of the Atacama Desert has a history of low rainfall, in some areas not one recorded drop of rain. An oasis had grass and palm trees, fed from an underground river coming off of the mountains.

Giant cactus plants are prized for their wood, used to make furniture. So many were being cut down, the government made laws to protect them. Only if they had burned were they able to cut them down. So, guess what, many of them seemed to catch fire. Another big tree made an excellent home if the base would be hollowed out, so again, they seemed to catch fire, but just at the base.

I was in a small community further inland before Christmas. It was odd to see Santa and a wagon pulled by a tractor, all dressed up in the 40-degree C sunny weather. It was a party for the kids and they were having a great time. That town had water with a very high level of arsenic, one place in the world where I did not drink the local water.

Some communities in the mountains had houses with no windows. It was explained that there was no need, as the whole family would be outside working before dawn, and not be returning until after dark.

In the early morning, we took a tour to some geysers in the mountains. We were there early because the temperature goes down to about -20 degrees C at night. The geysers freeze, leaving steam coming out of the ground, around the frozen ice spouts. As the sun comes up, it warms quickly, melting the ice and allowing the steaming water to spurt up again. Soon we were in the hot pools for a swim.

As we travelled up, we had to take precautions against 'altitude sickness.' This was very real. The altitude at Colca Canyon can reach 4800 metres, or 15,800 feet, where we were viewing the giant Andean Condor. One of the young Peruvian ladies on the bus passed out from lack of oxygen. We found her phone and camera, and had her lay down to recover.

We were encouraged to drink coca tea, a drink made from hot water and coca leaves, the very ones that cocaine is made from. Everyone drinks it, especially the people living on the coast in Argentina. It works, as does Ibuprofen.

The animals of the high altitude, such as the llama, and the never-domesticated vicuna and guanaco, can be seen on the hillsides. They have an animal that is the same as our jack rabbit, but with a long tail. Lizards were abundant. Salt flats in the valleys have water that is perfect for growing shrimp, so also perfect for flamingos. The salt is harvested by the area residents to trade for other goods.

We dropped into a big valley, to the ancient city of Cusco, a gathering place for native ceremonies for more than 1,000 years. The whole city was vibrant with entertainment and tourists. While my very extraverted and attention-seeking friend Gerty was gathering fame and fans, people gathered. It was a great situation for pick-pocketing, and sure enough, they got my wallet, right after I was at an ATM.

They are so skilled, opening the zipper on my pocket and getting the wallet out as I was being bumped around, I didn't notice it was gone for many minutes. I was not happy. I had an old warn wallet in my bag, which I wore for months with a note saying "F**k You," and no money in it, but was never robbed again. I got some more money, with a card I had hidden, and put some in my bag. It was removed too, likely by the cleaning staff. I'm over it now, but I still hate tourist places.

I believe it was in Cusco at a big Catholic church where centuries ago the natives were given a choice. They could become Catholic, or go through a door leading to the back garden where they were executed.

A usual thing in the churches of South America is to have a beautifully sculpted pulpit with a matching cover set above, over the top. On the peak of the cover, you may find a skull. It will be the skull of the architect who built it. The bigger churches will have a set of pipes for the organ, really large and showy. Of course there will be lots of exceptional statues and stained-glass windows.

The natives who showed to have artistic talents were shipped off to Spain, where they were given lessons on painting murals in the churches. One church had a painting of the Last Supper, obviously done by one of these natives. It was a dead giveaway. He had painted a cuy, or hamster, as the food on the table for the Last Supper.

A train runs from Cusco to the town of Machu Pichu, which is the site of ancient Incan ruins. There is a trail that a lot of trekkers take, but I wisely chose to take the train. Many houses along the track had a little cow placed on the roof, apparently a Catholic symbol for protection. The train must climb out of the valley to get to level track. It does so by climbing, then going in reverse up a section, going forward up, etc., until it is out of the valley. The ride is very scenic through rugged hills. We arrived at the town of Machu Pichu and stayed overnight.

The ruins of Machu Pichu were amazing, walls made from intricate stonework, steps for growing vegetables, holy places, unbelievably done in that era, with little tools and technology. I can't begin to describe it. The whole area has so much history, with the Sacred Valley, their storage places in the high hills, their burial places in the cliffs, and the Inca Trail.

We left Cusco on a bus enroute to Bolivia, with adventures along the way.

The bus into Puno was greeted by the nastiest looking people ever. Fortunately we moved on to the bus station. I haven't been afraid ever, except for those guys. They looked pretty dodgy.

Have you ever felt uncomfortable around certain people? Multiply that by 10, knowing you are a tourist target in a strange country with nowhere to hide and no one to turn to. I had to be aware of my surroundings and my safety at all times. These guys sent shivers and I felt the danger.

As luck would have it, the day before we went on the road to Bolivia, some people decided that the cost of electricity was too high. To protest, they had gravel trucks spread big rocks on the highway for about 40 miles. They had to be cleared before we could go. I think it's part of that 'demo-crazy' thing.

We spent a day touring the floating islands on Lake Titicaca, built by gathering and binding reeds, to be replaced every ten years or so. Their dragon-shaped boats are also built from reeds.

The Lake had been stocked with fish from Canada, a couple of species including trout, which rapidly took over and killed the native fish. Big mistake again, trying to help nature.

With one lane being opened, we proceeded on the long slow trip, one flat tire, but we made it, all the way to Copacabana, Bolivia.

Bolivia

We took a side trip to Friday Island on Lake Titicaca. They greeted us with beer and a dance party in a hall. The residents of the Island are native people, who make their living by knitting caps. Only males do the knitting, very fancy, especially if they are wedding caps. Only males wear them.

The residence we stayed at had a front door that was only about 4.5 feet high, plenty high for the locals. As the night got colder, I added heavy blankets, seven in total. The main home had a wood-burning stove with no chimney. The smoke just drifted through the thatched roof, accounting for the average life span of the women there to be about 37. The woodpile of sticks to burn had hamsters living in it, readily available for special occasions, like Easter.

It is celebration time in Copacabana, Palm Sunday. All vehicles are being blessed, cars, trucks, bicycles. It was a process where beer is sprayed inside and out, the trunk and the engine, then flower petals strewn all over it. A priest or bishop would then come to bless the vehicle. Whatever beer was left over, and they made sure there was lots left over, would be imbibed by the family owning the vehicle. It was quite a sight with messy vehicles and drunks everywhere. This was a Catholic celebration. Flowers were beautiful and everywhere, particularly in the impressive 16th century cathedral.

We toured a place near La Paz called the Moonscape, which was really out of this world.

A street in La Paz was set up for trades people with their tools, advertising their availability, including electricians, plumbers, painters, carpenters, laborers, etc. If you needed work done, you went there and got the people you needed. A man on the curb was typing a letter for someone, making a living doing a service with a typewriter.

Bolivia has no access to the sea, so it is difficult to export their goods. The Chilean government refused to grant access, a corridor to a port on the sea. There was good reason for revenge.

An important soccer match was scheduled between Chile and Bolivia. Usually, the visiting team is at a big disadvantage by coming to such a high altitude, making it difficult to breathe, while the locals are accustomed to the diminished supply of oxygen. The altitude in La Paz is 3,640 metres, or almost 12,000 feet

The city was shut down the afternoon of the match, with most stores and businesses closed. Stages were set up for band music and all sorts of celebrations in anticipation of a Bolivian victory. We got our faces painted to the local team colours and went to the packed stadium.

The Chilean team won two to one. The streets were empty, all the venues for celebration were taken down. The next day business returned to normal.

On the return from Bolivia to Puno, Peru, the same road with rocks had another problem. A small town near the border has a bridge on the only road crossing the river. It seems the mayor grabbed the town's money and ran off to Lima. To rebel against the mayor, they dumped a load of gravel on the bridge, so no vehicle could cross. So there we were, walking a couple of miles down the road to another bus that had been arranged for us. Thank goodness the local kids were there to carry our bags, at a cost of course.

On Good Friday, there was a Catholic vigil happening, the Stations of the Cross, 14 stops of events through the Crucifixion of Christ. Thousands of people were in a night-parade, all carrying candles protected from the breeze in plastic pop bottles. There was a man dragging a big cross, a man hanging from a cross with thorns on his bleeding head, the BVM with a donkey, priests dressed in robes and attire depicting that time. It was amazing, but with so many bodies everywhere, I didn't dare carry a camera.

Easter Sunday is a big day in the Catholic religion. Every church and cathedral, and there are many, are filled. An odd thing I saw, was a bishop entering a cathedral, while a man pushed his way through the crowd to have the bishop touch a big pop bottle filled with water. It then becomes "Holy Water". He was really happy and a big grin on his face. The Easter ceremonies are very colourful and serious, something to see.

Back to Lima, my friend Gerty left for Canada, and I settled in at a hostel.

RETURN TO LIMA

I found a nice little hotel, more like a hostel, at a very reasonable rate. The staff were excellent, the owner not so nice to them, even withholding a pay cheque if one of the staff wouldn't go to bed with him. Thankfully the entire staff got on his case and she was paid, but you knew this would happen again. There was a pool and an Argentine-style barbeque, and a butcher shop a block away. It was a great way to socialize with the other guests, and get to know the staff.

One of the guests joined me for breakfast one morning. Of the many pathetic people I have met over the years, this young woman was over the top. She had a room reserved and paid for at the Sheraton, where I had been staying, on a street with a 10-lane highway in front of it. She was saving money by taking a budget cab ride to the hotel. These cabs become cabs by displaying "Taxi" on a piece of cardboard. Anyway, he took her down a back alley where a load of gravel had been dumped. He told her that the road was blocked and he would not be able to get her to the Sheraton. So he found another place for her, where I was staying. She said she was a supervisor in charge of about 20 people at her job. I wondered why she was travelling alone. She is so very fortunate she wasn't robbed or raped or both, but she thought it was no problem.

A couple of Canadian girls from Calgary just out of high school were standing on the sidewalk outside the hostel. The backpacks and things attached were so heavy they couldn't move. I asked them what they would do if someone was about to rob or hurt them. The explanation was, their parents had packed for them. They had just checked out, heading to Cusco and Machu Pichu. I convinced them to leave some things in storage at the hostel, to pick up when they return. They unloaded many rolls of toilet paper, 15 changes of clothing, six pairs of shoes, makeup from hell, lots of canned food, and whatever their mothers thought would not be available in such an underdeveloped country. We had a good laugh about it, and they were much relieved. Nice young ladies.

Previously in Tacna, I had met an interesting and lovely Peruvian lady named Martina. I got in touch with her when I had returned to Lima. She was working at responsible jobs, handling money, selling cars at a dealership, selling jewelry, real estate, and who knows what else. Anyway, she was a responsible and respectable lady, who made friends easily. We became very good friends, travelled together, as she continued working. I moved into her suite with her, her mother, and her son.

Latinos tend to look after their parents, and their children don't just run off and find a place of their own. It is not unusual to find three or four generations living under the same roof. Many of the youth live at home for years. This is why one-hour motels with discreet rooms are common and so successful.

No English was spoken at their home. My weak Spanish was about to take a giant leap forward, but not quite fast enough. Martina's mother, who didn't like me anyway, was always trying to trap me with the language. One morning she asked me in Spanish, "where in the world did you find the best beer?" I thought for a moment, then gave a safe reply in Spanish "In Europe." I felt good about my reply, until she asked, "Why??"

I pondered how I could escape this question. I thought, well, maybe I could say that it had no preservatives in it. That was easy, because Spanish words generally follow a pattern, so conservative is 'conservativo,' so it must be 'preservativo.'. So I proudly proclaimed, "No hay preservativos!"

Gramma stared at me, giggled, and then laughed hysterically. Martina just stared, while her son smirked. I knew I had said something wrong, but what was it? I whipped out my Eng/Span dictionary. Oh-oh, preservativo is a condom. So I was telling Gramma that beer was better in Europe because it had no condoms in it. She laughed at me for days…gringo estupido.

Martina took me everywhere around Lima, making the city a favourite place in South America. We went to beaches, shopping, shows, and all the things the local people normally do. One of my favourite events was her cousin's little girl's birthday, three years old. She was dressed up like a princess. About 30 relatives were there, a weekday afternoon, dressed up for the occasion. We all ate, drank, danced and sang well into the evening. I was treated like one of the family. They do know how to enjoy themselves. It was another example of how much the family is revered.

We travelled up the coast to her favourite beach where we met her friend Alicia, a Supreme Court judge's widow. She was a delightful lady, but a disaster as a cook. I was warned, and she was right.

All along the coast, seafood was the mainstay meal. I love fish, so had fish at least once a day. There are so many species, cooked so many different ways, I could not get tired of it. The cold Humboldt Current from the Antarctic makes the fish firm and delicious. The seafood section of a big grocery store had more than 100 species of fish on display.

I left Lima, and Martina returned to work. I would be seeing her again.

Colombia

I left Lima, on a flight to Bogota, Colombia, where my brother was working. A lot of security was required, as the FARC group of revolutionary armed forces was very active at that time with kidnapping and bombing. I was a target because I was a foreigner, and my brother was working for an oil company. I travelled in a bulletproof car with an armed guard on a motorcycle.

Having the perfect climate, many miles of greenhouses grew flowers, mostly roses, which were being exported all over the world. The greenhouses were secured by armed guards of course, to keep their secrets. Trees were taller than big buildings. The countryside was amazing, deep valleys and lush forests with lots of rivers, armed guards behind sandbags at some bridges.

We spent a couple of days away from Bogota, in the Colombian Hills. Every place we went was loaded with flowers. Markets had fresh vegetables, lots of pottery, and artisanal goods made by hand and painted, all selling at far too little. A ceramic wind chime was 50 cents, and likely took days to make and paint.

We visited an awesome salt mine, where giant caverns had been dug out. Stations of the Cross were in big rooms, even a church with an altar. We took a chair lift up to a restaurant on a mountaintop with a magnificent view onto the city far below. Another restaurant had a horse show, with the little horses that take many small steps very quickly. It was quite impressive.

I had a nice afternoon at the Bogota stores with their Spanish language teacher. She was an interesting lady with some good stories.

I flew back to Lima, just in time to see a big gay parade. I spent some time with Martina, then returned home to Alberta, end of May, 2004.

It was an indescribable experience to be in South America for seven months, doing so many things and meeting so many marvelous people. I knew that I would return.

Czech Republic with side trips to Switzerland and Greece

THREE MONTHS, SUMMER OF 2004

I met a young lady in Costa Rica by the name of Marie, whose home was in Prague in the Czech Republic. She had done extensive travelling and was interesting to be with. I was invited to visit her in her home country. I was home for a short stay after the Pacific tour in South America, then headed off to Prague. It was my first experience in a country that had been under Communist control.

If you have ever watched a Russian coach yell at his team, scolding the players vehemently, that is the way locals were treating each other. My friend did that to me a few times, indignant and disrespectful. It was happening to others, so I just sucked it up. I trust it has since changed.

The cities and countryside are scenic and filled with history. There was very little damage from WW2. Towns without a river had man-made lakes for a water supply, stocked with carp, which was their special meal for holiday occasions like Christmas. The towns are spaced within a few miles, some roads having apple trees planted along the way. Fresh fruit was new for them, as the communist government forbid imports, wanting to be self-sufficient.

Along the roadside we found a small wedding chapel for three people, everyone else had to stand outside.

The Republic had joined the EEU not long before this. It was sad to see, as they were not used to the ways of the capitalist world. European countries were taking advantage of them. The new rules required bee hives to be a certain dimension, which required replacement of all Czech hives. The whole honey industry in the Czech Rep shut down. A thriving yogurt industry shut down because they couldn't get a license for a quota.

I found the two best beers in the world. In the town of Pilsen, a 900-year-old brewery makes the original Pilsner beer. The city of České Budějovice has the original Budweiser brewery, also 900 years old. A sad story: the American Budweiser company patented the name in the Czech Rep, meaning the original brewery of 900 years had to change their name. I have not had a Bud since, unless there was nothing else. Years later a court straightened out the debacle. The American company can now use the word 'Bud,' but not Budweiser. The proper brewery name has been restored to the original Company. Thank goodness, as there is no comparison in quality or taste.

Everywhere you go in Prague, you will see a cow statue on the street. If a donation was made toward homeless people, you are entitled to decorate a life-size cow. Some have advertising, others are an object of art, and all are interesting. I never saw a homeless person on the streets. A tall water tower has figures of men climbing to near the top. It looks real.

The town square is the home of the famous astronomical clock, known as the Orloj. It was built in the late 1400s. Its many features include telling the time, the date, astronomical and zodiacal information. This includes the relative position of the sun, moon, zodiac constellations and other planets. Each hour it puts on a show with animated parts. The most popular time is the spectacular performance the clock does at midnight on New Year's Eve. A crowd fills the square to see it.

The Prague Castle, built around the year 880, is the official office of the President of the Czech Republic. It is located on the edge of the Vlatava River, across the Charles Bridge, a popular tourist area. It is listed as the 'largest coherent castle complex in the world' according to Guinness World Records.

Venceslas Square is a popular gathering place for tourists and locals alike. It has businesses, restaurants, hotels, bars, and houses of ill repute. It is nearly a kilometre long by 180 metres wide. It rises to the National Museum at one end. There are statues of the good King Venceslas, and of a martyr who set himself on fire to protest the Soviet invasion.

My friend Marie told me a scary story of an anti-communist uprising, a gathering of nearly half a million people in Venceslas Square. She and her friends had skipped out of high school to attend the rally. The Soviet military went so far as to move tanks to the top of the hill, where the museum is now, ready to fire upon the mob to quash the uprising. Eventually, the tanks were ordered to back down. That was the beginning of the end for communism in the Czech Republic, then known as Czechoslovakia. They later divided the country into the Czech Republic and Slovakia in what was known as the "Velvet Revolution".

Another side of the Square is the open drug market and the brothels. The legalization of prostitution allowed street hookers in abundance, and lots of hawkers to attract men into their clubs. One such club of note was in a multi-story large building, offering limousine pick-up for clients. Yes, I went there one evening.

I sat in a large room where they brought drinks and made sure I was comfortable One after another, the ladies filed in, sat down with me to display their virtues and entice me with their charm. I never saw the same woman twice, perhaps a couple hundred working at that time. Most were okay with me not having money but that I would return, except one Russian woman. She scolded me with, "Wot you doink here, you got no money??" I said "Wot you doink here, you got no boobies??" That wasn't a real good idea, remember what I said about them yelling? At that point I left, but it was an interesting evening.

The Prague National Theatre was built in the year 1867, entirely from donations. It was damaged extensively by fire in 1881, considered to be a national disaster. Very quickly private collections for rebuilding were raised, with no assistance from any government source. This opera house is a beautiful edifice, on the Vltava River, facing the Prague Castle, near Venceslas Square.

The Czech appreciation for music is evident. We went to many impromptu events at churches and parks, featuring tenors, singing groups, string and brass instruments. They were all professional grade. I got a talking to for chewing gum at a performance. They are very serious about their culture in the arts.

My buddy Marie showed me around Prague. The vestiges of the communist era were prevalent in their way of life, the stores, businesses, buildings. There was a lingering sense of mistrust, especially with the older people, from the system of having people spy and report on their neighbours and opening of mail. The subway system seemed to work well, but was very confusing to me reading the names. I was asked to produce proof of ticket purchase after a ride. The ticket was in my wallet, which I took out to show the policeman. This was followed by a fierce tongue-lashing from my friend for showing my wallet in public, because of so many Gypsies who would steal from me.

All the yelling, scolding, and tongue-lashing was not a problem. It was recognized as a part of their culture, what they saw and learned. I saw it happening to other people, but mostly men doing the dominating. They always reverted to being nice people when the chastising was completed.

High-rise buildings are identical, in groups of many. Marie took me to visit a doctor friend of hers. She lived in a sixth-floor apartment. Marie phoned to say we were at the door. The keys were tossed down to us from a window. On every second floor a locked gate blocked further entry. Finally on the top floor lived this lovely mild-mannered doctor. We went to a Czech restaurant, with cuisine that was simple, but very tasty.

We left the city to see castles, medieval, ornate, and filled with interesting history. The *Karlštejn Castle* is just outside of town, and had been restored to the original medieval state, one of the best castles I have been in.

We went on a camping trip along the Vltava River. One night was spent tented near a dance hall, where I discovered that I was not as talented a dancer as my partner, but it was fun and different.

We had met up with a couple of Marie's lady friends at the campground. The four of us got on a raft to float down the river, a popular activity. Signs indicated where the bars were set up along the way. I don't think we missed any. We passed small towns along the way, most having some big buildings. At the end of the day, a van was there to return us to the campground.

We spent a few days camping, touring the countryside. We visited the breweries of the best beer in the world, the Pilsner and the Budweiser breweries. We stayed over in a town that was designated a UNESCO heritage site. There were no rooms available in the whole area, until Marie used her charm to get a place. Funny thing, I asked her a question in English and the price doubled. Marie got the price back down, but I got another small thrashing. I should have known better.

We were at restaurants where they had old crests, a coat of arms, on the wall. They had been painting around them to preserve the amazing artwork. One was from the year 1688, and the other was from the year 1379.

A museum had a poster from a demonstration. It was titled: "It was a time of happy shiny people. The shiniest were in the uranium mines".

Switzerland

We took a long bus trip to Zurich in Switzerland to visit Marie's friend. She was married to a Cuban national who was putting pressure on her to have his brother sponsored for Swiss citizenship, and be living with them. He was jealous of Marie spending time with his wife, which annoyed them both. I stayed out of it.

We noted dozens of jet trails from airplanes all over the sky. Marie called them 'Cones.'. She said airlines were making extra income by taking hazardous waste and unloading it in the sky. I still don't know if that is true. I know it is not normal for trails to stay in the atmosphere for days, and there were dozens of them.

Needless to say, the Swiss experience was one of the nicest trips I have taken. The people were friendly, the scenery awesome, the history great, and our activities were unusual and so enjoyable. The buildings throughout the country were laden with bright flowers in planters at every window.

We swam in Zurich Lake, on the edge of the city of Zurich. There was a fig tree near the third-floor window, where I could reach out and grab fresh figs. Everything was expensive, a plain t-shirt was $90. Apparently personal income was also very high. People were moving from Germany to Switzerland for financial reasons.

We drove to their cabin in the mountains. It was quite a drive. We went through the Gotthard tunnel where an explosion with fire, the result of an accident, killed 11 people four years prior. They let one car every five minutes go through the tunnel. We were in Interlaken, a city between two Lakes. The Matterhorn was visible from there, or somewhere along the way. Bern at lunchtime had an endless line of people sitting on the sidewalk curbs to have lunch. We stopped for a night at Locarno, and attended an international film festival.

Next day we reached the destination, a small town high in the Swiss Alps. I don't remember the name of the town. Students from a school for sculpturing, left their statues all over the town. I recall one of a man upside-down, buried from the waist up. There was a lot of stonework in the area, like one church with an alternating black and white pattern. Another had rose-coloured marble. Many beautiful colours and designs came from a number of active quarries.

The house we stayed in was over 400 years old. The roof was covered with pieces of slate laid like shingles. How did the frame hold up those heavy rock pieces for centuries?

Some buildings had base pedestals of cement, raised up to a mushroom shape. The idea was to prevent mice from getting in, on buildings where they were storing grain or hay for their animals.

Near the town was a pool of glacier water, fed from a little waterfall, draining as much as it was being fed. They encouraged me to go for a swim in that icy water. "No swim suit? Don't worry about it, no one cares." I stripped down, walked to the pool and jumped in. Sure enough, no one cared. Then I thought, why didn't I walk to the pool, then strip and jump in. Anyway, it was icy cold but very refreshing. I swam around for more than a half hour. When I got out, it didn't matter.

We toured the area to see the quarries, a dam with a generating station, amongst high jagged mountains. A few days later we returned to Zurich.

We went back to Prague by bus. Marie had things to do, so I booked a trip to Greece for a couple of weeks.

Greece

I stayed in *Leptokarya* at a resort on the beach, Mediterranean side. The beach was rough gravel, as per usual on the Mediterranean. It was a Czech area, with the Greek merchants speaking Czech. The restaurants served the delicious food that the Greeks are famous for. I stayed in a motel suite with two young lads next door on one side, and two lovely Czech ladies on the other. One of the ladies, Ivana, liked to have breakfast outside in her panties.

The other, Lucie, had a penchant for large hats. We hung out some, but not for breakfast.

I went to a dance by bus, then almost missed my stop on the way back, pretty scary. The lads and I got a car and went to Athens. The Olympics were on at the time. Traffic was terrible, could not park or find a restaurant, so returned.

I went on two other trips. Meteora is a rock formation of vertical peaks with six monasteries perched on top near Thessaly. Construction of the monasteries started in the 14th century. Hermit monks were living in caves on the peaks from the 9th century on. It looked impossible to climb, much less build on top of the towering rocks. The site is amazing, well worth seeing.

The second trip was to a number of the islands that Greece is so famous for. On one of the islands, I saw a man with a loaf of bread and a bottle of wine, and a woman sitting across, legs up on her suitcase. They seemed relaxed and happy. After touring the island for a couple of hours, I came upon this couple again. By then, the bread was almost gone, a second wine bottle almost empty, and her feet still up on top of her suitcase. I believe that explains the lives of the Greek people.

I returned to Prague on a flight with the same two ladies. The plane was an old Russian model, which leaked water through the window as we flew through rain. One of the overhead bins had the door fall off in midflight. As we went through a bit of turbulence, people were gasping with fear and hanging on to each other. When we landed, everyone applauded enthusiastically.

BACK IN PRAGUE

I spent some time with Lucie in Prague. She was an interesting person, with a father well-off in a high position. She had no job at the time, was slightly spoiled, but a very nice lady. We went to a hockey game in the new arena, world class venue, with the Czech national team playing. They love their hockey there.

The most famous hockey player out of the Czech Republic is Jaromir Jagr. He has a famous bar in downtown Prague, with a display in the middle similar to the one above centre ice in an arena. The story is that he married a famous pretty newscaster, but it quickly broke up, something to do with his mother. None the less, he was still the hero and one of the most beloved people in the Republic. He was still living with his mother.

Lucie took me to the most famous tarot card reader in Eastern Europe. She used three sets of cards, they all agreed with her readings. She talked, Lucie translated, and I wrote down what she was saying. She read that I had two children, boy and girl, their ages, their professions. She knew that I was divorced and why, what my profession was, my financial situation, my love life, and that I had just lost some money on the stock market, but would more than recover in the coming months. She read my past and my future with great accuracy. I still have the notes I wrote. She made one mistake, that I would very soon have a major love event happening. . . . . . .still waiting.

Marie and I met up again. She was planning another trip to Central America while I was on my way back to Canada. It had been a very satisfying experience in all three countries. That was the summer of 2004.

South America - Argentina, Brazil, Bolivia

SIX MONTHS, DECEMBER 2004 - MAY 2005

This trip to South America is to the Atlantic side. I landed in Lima to meet my friend Martina. We travelled up the coast to the beaches north of Trujillo, in Huanchaco. After about ten wonderful days of beaches and seafood, we returned to Lima for Christmas.

I caught a flight to Buenos Aires.

Argentina

Buenos Aires is a beautiful city with a rich history. The language is Spanish with infused Italian. The cuisine is centred on meat, all kinds, cooked on their special barbeques. The people are nice, but appeared to have a bit of "upper class" attitude. The coca leaves tea tradition from the high Andes to prevent altitude sickness was everywhere in that part of the country. We were at sea level, okay, doesn't matter. Everyone had the fancy cups and metal straws with the filter.

The barbeques they use were the inspiration for the "George Forman Grill." They are the central point of a lot of restaurants, cooking meat from every available edible type. Along with a great variety of vegetables and greens, we would fill our plates and pay according to the weight.

The street in front of my downtown hotel is famous as being the widest avenue in the world, Avenida 9 de Julio, at 140 metres or 460 feet. There are six lanes each direction, then a roadway on each side with three lanes, and giant medians. It takes three sets of street lights to cross it. It was named after their Independence Day of July 9, 1816.

The main river in Buenos Aires is the Rio de la Plata, fed from the Rio Salado. I was told that if I drank a half glass of water from the river, I would be dead in 10 hours. It has been poisoned from industrial waste. And yet they have a scow that runs offshore to collect garbage from passing ships, rather than allow them to dump in the ocean.

A very sad event happened on New Year's Eve just before my arrival. A nightclub in Buenos Aires, hosting a rock band, had about 3,000 in attendance, double the venue's capacity. They suspect that someone lit a flare, common for NYE celebrations. The flare lit a plastic netting on the ceiling, raining flames onto the crowd. Four out of six exits were locked shut. 194 people died, while 1,492 people were injured. It was a tragedy the public blamed the government for. Read about it, the República Cromañón nightclub.

The people love to show off their Flamenco Dancing. They say the dance originated on a particular location in Buenos Aires. On that street people were lined up to dance, and many more to watch. I know people from my Island who holiday there every year to take lessons and to dance.

The movie, *Evita,* with Madonna playing Eva Peron and Antonio Banderas, is one of my favourite movies. I had the good fortune to be in front of the Casa Rosada, where Eva gave her speech from the second story balcony. The story became very real at the cemetery where she is laid to rest with her husband Juan Peron, then President of the Republic of Argentina. The people tried to have her remains moved to another cemetery because she was a commoner, and not good enough to be where the elite were buried. She died at the age of 33 from cancer. To this day her remains are with the rest of the Peron family in that cemetery.

The cemetery was an amazing place, as so often is the case in Latin America. Some mausoleums were built like a small church, some cases maybe better than the homes they lived in.

I was enjoying my dinner at a fancy restaurant, when a nice lady named Nataly asked if she could join me. She was from Panama, travelling alone, recently widowed. We toured in Buenos Aires for a couple of days. She changed plans to return to Panama, and decided to travel with me to Brazil.

At the railway station in BA, we met a gentleman who used to work for one of the rail companies. He could travel for free, and loved to take tourists to see the countryside. Well, he found us. We spent a totally enjoyable day travelling the countryside, even to where the Caballeros were riding the range to look after their cattle.

Getting a visa to Brazil was exasperating. Their consulate in BA was lined with people, half of them angry. The visa was very expensive. The form had to be signed by a legal person, more money. If there was a mark on the paper, I not dotted, t not crossed, it was rejected. Start over, more cost. It was like they didn't want anyone to go there. One fella tried to suggest something to his wife, her reply was that he should just shut up, he was too stupid. He looked so down-trodden, I had to tell him he didn't have to put up with that. His eyes lit up. Couldn't help myself. I don't like bullies.

With visas in hand, we arrived in Punta del Este, Uruguay. That city had beautiful beaches, and is a famous tourist destination.

The next day we were at Iguazu Falls, on the Argentine side. Crossing the Frontier to the Brazil side, the falls were never-ending. Iguazu is the world's largest waterfall system, even surpassing Victoria Falls. There are 275 different cascades, falls, and drops. There are 14 falls that drop to a height of 350 feet.

Brazil

Brazil is an amazing country, and beautiful to visit, while being a bit scary. It is safe if you behave and have some street sense. The country is so large, you could pick up the continental United States and place it inside Brazil, with a little twist so that Florida fits. The language is Portuguese, understandable from Spanish to read and with some work to know the appendages to their words. I understood enough to get by, and Nataly understood much better than I.

The people range from black to white, and all points in between, from integration over the centuries. There seems to be no separate groups, except

German communities still schooling in German. Near as I could tell, they live in harmony with no colour or race distinctions. However, it was evident how expensive a restaurant was by the tone of colour in the clientele. There are a lot of poor people in very crowded conditions living in really close-knit communities. They are proud of their heritage and do a lot to support one another.

The lack of opportunities for employment had resulted in a rise in the sex trade. One lady told me to get rid of Nataly and go with her, in a bar where all could hear. Another one on a bus said she was going to grab me, as translated by Nataly. She moved right on me while I covered my wallet. I witnessed one know-it-all tourist get tossed and locked out of a woman's hotel room, without money or clothes. Who do you complain to when you are locked out naked? It was a common occurrence, and of course the police always side with the resident people over tourists. The beaches were beautiful, but fraught with thefts and scams. I only went with my Speedos, so not much to steal from me.

The country still lives under the cloud of a decision made many decades ago. It so happened that a deep recession hit the country, so much so that families would send one or two of their children onto the street because they simply could not feed the whole family. These children formed groups who did what they had to do to survive, becoming a menace. When the government was forced to do something, they decided to send out a squad to rid them of these kids, in other words hunt them down and shoot them. They still live with the consequences of that decision.

The hotels and other buildings along the beach are high enough to disrupt the natural air flow from the sea to the centre of the city, causing a considerable rise in temperature. Downtown is situated in a rain forest area, which has degraded from the extra heat. This started a trend worldwide to limit the height of buildings along a seashore.

We arrived in Rio de Janeiro prior to the Carnival, and spent about a month there. The beaches were as nice as anywhere in the world. We stayed at a hotel on Copacabana Beach. The immense Christ the Redeemer statue stands nearly 100 feet high atop a mountain. A cable car goes up to the statue. It is one of the new seven wonders, and increases housing value if there is a view of it.

The Carnival was the greatest and most spectacular event I have ever seen. The whole city was involved, every store had people dressed up in fancy hats and costumes. The whole country was in a party mood. It is a celebration starting on the Friday before Ash Wednesday, and finishes on Ash Wednesday, before fasting for Easter. The country is 65 percent Catholic, or 143 million people.

We were able to get tickets for both parades, both nights. They ran all night, starting before dusk and ending after sunrise, along a street about half a mile long. The floats, or groups are represented by more than 1,000 different samba schools, with millions of dollars spent on costumes and sponsors. Each school can employ thousands of designers, painters, musicians, dancers, and seamstresses. It's a real neighbourhood affair! The costs are paid from City Hall, for millions of dollars, the rest is from fund-raisers.

I took about 3,000 pictures. The floats were exotic, the costumes exquisite and colourful. Each and every one was magnificent. I find it impossible to adequately describe this event. If I were to recommend one thing for you to do in your lifetime, this would be it.

An incredible month later, Nataly flew back to her home in Panama City from the airport in Rio de Janeiro. I would be seeing her again soon in Panama.

I flew on to more incredible adventures inland, to the city of Manaus with a change of planes in Brasilia. Brasilia is the federal capital of Brazil, a designed city from scratch, planned from nothing. The flight connection had a wait time of three hours, perfect for taking in a movie at the theatre in the airport terminal.

Manaus is situated at the mouth of the Amazon River, where the two main rivers from inland feed into the Amazon.

THE AMAZON BASIN

The Amazon River System is the longest and largest by discharge volume in the world, more than the total discharge of the next seven largest. It is fed from rivers in Brazil lowlands, Peru, Ecuador, Colombia, and Bolivia. The name Amazon is said to come from a legendary event hundreds of years ago, when some marauders from Europe tried to take over the land in the area. They ran into resistance and got beat up badly. The explanation to their king was that an army of very large women got them in a surprise attack. They became known as the band of amazons, and thus the river's name.

MANAUS

Manaus is a city of about two million people, located at the headwater of the Amazon River, where two major rivers combined to be the Amazon. It felt more like a small town, as the people were friendly and happy.

I became friends of the manager of the hotel where I was staying. He and his friend who owned a tourist business took me for a boys' night out, which I am sure their wives would not appreciate, but such is life in their world. They took me out fishing for piranhas at night. After catching a couple of fish, we changed our focus to alligators. If you are quiet with the canoe gliding forward with a flashlight, baby alligators will not move. When you pick them up, they go limp and do not struggle. It was much fun. They arranged for me to go on a boat trip up the Rio Negro, the smaller of the two rivers into the Amazon, being only about five miles across.

I got food poisoning from a hamburger at a food stand near the hotel. Recovery took about three days. By this time the boat was gone on a tour, so my buddies found another boat for an eight day trip. I was the only client on the boat, a 50-foot double decker, with a captain, his helper, a cook, and an indigenous guide who spoke English. The cost was less than the hotel, and included meals, great meals.

RIO NEGRO

The boat was comfortable, and as I was the only client, they were at my beck and call. We did what I wanted and when I wanted. Actually, I was so easy on them, they got lazy. There was a hammock on the upper deck, the sun shone all the time, and the temperature was moderate. I got lazy too. But we did some awesome things.

The river was about five miles wide in spots, with a few islands, and quite placid at that time of the year. The name Rio Negro, or Black River, comes from the water colour. It is not black, but a very dark red that appears black. I got some awesome pictures of reflections in the red water.

They taught me how to fish for piranhas. We caught many, and although they are quite small, are very tasty. The cook cleaned a set of teeth for me which I still have. Now here's the surprising thing—after catching the piranhas, the boys went swimming in the same water. They didn't get eaten, so guess it was safe for me to swim also. It was scary at first, not something I thought was a good idea, or even possible.

They took me by canoe to some of the islands. The lack of wildlife was a disappointment. They said most of the birds had been taken for their feathers. I had seen these missing birds and animals in abundance in Costa Rica.

We stopped at indigenous villages. Being the only tourist was good, I could talk to them with my interpreter guide. They were very friendly, happy to have me there. They showed me some really interesting nature things in the jungle, their homes, how they made a living. I was pleasantly surprised, as I was aware of the really horrible treatment they had been given.

We went ashore at another village where there seemed to be a lot of activity. My guide explained that the mayor was voted out of office six months prior, but refused to give up his office. A young fellow ran past us, turned back and angrily shouted something in his native language. I asked my guide what he had said. He replied, "The Mayor is an asshole."

In another village they were feeding dolphins, fresh-water dolphins. This is the river that is dark red from the minerals in the soil which rubbed off on the dolphins, making them pink. Being the only Gringo around, I became Star of the Show. From my seat on the pier, the pink dolphins swam around my feet as I fed them. They were so gentle, I jumped in and swam around with them.

THE AMAZON RIVER TRIP

Time to leave Manaus. My buddies, aware of my adventurous spirit, suggested taking a boat back to the coast on the Amazon. This really was an adventure.

The boat had four levels of passengers, with many dozens of hammocks on each level, except the top level that we were on, the Penthouse level. It would be a four day trip. A bar was open for the "Penthouse" people. We had a great view from the top of the ship. Our penthouse suites were bunkbeds in a space about six feet wide by eight feet long. Every meal was provided and served on the lowest floor by the engines, which meant we would be paraded past the glaring eyes of hundreds of hammock people. It was uncomfortable, but the food was great. It was an experience like no other. We moved as a group, so not so bad.

The people on the palace level included a couple of Latino tourists, a couple of Brazilians, a couple from Montreal, and me. The Montreal couple were on a year leave of absence from their jobs, she a teacher and he a Canadian Customs supervisor. She was pregnant. They planned to get married when they got home. The others were pleasant people, good to be around.

The Montreal couple, nice people, she spoke French, he spoke French, English, Spanish and some Portuguese, while I spoke Spanish, English and some Portuguese. We had all languages covered with the other penthouse people as well. On one of the meal trips to the engine room, the French guy (can't remember their names) and his girlfriend saw a young woman with a baby right near the extreme noise of the engines. They enquired whether a penthouse suite was available for them. There was, and the three of us split the cost, and the child and her mother were removed from the noise. She was shy, but fit in with the rest of us. Of course everyone fussed over the baby.

The boat was not real speedy, so local villages along the shore sent fresh food in canoes to run alongside the boat, to sell to the passengers. Remember, only we, the penthousers, were provided with meals. One small boy in a big canoe filled with veggies was definitely not more than five years old.

The Amazon River level fluctuations are caused by seasonal snow melt off the Andes, and the dry and rainy seasons. The water level can change by 50 feet. We obviously were in a low-level situation, as there were houses up on the hillside built on stilts. More often, we would see floating houses with gardens and trees. They would have a boat alongside. For them, there was no worry about flooding. You had to be there.

We made one stop halfway out. There was a large agricultural mill there and a few shops. We stepped off the boat, amidst the evil glances of the hammock people. A New York woman from a small cruise ship paused to express her condolences to us for having to travel under such wretched conditions. Little did she know how much we were enjoying it.

BELEM

The boat dropped us off at Belem. At this point, I'm thinking the Amazon River is about 250 miles wide. We had passed Parrot Island, where large numbers of parrots were returning from feeding. I regret not spending time there, but you can't do everything. The Montreal couple regrettably moved on, while I stayed in Belem for a couple of days. There I met an interesting fella from the Bask area of Spain. He was in Brazil as a supplier of costumes for the Carnival parades.

SALVADOR DE BAHIA

He wanted to go to Bahia, as did I. We arrived in Bahia and said goodbye. Guess what happened next – I ran into the Montreal people. We happened to be staying at the same hostel. We hung out for a day and then ran into my Bask buddy. He had rented a car. We all got along so well, we spent most of the next week doing things together. Despite the language differences, we were able to translate every word said to everyone's understanding. We went to night clubs, got invited to private parties at peoples' homes, and got to know the fabulous city and some of the people. We went to a peninsula surrounded by a reef. The trapped water was bathtub warm and not refreshing at all.

Then a French woman wanted to come along. We said sure. She spoke all the languages, but when she discovered somebody spoke French, she would speak nothing else, destroying the chemistry the rest of us had built. So that broke us up, everybody headed out.

I flew back to Buenos Aires in Argentina.

ARGENTINA ONCE AGAIN

The bus terminal in Buenos Aires had more than 100 departure stations, spreading to all places in Argentina. Nearly 200 kiosks sold tickets for dozens of bus companies. I took a bus to Catamarca, a city inland enroute to Bolivia.

I joined a group of young people from Buenos Aires on a tour of the area. They were an actress, a singer, and two more free and happy people. It was so enjoyable, typical of the young people in Argentina. The mountains and hills were amazing in their variety of colours, with many shades of red, yellow and brown. The hills were jagged with crevices and caves. We found a place for the singer to play his guitar and sing love songs.

We toured a quiet and peaceful town called Maimara, with a good hostel and interesting museums. The trip was most enjoyable, and while my friends returned to Buenos Aires, I caught a bus to Salta, enroute to Potosí in Bolivia.

The bus arrived in Salta around 3 a.m. It happened that five of us were looking for rooms, and only one taxi available to get there. This was a most disgusting event. Besides me, there were a young Norwegian woman, a

German doctor, an Aussie guy, Pandy and a Czech woman, Moldie. The doctor had a medical practice in Germany where he owned a home as well as a vacation home in Algarve, Portugal. Pandy and Moldie were travelling until all their money was gone, so they stretched every penny.

The taxi driver gave us a price, to which the doctor countered with the idea that we had power and could negotiate because there were five of us. He wanted to save a grand total of about six cents for each of us. He threatened to have us take another taxi, of which there were none available. I told the taxi driver that I would take his ride. The Norwegian lady immediately said, "Me too." The other three piled in, mad as hell, and let us know how pathetic we were.

After about a 40 minute ride costing about 55 cents each, we arrived at a hotel. The manager was awakened. He gave us a very reasonable price, to which the good doctor responded with our solidarity in numbers, demanding lower prices. Again, the Norwegian lady and I both said we would take rooms. Angrily the others said okay, but wanted the best rooms. The manager said no, they go to the other two. And, your price is not the same. Really, the rooms were cheap anyway.

So, in retaliation, the doctor stole the sheets and Pandy and Moldie stole the pillows when they left in the morning.

As it happens, all of us except the Norwegian lady would be catching the same bus to Potosi in a couple of days. That would be another adventure.

Salta is a great place to visit, a city of about 600 K. There is a large presence of Indigenous people. The markets are fabulous, with native crafted goods, and fresh fruits, vegetables, and meat. The countryside is still covered in fantastic colours. There was a lot of furniture made from the cactus plants in the area. Cactus wood looks like expanded metal.

The hills heading toward the Andes were covered in greenery, being on the rainy side of the mountains. Precipitation only falls on the east side of the peaks. Cacti grew very big there, making it ideal for furniture. Like our "old growth forests", they were being over-harvested, so a law was passed that only dead ones could be cut down. As a result, a lot of cacti mysteriously caught fire, and then were cut down.

Still recovering from the taxi and hotel episodes, I was getting on the bus to Potosi. A young lady was collecting a tourist fee, the equivalent of one penny. Pandy and Moldie refused to pay, and knocked her over in the process of getting on the bus. I picked her up and paid their fees and mine, a total of three cents. She was crying. I got on the bus, and there was the doctor, still mad at me, carrying his sheets.

The bus was ancient, in bad shape, noisy, overcrowded. It would make a chicken bus look good. I sat down as the seat slid off its base. I got that fixed by placing the seat on my luggage. I was on an aisle seat, with kids laying on the floor.

The route was long and had lots of steep hills to climb. It was hot and the windows were open. The gentleman sitting beside me had luggage in the overhead that kept falling into the aisle, onto the kids laying there. I would pick it up and put it back in the overhead rack. The man behind me thought it was my bag, so he yelled at me every time it fell. There was no explaining.

It started raining on me, coming in the open window. I wondered how it could be raining, as it was hot and totally sunny. When we finally arrived in Potosi, I found the answer. There were two sheep tied to the roof.

Bolivia

It was a pleasure to be back in Bolivia again. The air in the high mountains was refreshing, as were the friendly people. Bolivia is one of the poorest countries in the world, and as I have said before, the poorer they are the happier they are. Their vast resources are severely underdeveloped. The inequality and the lack of human development has hindered progress. Deforestation and soil erosion are problems.

The *Nestlé* company, funded by the World Bank, was to clean up the water supply in Bolivia. They took over the wells that local people had gotten their water from for centuries, closed them and forced the locals to buy their bottled water. The people are very poor, forcing them to walk for miles to get water from other sources.

We managed to get to Potosi, got the potatoes and sheep off the roof, and left to find a hostel. The streets were steep and narrow, and the air was thin from the elevation, 13,400 feet, making me dizzy walking short distances. The city was founded in 1545 and grew to more than 200 K, one of the bigger cities in the world at that time. The Spanish had discovered silver. The mines there provided silver for Europe for centuries. A museum of interest is the mint that made coins for Europe. The mines were open for tours.

Thinking I would be free from the intolerable hassle from my buddies, I went to the mine area where they were selling tours. Who should I run into? The doctor and the other two scabs were trying to get bargain tour tickets. They were so happy to see me, as now they could negotiate an even better price. I declined and finally got rid of them. Looking at the mine entrance, the tour people said there were very narrow passages that I would need to squeeze through. I don't like claustrophobic conditions, so declined to go in. There was a story about a Japanese tourist saving money by not renting a headlamp. He took a wrong turn, falling down a shaft to his death.

SUCRE

I was on a better bus to Sucre, the capital of Bolivia. The government sits in La Paz, but Sucre is the capital city. The city is a World Heritage Site, population about 300 K, and is indeed a beautiful city. I found a room with air conditioning, television with about 40 channels, a kitchen, and room service, for a very small fee. It was a comfortable place to relax and recharge. The markets were exceptional, the restaurants great, and the weather perfect.

I happened upon a tour business. The tour agent was a French lady, who was also my tour guide for a trip in her car to an Indigenous village. It was very insightful and interesting. One part of the tour included seeing a cemetery, which I have always found interesting. Before we arrived there, she gave me the option of either going to the cemetery, or going to a by-the-hour hotel room for a while. Some of those headstones were really interesting!

Next stop was Santa Cruz de la Sierra, with about a million people at this time. I have a painting of the Piray River in the jungle, painted while I waited. An interesting city bylaw was that a man cannot be having sexual relations with a mother and her daughter at the same time. Maybe something happened in the past.

I didn't spend much time in Santa Cruz, as I had a call to return home on a family matter. The flights would take me from Santa Cruz to La Paz to Lima to home, just a few days before my scheduled return.

I got the last ticket from Santa Cruz, a seat by the toilet. One of the stewardesses was a beauty. As she walked from the back to the front of the plane, heads popped out from every aisle seat as she passed by. She knew she was good, changing into different clothes and shoes, three sets on the short flight to La Paz.

In La Paz, customs held everyone up, just not doing anything. When time to takeoff came near, no one was moving, so two of us went to the front where they stamped our passports. We ran to the gate where they were about to close the door on the plane. We made it, but there were only three passengers. It should have been at least half full.

That was the end of another most memorable trip to South America, an unforgettable six months.

DOMINICAN REPUBLIC

November of 2005

As the result of a motorcycle accident, I went to the DR to help recover. On the last day of May 2005, I had a minor accident that had major consequences. I was returning from the Island to Alberta, in a heavy downpour on my bike in Vancouver. Traffic had stopped, but I couldn't. I hydroplaned into a van just hard enough to fall off the bike. I had a hairline crack in my hip, not visible on X-ray but causing extreme pain. An MRI showed the crack. Blood clots gathered on both sides of my lungs, making surgery to insert a pin not possible. Unfortunately, that meant a long summer in a wheelchair. I was finally able to walk on crutches when the snow and ice made that difficult.

My plan was to build strength by walking in the warm sand of the Dominican Republic at a resort for two weeks. That worked so well, I returned to Alberta with a plan to leave for the winter. A couple of weeks later, I was on my way to a great adventure in Africa.

CHAPTER 10

Africa, Seven amazing months in eight amazing countries.

DECEMBER 2005 - JUNE 2006

Fortunately I was able to find some notes about my travels in Africa, providing some interesting detail that I had forgotten. Some times were scary, but most times were precious and exciting, most definitely memorable.

There are many different languages in Africa and they include Dutch, French, Portuguese, as well as the local native tongues. English is spoken in most places, so it was only a minor problem to communicate anywhere I went. Some languages use a clicking sound, not something I could have mastered. There seems to be a lack of words describing numbers, so you will hear a number in English coming out of a conversation in a native tongue.

Africa is a beautiful part of the world. Everywhere you go, the cities, the countryside, rivers, lakes, and mountains, beauty abounds. Unfortunately, all you ever hear about or see on TV is wild animals and starving people. It just is not that way.

South Africa

With stops in Lesotho and Swaziland

There are 11 official languages in the Republic of So Africa. Many people speak all 11. The most common are Afrikaans (Dutch-African mix), English, Xhosa, and Zulu. The cities look wealthy, but some adjoining townships are very poor. In one case, there was a BMW dealership right next to a township. There was 37 percent unemployment, much political corruption and false promises, and progress was slow. That leads to a lot of crime and is dangerous in some areas.

The food is great. They are meat-lovers, and are serious about their *braai* (a So African bbq) and their *poikies* (bbqing a large pot of layered meats and veggies, no stirring allowed). The lamb is delicious, like none I have tasted elsewhere. This is the only place I found the calamari to be not rubbery. Calamari steak is delicious, as are the ostrich steaks, crocodile, and varieties of antelope. Seafood is delicious. I was deep-sea fishing, caught a three foot shark and some red romans, very good on the braai. Restaurant food was good, but expensive.

The first words of warning upon arrival in Johannesburg were to stay away from the downtown area. One story has a tourist who thought downtown must be the safest, so that's where he went. Soon after he was standing on a street corner in his underwear. Having no clothes, luggage, money, passport or even chewing gum can be tough to recover from.

It was sunny and warm, perfect to do lots of walking, while recovering from a hip injury. A kiosk in the airport directed me to a safe comfortable room at a quiet hotel. I took some money, the Rand, from an ATM at the airport. The taxi was subsidized by the hotel.

I was the only customer at lunch in their restaurant one day. There was a cricket match on TV. The waiter spent the next hour or so explaining the rules of the game to me.

Cricket and soccer (sorry, football) are the two important sports in So Africa. The country was in the process of building stadiums to host the FIFA event, which many predicted to fail. Apartheid was still a huge problem, with many countries boycotting So Africa. While apartheid was formally declared gone, its effects were still very much in place. The games were played successfully a couple years later. You may recall those noisy horns.

Nelson Mandela's home and the jail he spent so much time in were the objects of an interesting tour. Another tour was to the parliament buildings. A museum showing apartheid history, explained the change to "Afrikaans" as the only language to be spoken and taught to the native students. That resulted in very little usable education for the coloured population, who did not speak Afrikaans.

Cape Town was the next destination. The 'Blue Line' ticket was $1,000, a luxury train that would have been interesting. But by plane, it was only $75. I took a hotel-subsidized taxi that should have cost about $15, but the driver had six inches and a 100 pounds on me, and he wanted $95. I paid.

Cape Town is a very different city, more open, safer, with more touristy things available. That was good for me, to take tours and do the things that made my walking stronger. I got into a hostel, or backpackers as they call it.

I took tours to see the penguin colony, wine country, Table Mountain, and a diamond-cutting shop. It was odd to see penguins in such hot weather. The wind was brutal, sandblasting the poor animals.

The wine country tour was much like the Okanogan region in BC, beautiful rolling hills with vineyards and wineries. Unfortunately, I'm allergic to some wines and never developed a taste for it.

The diamond-cutting shop business surprised me. I had never seen diamonds in the raw. Before cutting, they are very different from what I had imagined. It was interesting to watch so many people focused intensely on their cutting skills. The shop was in the wharf area, with many seafood restaurants.

A cable car ran to the top of the flat ledge known as Table Mountain. From that vantage point, different areas of the city as well as the penguin colony can be seen. It was very dry at that time, and always windy. A young British tourist threw a cigarette butt out the window, starting a fire. He took off driving, but someone got the licence number, and they stopped him at the bottom of the hill. Unfortunately, a British lady was hiking up the hill and got caught in the smoke and died as a result. The young fella was charged with manslaughter.

A horse race event was happening a few miles from Cape Town. Women dress up in formal wear, full dress and fancy hats, and are judged for prizes. A Canadian woman was one of the finalists. Everyone was having a blast. My one bet was on a trifecta which I won, but those horses were favourites. The payout was just enough to pay for the cab ride back to the city.

The backpackers where I stayed had a transportation arrangement with Baz Bus. Baz Bus is a hop-on hop-off shuttle from Cape Town to backpackers all along the coast to Mozambique, then inland to Swaziland, Pretoria, and Jo'burg. It was perfect, with a word to reception wherever you were, the bus would pick you up and deliver. When you are tired of one beach, on to the next, and they are all great. Rooms were inexpensive but comfortable. Dorms were really cheap, with multiple people to a room. I always tried to have a private room. I ran into the same people many times. In particular, there were two young ladies from Salt Spring Island and some Europeans from Germany.

Thousands of young people were in Africa volunteering, for the most part in health work, especially AIDS education. A lot of them were from North America. They liked to take time off to visit the beaches where we were. The tourists were mostly Germans, Brits, Swiss, and Canadians.

At one of the stops, Mossel Bay I believe, a very private set of cabins was perfect for a restful few days. A *braai*, or African barbeque, was heating up. A pleasant couple invited me to join them for some steaks they were cooking on the *braai*. They were great people, the food was great, but when I got back to the cabin my shoes were gone. Other items had also been taken, but I had just bought the perfect shoes, very expensive, very annoying. Someone had been seen skulking around earlier. He climbed through the window and escaped in his new shoes.

I have strange recollections of the next stop. British boys were getting drunk and trying to impress the girls. No one was impressed. The other thing was the hordes of geckos, with no cats to clean up in the room. They are cute, but poop everywhere.

I took a side trip to Oudtshoorn, famous for its caves. I stayed for a week for two reasons – visiting the caves, and the food. The caves were massive, endless, and beautiful with pillars and colours, an amazing variety of calcite deposits. The food was amazing, made me stay longer just to eat. They served the best lamb I have ever tasted, having to do with the nutrition in the grass they ate. Steaks from the local ostriches were the tastiest ever. The calamari was really tender, not rubbery as I have become accustomed. They had ostrich races, with not so small riders. I watched an ostrich hatch from the huge egg.

After a week I caught a ride with a rich girl from Toronto who had a rental car, back to George, and on to Knysna. The backpackers place had great service from comedic employees, like the 'Bitch Breakfast' for three rand. A large Monkey Park took up a day, while going deaf from the howler monkeys. I had to be careful with the tamed zebra, who would kick the hell out of you if he got a chance. A tamed elephant followed me around, and I fed a couple of tamed kudus, a species of antelope.

It was a short hop on the Baz Bus to Plettenburg Bay. Plett Bay was a most interesting stop. I learned about 'blood diamonds,' went fishing in the ocean, had a couple of evening *braai* meals, and spent time with the local people, and the guests and some volunteer workers at the backpackers.

The first backpackers in Plett Bay had a quiet owner who did not talk to me for a couple of days. Once he started, there was no stopping. He was spinning many yarns about many things, incredible stories. He spoke about how he and his partner were involved in shady schemes of phony technology being sold to different African countries, whose leaders were not savvy about new technology but hoped for a power grab. I wish I could remember more; they were unbelievable. He explained to me what blood diamonds were and the humongous amount floating around the continent.

One amazing story was of a family who had hired them to steal a big jar full of raw diamonds. When an inheritance is passed down, it all goes to the eldest son. The rest of the family members wanted their share. He went into his shop and showed me a small jar of raw diamonds, his payment for the job.

After about three days, I moved closer to the beach, to Amakaya B/P, owned and operated by a very pleasant and sociable young fella. His father dropped by and we started a conversation about his life in So Africa. He eventually related to when he and his partner were selling phony technology and stealing blood diamonds. I'll be darned, he was partners with last B/P owner! We became friends, and the stories continued. He took me fishing in his little boat in a rough sea. Despite being sea-sick, I caught a few fish which we cooked for dinner on the *braai*. The parties went on each evening, very pleasant meals, lots of booze, and great company. Time to go.

Baz Bus advertised by handing out condoms, with various sayings, actually quite amusing. I'm not sure what brought that on, but Baz Bus took me to Port Elizabeth. I met a couple of local gals who showed me around town the next day, and we attended a Garlic Festival. It was everything garlic.

I ran into a couple of guys, having a beer. We ended up at one of their homes. The next day was Sunday and everyone was going to church. I said I couldn't go as I only had short pants. This guy said okay, I'll go in shorts too.

The most amazing thing happened in church. That fella was a part of the ministry, and all the parishioners were looking to him for spiritual guidance. One man, about 50 years old, asked for his blessing. He placed his hand on the man's forehead for a few seconds and gave him a little push, and the guy fainted. I asked him what happened. He just tossed his head and said, "It happens all the time." It was weird.

Coffee Bay was the next stop. The backpackers had a lot of guests, a large space with multiple beds, and many cabins. My cabin was across water, accessible in low tide, or across a bridge at high tide. I hung out with a few people I knew from other stops on the Baz Bus route, like the Salt Spring girls and the German girls. Some locals were having a party, pretty wild, lots of booze and weed. Weed there is acclaimed to be some of the best in the world and readily available in the wild, so I was told.

We also took a tour to Jabulani. A group of kids about 12 years old had been taught to sing, to perform for the tourists for money rather than begging. American volunteers were doing that. We visited the countryside, smeared red mud on our faces (don't ask), and had a roasted lunch on a fire pit from seafood that kids were getting from the beach. It was good

We went to a local bar that was different. Beer was brought in to the pub in two-litre containers, then poured into a pail. The pail was passed around for everyone to have a few swigs, then more containers were brought in. No surprise, two very good-looking women were there, obviously getting the guys to buy beer for them, and lord knows what else.

I was able to be an observer at a polling station, where they were having a local election. Everything was very official and efficient. They were checking every detail. Now that I think about it, there was not a white person to be found anywhere.

The little country of Lesotho is near to the backpackers at Coffee Bay. It is a small country within the country of South Africa.

Lesotho

We went on tour to Lesotho. Interestingly, the husbands have a little round house with a thatched roof, same as the wife's house. If the wife is unhappy with him, he lives in his own house until she lets him back. That was the only time in Africa where I saw women get some respect.

We were invited into a home for lunch. There was a tub with a chicken in it, laying the daily egg. The floor was highly polished, made that way with cow dung, believe it or not. Lunch was very good, and the ladies were very kind and happy. It was part of the tour.

BACK TO SO AFRICA

Durban was the next stop on the Baz Bus tour. The city has a high percentage of Indian residents, as a result of slave labour being brought in from India. They are more than a million, or one third of the total population.

I was taken to a B & B, nice place, alone for a change. There was a cricket match in town that I wanted to see. The national team from Australia was there to play the national team from So Africa. Competition is fierce between these teams, as well as with India, Pakistan and a couple others.

It was a one-day test match, sold out a couple of weeks before game day. A scalper's ticket cost me $50 for a seat on the grass, where about half of the fans were. The game ran on from two to nine p.m. I sat next to a couple of surfers from Dublin, crazy guys. They liked me because I gave one of them my chair, as he had a bad leg and didn't have a seat. We became friends for life. He had a devastating morning that day, as his girlfriend in Belfast had crashed his new Mercedes and she didn't have a licence, so no insurance. The fans were crazy, drinking hard in the heat, then fighting with each other all night. Good looking girls were delivering beer, making big tips, and driving the men crazy. The Irish gave me a ride home after the game. Stopping for a red light, they laid out lines on the console and did the straw trick on some coke. I declined, as I have never done drugs and never will, but is always interesting to watch others. I arrived back to my room safely.

The match was not what I expected. The game itself was exciting, very competitive, but I seemed to be one of the few who noticed.

I left Durban, to other stops along the way, but I can't remember where. I recall some good memories, too numerous to mention, as well as being pretty sketchy.

The last stop along the coast was St Lucia, on the border with Mozambique. There was a large lagoon, half sea water and half fresh water as the tide went in or out. The sides were lined with trees that appeared half dead, but were actually that way from filtering salt. There were more than 500 Indigenous plant species along the lagoon, so I was told. The water was loaded with hundreds of hippos.

The hippos come out at night to forage, walking 10 or 20 miles a night. They are very dangerous, as many people have died trying to chase them out of their garden. We spotted one a couple of times walking through town. We also came across a baby python, cute like all babies are.

I was on a boat touring the lagoon with a couple of Dutch girls. We had to dodge the hippos on the water, there were so many of them. The girls asked if I thought it was okay for them to sunbathe topless. I agreed, for sure, but told them about the men being very dominant, and would take that as an open invitation for sex, so not a good idea. (Trust me, I saw the male dominance many times).

One disturbing meeting happened there. A man offered to take me on a hunting trip, any animal I wanted to shoot, lion, elephant, whatever animal I chose, I could shoot, have the head mounted and delivered to my home for $500. How sick is that??

Swaziland

Like Lesotho, Swaziland is completely enclosed within So Africa. The country has 12 states, requiring the president to have 12 wives, one representing each area. The appropriate wife would accompany him to that state whenever he would visit.

They put on a show for the many tourists, a troupe of ladies dancing. Normally, they would dance topless for the king and the local people, standard tradition, but they were in full dress for us. One of the ladies had her top fall off from the energetic body movements. She just continued to dance. Some idiot and his wife stood up pointing and laughing, shouting "Look at that!!" They had obviously not been accustomed to the anatomy of the human body, and had never been beyond the lawn mower section of the hardware store that he must have worked in.

BACK TO SO AFRICA

I caught the Baz Bus to Pretoria. I arrived on Friday to discover that I needed at least three free pages in my passport for every country I was going to, plus a page for each visa. I would run out of room, so needed a new passport. Monday morning, I went to the Canadian Embassy. They had been processing passports locally on a two or three day wait, but the rules effective that Monday were to require passports come from Ottawa. So instead of three days wait, I had a three week wait. I didn't mind, as there was great drama at the backpackers and in Pretoria.

The owners of the backpackers were exceptional, and we were soon friends. Six young fellas from India had come to play cricket. Their agenda for playing didn't happen, but they decided to stay for a few weeks anyway. A student from Ivory Coast was beautiful, driving all the guys crazy with her secret agenda. Two ladies from Cameroon, sisters, one married, were there long term. A young doctor, a local just graduated, gave me an insight on the AIDS situation, at its height at that time. A German medical student, Andreas, was doing research, inviting me along on his safaris to study the dung beetle for possible medical properties for a cure for cancer.

Another fella ran a safari business, and was a frequent visitor to the place. He complained a lot about how he was treated in the US. They wouldn't let him on his flight, then guarded him until they put him on the flight they wanted him on, all this because he was a citizen of the apartheid country. I went on Safari with him half a dozen times with Andreas to the Pilanesberg area. Dung beetles are cool.

I don't remember names, but I remember the crazy activities and the crazy people like it was yesterday. Everyone got up in the morning and headed to the kitchen, looking for what trouble they could cause on that day. Everyone had way too much time on their hands. It was so much fun following the drama. Other guests came and went, adding strings to the web of mystery, while the long-termers suspiciously guarded their territory, whoever that might be at the time.

The Doctor told me about Aids in So Africa. Forty percent of the men in the military were HIV positive. The Vice-President of So Africa was caught with a hooker. He denied it, but there were many witnesses. Then it was uncovered that she had AIDS. He said it was okay because he had a shower right after. This was a typical attitude, as the government had refused international help, saying Aids was a Western hoax trying to destroy them.

A group of us went out to a bar one evening. We sat outside at a dimly-lit table, having some drinks. My bill arrived, with light printing. I paid with Visa. About five days later, I looked at the receipt. The server had added a one in front, changing it from 110 Rand to 1110 Rand. Too late, cost me 1000 Rand. Silly me!!

On the way home, a lady from Cameroon and I stopped at a nightclub. As soon as we entered, several whiteys gathered around, telling me to get that black @#*& out of there. We left. Down the street, a house with several black people yelled a warning to me to keep away from their women.

The only really scary time was in Pretoria, when I was escorting the lady from Ivory Coast to the Plaza. She could not reach a taxi by phone, and was uncomfortable walking alone at night. As we were walking in the middle of the street in a higher class part of the city, we heard grunting noises behind us. Upon turning, a five-foot machete was aimed at my head. My friend backed up and screamed, catching the attacker by surprise. I joined in with my best karate yell, and he bolted with his buddy. Within seconds, residents flew out of their homes to give them chase. When I told the owner of the backpackers I was staying at, he reached to his boot and flashed a pistol in my face, telling me that if it happened to him, that kid would be dead.

They were a couple of coloured kids, about 15 years old. The war wages on, and apartheid was not done and gone, not forgotten nor forgiven.

This was happening in Pretoria, in a high-end neighbourhood, as safe as you will find. It was definitely unsafe to mix colours, from both sides of the spectrum. Apparently, this same lady was walking with a white fella when a truck with two whites stopped to beat up the guy, putting him in the hospital.

I took a trip to the Bakubung Bush Lodge, near Pilanesberg. As usual, the safaris were exceptional, the staff wonderful. On one of the safaris out of the Lodge, several of us were in the back of a truck. An elephant approached and stuck its trunk very close to me as I backed away. The guide stood by with a loaded rifle in case of trouble. Many of the trees there have these long hard sharp needles, one of which cut my shirt sleeve and a slight cut to my arm as we drove by. The elephants wrap their trunks around these thorny branches, break them off and eat them.

From there, Sun City is about ten kilometres away. Sun City was built because gambling was allowed there, the same as the way Las Vegas started. One of the beautiful hotels there had a beach with a wave machine, a professional class golf course, and everything high end. I asked at the desk how much the rooms were. Prices ranged from US$3,500 for a room to $12,500 for a suite, per night. Then he said "But I'm sorry, we are all booked up". I said "Damn, I wanted to stay for a week". An LPGA televised golf tournament was on at the time.

One amazing plant, found in So Africa and Zimbabwe, was the Baobab tree. It has a huge trunk, hollow inside, with small branches on top. The trunk holds water gathered up during the rainy season to survive during the long drought periods every year. Some animals are dependent on that water, as well as some people. Another plant, the sausage tree, stands alone in great plains of grasses. The fruit resembles large sausages in shape, and is the source of nutrition for a multitude of animals.

My new passport was in finally after a couple of weeks wait. That afternoon I was on my way to Harare.

Zimbabwe

The flight from Pretoria to Harare, the Capital of Zimbabwe, was uneventful except for the peacock-haired student I sat beside. When asked if he knew of a good place to stay, he said his father had a friend with cabins for rent. His father drove me there. They had been removed from their livelihood by the government, and were friends of another family who also lost their farm, my new landlord.

The name Zimbabwe can be translated to 'Houses of Stone.'. A 35 foot high wall built of granite and no mortar, known as the 'Great Zimbabwe,' is believed to have been surrounding a royal palace.

At this time, the political situation was extremely bad. Five years prior to this, the Robert Mugabe government had confiscated all land farmed by white people and gave it to black people. The economy collapsed, but most of the people were very happy to get rid of the whites, especially the ones who were given the farms. This model of behaviour was much admired in Malawi, and became popular in Zambia.

There were many groups of young people who spent their days dancing and singing in the streets, wearing shirts with severe anti-white slogans. I missed many camera shots for fear of being taken down, not even making eye contact. After the whites were removed from their farms, the land was given to black families. Typically, they would do the harvest, mostly tobacco with some cotton, sell the goods and that would be the end of the farming. A lot of the money would be used to buy cars, perhaps a house in Harare, and party-time.

Their currency was being inflated at a rate of 1,800 percent per year. We went to a restaurant in a hotel and paid for breakfast with notes from a bag, larger than a grocery bag. The next day we needed a bigger bag. The export of agricultural crops had fallen to next to zero. With the loss of crops to export, there was no money for imports, so gasoline was hardly available. Once a week a truckload of gasoline would come in to a gas station near Harare, while cars lined up for days, for miles, to get a couple of gallons. Employment was at a rate of about 10 percent, while they walked many miles to work, as buses couldn't run without fuel, and no fuel for cars.

A market along the main highway, miles long, provided an income and a home for many people. Mugabe decided the market was an eyesore, so had ordered it removed. A bulldozer removed the entire market, leaving the people homeless and without a way to make a living. Lots of people were unhappy with Mugabe, but their beliefs were that the leader is always right, and he should remain their leader until he decides to go.

Zimbabwe used to be Southern Rhodesia with the capital Salisbury, now called Harare. The government under Mugabe was wanting to take the tourist to the cleaners, especially if white. Costs were many times what the prices were for a national. Example, to see the Zimbabwe Ruins, it cost me US$21, for a national, about 80 cents. Meikles Hotel, one of the best in the world, was hurting so much because of no tourism and offered me a room for US$250 a night, for nationals, $75. It cost me US$85 for a visa to enter the country one time. As a result, there was no tourism, employment was about 10 percent, and inflation 1800 percent a year. The zim dollar used to be six to one US dollar. It was now 200,000 to one US dollar, and sliding fast.

Harare is home to some amazing architecture. The Eastgate Centre is an ultra-modern building, with first-class design for natural cooling. Mugabe's palaces are magnificent, while his subjects live in squalor. I wanted to take a lot more pictures, but it was too dangerous if any local was in the photo.

I moved into one of the cabins I had been taken to. The owner, Bob, was a prince of a gentleman. I was incredibly fortunate to have been directed his way. He did everything for me, including driving me all around the country, showing me things otherwise not available, as there was next to nothing for means of transportation. The countryside was beautiful, the climate perfect, and there was very little traffic. The older local people were very kind and honest. Bob had lost his wallet with lots of cash in it. He called where he thought he might have lost it. We drove back there where it was recovered with all the cash in it.

Bob was about 22 when the government took his family's tobacco farm from them. He drove me to the farm they lost. The farm workers had a village of about 300 black families, a clinic with a doctor, and a school. The new black owners got the harvest and sold it. The village went to ruin, no one remained, as no farm work was done after that harvest.

When the government troops came to take over the farm, they tried to break down the big gate. Bob's sister was home alone, and not knowing what was happening, fired a shot in the air to scare off whoever was breaking down the gate. They did break the gate, arrested his sister and charged her with attempted murder. Only by paying out a lot of money were they able to get her out of that mess. The place was a disaster. It was incredible to imagine what they went through, and yet they still wanted to live there. Some were invited to set up farms in Zambia, which in the end did not work out so well either.

Bob gave me an incorrect email address, so was unable to contact him again. If you ever read this Bob, I am forever indebted to you for your incredible kindness. I understand why you love your beautiful country, Southern Rhodesia as it was called.

Kenya

Giraffes were being chased off the runway as we landed in Nairobi. Kenya was different. It appeared so wealthy after being in Zimbabwe.

The people were very nice. I felt like a grain of salt in a pepper shaker, as only about one percent of Kenyans are white. They mainly spoke Swahili and English. There are 72 tribes, some Muslim, and about 80 percent Christian. Most people were religious. I had breakfast with a black Anglican bishop one morning.

I went on many safaris, not far to go with so many animals in the parks, and most still roaming free. We saw the 'Big Five,' named so because they are the most dangerous animals in the world to hunt. They will double back and hunt you if you go after them. The club includes the lion, leopard, rhino, elephant, and Cape buffalo. My buddy from Denmark expanded it to six, to include the African Woman.

The Maasai tribe, usually dressed in bright red clothing, are a wealthy people, famous for Olympic marathon runners. They are known to go for a spontaneous walk to somewhere 50 or 100 miles away. They owned most of the land around Nairobi which they sold to the city including the airport. They have a lot of cattle, and a lot of wives. It costs 10 cows to buy a wife. It was surprising to see white women in their homes, but apparently, they were lined up waiting for a chance to be chosen. They live in the typical round homes with a thatched roof, only bigger—after all, they are wealthy.

The Maasai lands had just gone through a drought while I was there. They were advised to sell off part of their herds, but that didn't fit the Maasai plan, so they kept them all. Half of their cattle died of starvation. To replenish their herds, they went across the border into Ethiopia and raided their herds to replace their losses. This caused a political crisis between the two countries. The Kenyan government loaded a plane with about 20 officials for a meeting in Ethiopia to divert a political disaster. The plane crashed, for which the President ordered two days of mourning for the whole country. Instead the people stayed home from work for two weeks.

There was some chaos at this time, but I hunkered down at a hotel. The bed was inside mosquito netting, but the little bug that carries malaria could get through. I woke up in the night to find my wrists and feet had been bitten badly. Thinking it was bed-bugs, I informed the desk. They informed me that it was mosquitoes. Apparently, more people were dying from Malaria than from AIDS. Fortunately, the doctor I had met in Durban had given me a safe prescription for malaria, a one-a-week pill. I had heard about the side effects of malaria pills, and had decided to use mosquito spray. Well, that would not have worked. See? Everything has a way of working out. I could have easily caught malaria.

I was in a higher-class restaurant, trying to get the attention of a waiter. While trying not to be rude, I was frustrated, wondering what I was doing wrong. A neighbouring table took note of this and helped me out. He very quietly said "psst," and the waiter across the room immediately turned and headed straight for his table. Who could know that??

One strange thing going on in Nairobi is for women to get foreign men to put them up in a place to live for three or four months for favours, while saving a place for the men to stay during that time when they come to visit Kenya. When you get three or four men lined up, a woman would be set up for the year. So when I went to a bar alone for a beer, it was like moths to a light. I didn't understand the commotion at first.

A grab-and-run thief was chased down on the street, caught and beaten to death. They returned the purse to the owner. The story was front page news and became the popular thing to do. Another story ran about a thief hollering for the police to come and rescue him from getting beaten up on the street. Maybe it wasn't right, but was very effective. I felt safe there.

A restaurant in Nairobi, called The Carnivore Restaurant, serves barbequed meat from every animal in Africa. Not knowing what they were up to at the time, a couple of ladies invited me. I ate crocodile, zebra, kudu, different kinds of antelope, buffalo, you name it they had it. It was cooked on skewers over a fire, upright and to a point in the middle. They served nonstop, until you threw a supplied little white umbrella onto your plate.

Just out of Nairobi, there is a large market selling chickens, grains, veggies, ornaments, everything imaginable. It is located by the Great Rift Valley. The valley was created by movement of the tectonic plates 20 million years ago, ripping apart the earth's crust creating a massive depression with very steep sides, for about 4,000 miles. The market is just out of Nairobi, on the edge of the cliff.

It was time to go on a tour out of Nairobi, to Samburu. We stayed in tents one night, in Maasai country. The meals were what the native people were eating, very different, very tasty. Hot water for a shower was from a tank outside heated with a woodpile burning under it. We went to a Maasai village, where we were invited into a home. This is where I saw the white wives.

They don't bury their dead, instead they have a ceremony to place the body for hyenas to dispose of. If the body is that of a more important person, they place fresh beef on the body to encourage quicker eating for the hyenas.

We had the pleasure of seeing new and different animals, and many recognizable ones. It was a big safari every day, with giraffes, lions, leopards, little dik-diks, zebras, elephants, hyenas, warthogs, and many types of antelope, snakes, rhinos, and many birds. I never did see a meerkat or an aardvark.

There was a crazy cop from Denmark on the trip. He and a couple of Danish women had burnt their faces climbing Mount Kenya, which is on the equator, to the snowy peak, freezing their noses. He had been travelling for a couple of years. His story was that some members of his division were doing things that he didn't agree with, escalating to a court situation. They had put him on paid leave so that he would not testify. I believed him, good guy. He and I were in a small town pub having a beer, when two ladies approached us to play pool with them. Their offer was "If you win, we buy you a beer. If we win, you have to f**k us." Pretty scary with all the AIDS floating around. Well, on with the tour.

Many crocodiles were waiting at the Mara River crossing for the migration of a couple million wildebeests, zebras, and other animals. It is on their way to better pastures in the south. The animals follow the rainfall to the Maasai Mara in Kenya, and to the Serengeti in Tanzania. The crocs can go for seven months without food, and appeared hungry when they saw us. There were no migrating animals in the area at that time.

Back in Nairobi, a couple of days were spent wandering the streets and shops, observing life in general. A business was offering a tour to a rainforest and butterfly garden. Butterfly you say?? Believe it or not, the place was amazing. We rode a Jeep-like vehicle on a very rough road for several hours to get there.

I was the only person on the tour. This is where I met my guide, Shani, a very intelligent lady, happy and full of life, a pleasure to be with. We explored the rainforest, where we got lost. It was going to rain; that was obvious. Shani finally recognized where we were. If it had been me alone, I would still be wandering around, just me and the monkeys. When we got to the clearing, it started raining, and we both got drenched by the time we reached the building 50 feet away.

The rainforest was dense. We were unable to see through the canopy in places, with lots of birds and animals, many monkeys very high up in the tall trees. You could be lost ten feet from the clearing.

We went to a nearby village by bicycle taxi, very uncomfortable but we got there. I loved the avocado trees in the wild, fruit ripe for picking. Men were gathered in groups, cigars and whisky, talking and laughing, waiting for their wives to have lunch ready. The wives were arriving one by one from a 10 kilometre walk to pick up sticks for firewood, carrying the bundle on their head, to be used to make lunch for their husbands. Shani explained that if lunch was late, or he didn't like it, the thing to do was to give her a beating.

Everyone had a cell phone. They had no power, but everyone had a cell phone. A small shack with a source of power had about 50 phones on the wall being charged. They had similar shops to charge phones in South America.

Back in Nairobi again, I planned to go to Tanzania, and on to Zanzibar. I asked Shani to come with me. Having a guide was very convenient, and maybe kept me out of trouble. We got on a bus heading south. We had to stop to allow a herd of giraffes to cross the road. I seemed to be the only person to be amused by this.

Shani told me a story about her uncle who had come to stay with her mother. He was dying of AIDS and needed care. He had six wives, who apparently didn't want to look after him. As the story goes, sex for six was not enough, so he strayed into the neighbourhood for more, caught AIDS and gave it to his wives. Of course, as he could not satisfy six wives, they also strayed into the neighbourhood, passing on the gift that keeps on giving.

The 'many wives' thing is easy to explain. The wives are happy, they keep each other company and go to work. The husband stays at home, he doesn't have to work, and can only annoy one woman at a time.

Tanzania

This country was the opposite of Kenya, with 80 percent Muslim population. It was hot, about 35 degrees C, very humid in Dar, cooler at night in

Arusha at higher altitude, near Mt Kilimanjaro, highest mountain in Africa at about 5,100 metres.

Arusha was the first stop in Tanzania. It appeared to be a modern city, with high rise buildings, modern apartment blocks, clean streets and well-dressed people. The Rotary Club of Arusha had a 'water bore hole' project that was co-sponsored by the Rotary Club of Vancouver, Canada.

We travelled around the country for a couple of days. It was interesting to see the world around me through someone else's eyes. We arrived in Dar es Salaam. Even with a guide, there was an uneasy feeling where I did not really feel safe.

A buddy that I met later, told me what happened to him in Dar es Salaam. He caught a taxi for the bus station. It went a block and stopped, while two guys got in the back seat, one on each side of him. They asked for his wallet and drove him to an ATM to get more money. He told them that he was already limited out for the day and couldn't get more. They believed him, and gave him a ride to the bus station. He told them that he couldn't buy a bus ticket without money, so they gave him some. Then he asked for money so he could eat, they gave him some more. He said he needed money for a place to stay. They said no, he would be on the bus all night. He said that his wallet would be of no use to them, so they gave it back to him with the credit cards and his driver's license. They drove away, everybody happy.

We got duped buying passes for a ride on a fast ferry to Zanzibar. We were on a vegetable run that took forever. I was allowed to be in a special room that was air conditioned, but Shani was told to stay out because she was the wrong colour. That error was corrected promptly when they saw I had overpaid for both tickets.

Zanzibar

Zanzibar, which used to be named the Spice Islands, had a great beach with a resort hotel, restaurant and a bar. The main industry is tourism. Interesting things happened there with dolphins and urchins, doctors and customs officials.

I went for a swim in the sea, only to step on something painful. I limped back to shore, finding some sharp needles in the bottom of my foot. The guy from reception happened by, and one look told him that I had stepped on an urchin. He said "I'll get the doctor." A minute later this young fella appeared, looked at it, disappeared and returned with some coal oil, or kerosene. He rubbed the coal oil on it, applied milk from a papaya, wrapped my foot in a cloth, then put my foot in his mouth and chewed on it. I don't know how that did anything, but it never ever hurt again. My first thought was to urinate on it, which is the treatment in the West Indies. Am glad I waited, apparently that treatment doesn't work there.

A couple hours later while sitting at the bar enjoying a beer, guess who shows up. "The Doctor must be paid!!" he said, and asked for about a dollar. I paid him, bought him a beer, and pleasant conversation ensued.

One day on the beach, dead dolphins appeared, about 500 of them. The locals were busy burying them in the sand. Dolphins are a big part of the tourist scene, so they needed to be disposed of quickly. They were not local dolphins, but a pod passing through. It was believed that a combination of low tide and heavy rains had trapped them inside a pool blocked by the reef. The water had been desalinated to the point of being unsuitable for them to live.

One of the employees of the resort took a liking to my friend, with staring and groping on her body. I stopped him, while other employees there tried to explain to him that it wasn't right to do that. He seemed confused.

An artist on the Island painted a picture of a Maasai warrior for me, a great painting, rolled up and in a sleeve. When I went through customs back to Tanzania, the agent took it out to look at. He then folded it several times and threw it into my bag. Of course the fresh paint couldn't handle that treatment, and it had to be discarded. …not impressed.

The Spice Islands had been a major port for buying and selling slaves for centuries. We went to where the holding cells and auctioning stations were still intact.

Malawi

We arrived in Malawi by bus from Dar es Salaam. We stayed in the capital city of Lilongwe, touring around the city of nearly a million people for a couple of days. Shani had an interview in Nairobi, so I got a flight for her and said goodbye. She got the job with a communications company in Spain, where she still is today.

Politically, Malawi had developed a mindset similar to Zimbabwe, influenced by Robert Mugabe. It wasn't much of a problem though, as there was no farming by foreigners, and not much happening for tourists. I was the only white person there, but was treated well, with the same respect that I provided to them.

Although my foot did not have any pain, I had visions of those urchin spikes going to my brain. A medical clinic beside the hotel could help. The doctor couldn't remove any of them, even after I suggested he use a light and a magnifying lens. However, one of the nurses wanted to see me after her work time. She was bright, educated, and pretty. We had dinner and good conversation.

As a note, an English newspaper had a story about the cost of education in Malawi. About half of the budget was used to pay for funerals of teachers dying from AIDS.

I took a taxi to a resort at Malawi Lake. Two young fellas drove me there in a crew cab half ton. In the middle of nowhere, they stopped and three more guys got in. The driver said, "I made a mistake, the price isn't 50, it's really 500." A little trick I learned along the way, is that if you are madder than they are, they will let it go. This wasn't my first rodeo. They don't really want to have to deal with a screaming lunatic. So I told him, "Yes, you did make a mistake. You three in the back, get out. You, driver, get me there right now or you don't get paid." Guy in the back said that was enough and that he wanted to get out. The driver scurried to the resort where I paid him 25 for which he thanked me, then apologized and rode away. Most times when I got into a taxi they tried to get more than they were entitled to. No one got more, and a couple didn't get paid. But again, most of the people were very nice to me.

Thinking of the lady in Thailand who died from a spider bite in her shoe, I had always been checking my shoes before wearing them. My shoes were left on the deck overnight at Malawi Lake. When I gave one a whack, a bat flew out. Imagine the bite I could have gotten.

I caught a ride back to Lilongwe with some Jesuit priests, who did not try to rob me.

Somewhere in Africa, a large gathering of people was assembled in the street. I believe it was in Malawi. What I clearly remember is how uncomfortable I was with the icy stares I got from some of the people. It was enough to send me quickly to safety.

I got on a minibus in Lilongwe headed for Zambia. It stopped every other street and waited for passengers. They had put me in the front seat. A couple of little boys spotted me. It became obvious that they had never seen a white person before. When the bus moved, the kids ran to the next stop and resumed staring at me. Each stop gathered more kids, until about 20 boys and girls stood there soberly staring at me, until I winked at a little girl. They nervously giggled a bit, but the next wink got them laughing uproariously. I laughed too. The adults were gathering also, looking at the kids and enjoying the situation, as did I.

Zambia

Livingstone is a tourist town in southern Zambia, near Victoria Falls. I found a really nice hostel there, staying a couple of days. The Falls were excellent, good to see, but when I returned the next day, they were still the same. If you wished to cross the bridge into Zimbabwe to see a different side of the falls, a visa had to be purchased for about CDN$125 at that time.

I talked to a helicopter pilot in the bar, who used to be a pilot with So African Airline, and flew in the air force prior to that. He gave heli tours of the falls to tourists. One of his stories was of the requirement to hire coloured people. One stewardess was not well, so her sister came in her place, and no one noticed. They had her empty the garbage can from the cockpit. They were about leave the tarmac to take off when a door light came on. Investigating the problem, they found she had opened the back door of the plane and dumped the garbage on the tarmac.

The Zambian government decided to offer land to the white farmers who were kicked out of Zimbabwe. They felt it was an opportunity to increase the country's wealth by increasing agricultural exports, so they offered big loans to get them set up. All was well until the government cut the value of their currency in half, but left the loans at the same value. In reality, they were doubling the debt. Once again, farmers were losing their shirts as the banks reclaimed the land for their debts. As in Malawi, Zambia has its own problems, heading the same direction as Zimbabwe. They believed that Robert Mugabe was a great hero for getting rid of the whities (and their economy).

Namibia

I left Victoria Falls and went on a camping trip into the oldest desert and one of the driest in the world, the Namib Desert. The irony of it all, we were camping in three days of rain, the first of any real moisture in 35 years. We camped not too far from a lake, fed from underground springs. Some shrubbery grew on the dunes there, while further away no vegetation existed.

We were in an area called Sossusvlei, trekking up giant dunes with a view of more giant dunes. Some big trees grew there, the roots going down hundreds of feet to underground rivers. We were shown plants with broad leaves, over 2,000 years old. One was dying as a result of a tourist setting fire to it to see if it would burn. A camping spot was where some young people had a fire to keep warm at night, ignoring signs all around that this plant was poisonous to burn. All four of them were found dead the next day. There was very little vegetation as a result of 35 years without rain, and now here it was, raining for three days.

We had to pair up in the tents. I shared a tent with a fella who worked in Ft McMurray until he had enough money to travel, then would go until he was broke. Then he would return to his camper trailer and his work as an electrician in the oil sands plants. He was the unfortunate dude who got robbed in Dar es Salaam. We travelled to the same hostel in the capital city of Windhoek.

Namibia was a German colony, obvious when a truck rolled by with sauerkraut advertising on it. Most of the businesses were German, with many Germans living there. The restaurant food was different from the previous countries, but delicious as always. The hostel was gated and guarded, but not hard to get into. We both made lots of friends during our stay of about 10 days. My buddy left to head home, out of money, never to be heard from again. Once again, the people were interesting and gracious, making the stay memorable.

The countryside had many outcroppings with semi-precious gems, diamond mines and uranium mines. I didn't find any gems.

I took a bus to Swakopmund, on the coast. I stayed at a hostel that was fancier than in Windhoek, but not as much fun. I was in Swakopmund at the same time that Brad and Angelina were there to have their "Brangelina" baby. Coincidence?? I think not. Guess they didn't know how to contact me.

I love the desert. It was solid sand dune from Windhoek to Swakopmund on the seashore. Tours available to the desert were in high demand by the locals, as none of them had ever seen the flora, only there 35 years prior. It was new to them, and fascinating to me. It had rained there as well, and when rain comes seeds sprout, flower, and go to seed in an incredibly short time, maybe two or three weeks. The seeds go to the ground and wait for the next rain to fall.

A two and a half hour flight on a small plane, a Cessna 210, toured us around the desert, with some amazing sights of dunes and shipwrecks.

It was inevitable, time to go home. I went to the same backpackers in Pretoria to catch my flight home from the Jo'burg airport. The drama hadn't changed. The Indian cricket players were still there, the girls from the other countries had set up roots there, and the owners still having fun.

I was not ready to leave Africa. I wanted more food like—crocodile steak with monkey gland sauce, Kudu steak with blue cheese sauce, ostrich steak with stuffed figs, German sausage, lamb chops, seafood like calamari steak. Everything comes in steaks. I wanted more safaris.

I took home a bottle of cream liqueur made from the nuts of a particular tree. The fermented nuts would fall off of the tree, getting the animals drunk as they ate them. I took great care, risking it breaking in my luggage. I got it home safely. The next day I went to the liquor store, only to find the exact same brand and bottle of liqueur I had risked to get home.

While in Africa, many things stood out for me. The beaches are amazing. The dominance of the men over the female population was disturbing; nobody should be bullied like that. The kids are beautiful (as always), and the adults generally very kind. Thousands of enthusiastic volunteers from North America and Europe are making a difference with the lives of the African people. Amazing animals and landscapes were everywhere, seen from at least a dozen awesome safaris. The time in Africa had to be especially memorable for me to be able to retrieve from memory so many events and people.

Canada and United States

VARIOUS TRIPS IN VARIOUS YEARS

I had made a couple of car trips in my teen years to California, memorable because I had never been anywhere. We were at Disneyland when there were not many rides. Haight and Ashbury was the scene of hippies and the psychedelic vans in San Francisco, and topless barmaids. Las Vegas had few casinos on the Strip, the Flamingo where we stayed, Caesars Palace, and a couple of others.

Since that time, work, marriage and having kids got in the way of travel. I remained bound to home until after divorce recovery. Then the trips in Canada and to the USA became good experiences between international romps. I have been to every province in Canada except Newfoundland and Nunavut, and to a lot of States in the US. North America is as interesting to see as anywhere in the world, maybe the culture change is not as great.

Having returned from Africa and recovered from the bike accident, I immediately headed to a motorcycle shop to buy another. All they had left were white bikes. No way I would ride a white bike. On the way to another dealership, thoughts in my head were that I had my fun, and it was time to leave the game. My last bike was a Gold Wing 1800. I wanted the same, but they are very heavy and high centred, difficult for me to hold up if I am off-balance. Good thinking; that was the end of my biking career.

Yukon and Alaska

July 2006 for 15 days

    I made the trip to the Goldrush in a car, following a friend from Alberta and his friends on their bikes. I hated not being on a bike, but that was the price. It was relaxing and comfortable. All roads were paved, but we ran into some loose gravel on the pavement. One of the boys wiped out. He immediately jumped up, pulled his bike up and started it, racing his way down the highway. As one in the group described it, "He took off like a raped ape." We met other people up the road. The injured rider was laughing and drinking away the pain, telling us, "No problem." The next morning, he called someone to pick him up to return to Peace River. He was not able to go to work for several months. That relieved some of my pain for having to drive a car instead of a bike.

    The scenery for the whole trip was amazing, pristine waters and jagged mountains. Remnants of the gold rush days were still there, as tourists panned for gold and still finding traces. Animals were everywhere, buffalo, sheep, goats, foxes red and white, moose, deer, and elk. In Whitehorse, a dam for power production had fish ladders for the salmon to go upstream.

    Dawson City was well setup for tourism. Diamond Tooth Gertie's saloon served the ice-worm cocktail. The history of the gold rush was well displayed.

    The roads were paved, and in good condition, until the border into the US, Alaska. There were holes you could lose a bike in. The pavement was made for California, not winter weather. The customs agent had a severe southern accent, hardly understandable. Unfortunately, there was one egg in a cooler in the trunk, for which he put a hand on his gun. Eggs are not to be transported across the border.

    From Skagway in Alaska I took a small ferry to Juneau. Whales were playing and salmon jumping in the water. Cruise ships were anchored and the town was filled with tourists.

    The only snag was in the Fort Nelson area, where no rooms were available due to the influx of workers for oilfield plant shut-downs for maintenance. It was a good trip.

San Francisco

November 2008

We discovered the advantage of flying out of secondary airports, which have much lower fees for the airlines, and therefore much lower fares. A friend and I drove from Kelowna to Bellingham, Washington, and flew to San Francisco for $48 return each.

We stayed overnight in Bellingham, attending a performance by a military band.

From the airport in San Francisco, we were picked up by her daughter's husband, who drove us through a tunnel that I didn't know existed, to a city on the mainland. We stayed at my friend's daughter's home, on an acreage with a vineyard. It was enjoyable, except I had a beer with the husband two days in a row, so I must be an alcoholic. She insisted that I join AA immediately. She wanted her son-in-law to go to meetings also.

Houston

April 2010

Gary and I drove in his car to Houston, Texas, for a curling bonspiel. We golfed at courses along the way, down and back, and a few days for curling in Houston. We were gone for 30 days. The golf courses were open, but pretty quiet with much reduced fees, so we could take our time and practice a lot. That didn't help my game, but was fun.

On the way down, a service station attendant saw the license plate from Alberta, shook his head and asked if we had heard of airplanes. I replied "We were going to fly, but the kids took the plane to Europe this week." He had no idea where Alberta was, or Canada for that matter.

We visited a town in Arizona called Oatman, which had a history that Gary's ancestors were a part of. The old mining town is famous for the "Oatman Massacre" of 1851, where the Oatman family of nine was killed by a band of Indians, except for two girls who were captured. A boy of 14 years was left for dead, but recovered and walked to the village.

Oatman was a mining town. A museum has a mineshaft and mining equipment. They say that Clark Gable and Carole Lombard spent their honeymoon there. Clark used to go there to play poker with the miners.

The cactus flowers were in full bloom as we travelled through the desert. If you have not experienced that, put it on your 'must see' list.

We followed the Rio Grande to the town of Tombstone, famous for the gunfight at the OK Corral and the Boot Hill gravestones. One read, 'Here lies George Johnson. Hanged by mistake, 1882. He was right, we was wrong. But we strung him up. And now he's gone.' We had lunch at Big Nose Kate's Saloon and Casino, which was in original condition.

Next town was Laredo, Texas, also on the Rio Grande at a border crossing with Mexico. It is a cowboy town where a multitude of western movies have been made. We pulled into a bar to have a drink with the local people. They were more than happy to greet us, big smiles with very few teeth. It seemed odd when another man came in with a big smile and had a full set of beautiful white teeth. They mutually expressed their opposition to the government, saying they opposed health care, and if the government wanted their guns, they would be in a gunfight.

On to Houston, where we stayed at Bill and Sharlene's place, Gary's friends, a small farm just out of town. Bill had worked in the oil patch in Alberta before being transferred to the US.

After watching the Winter Olympics in Vancouver, Americans were going crazy wanting to play the game of curling. There were enormous waiting lists to learn how to play the game. Their facilities were nowhere near up to par for decent ice to our standards. They used a Zamboni to prepare the ice surface between games. The spectators passionately discussed how they were calling the wrong shots and strategy.

They had set up a bonspiel, and Bill had entered a team, including Gary. I was there to bonspiel, never missing a shot. All bonspiels are a great time, and everyone got the greatest enjoyment from it, especially the locals.

We headed back to Arizona, to Sedona to golf. Bill and his wife joined us with their motorhome. The scenery at Sedona is spectacular.

The weather report called for an impending snow storm to the north of Sedona, around Flagstaff. That's when Gary decided we should head southwest to San Diego for a couple days of night-clubbing. The Padres were not playing at home.

Going north, we drove to San Francisco. We stayed in a safe part of the city and did a pub crawl. We were fortunate enough to have a baseball game scheduled while we were there. I had been to Candlestick Park to a game, but had never been to their new stadium at AT&T Park. We sat beside a couple from out of state who travelled to ball games all around the US as their form of recreation. It was a fine sunny day and a good ball game.

Chicago

June 2012

I had met a young lady in Florida, who was retired and lived in a small town near Chicago. I always wanted to see Chicago, and was not disappointed.

I booked into a small hotel near her home, where she picked me up each morning. We would drive to a train terminal south of the city, and have a 20 minute ride to downtown Chicago.

We went to a dance in the country. She decided that I didn't dance well enough, so moved on to dance with other men. All the women were asking men to dance, while all but a few were more interested in drinking beer and watching the women.

A situation of mouse invasion had occurred at the O'Hare International airport terminal. The remedy was to introduce a load of cats. Poor parent planning resulted in a severe problem of overpopulation of cats that they couldn't catch, so goes the story.

It was an interesting week, a different lifestyle and different attitude from the people I ran into there, too busy, and not really friendly.

Arizona

December 2012 to April 2013

Friends staying in Florence, Arizona, invited me to join them for the winter. They had no one to dance with. A little trailer was arranged for me to rent for my stay of four months. I had heard from people who spent every winter in some part of Arizona, and they seemed to love it. I was skeptical, but thought I should try it. I loaded the car and drove there.

The complex was gated and well patrolled, with a large and active clubhouse, a nine-hole golf course, two swimming pools, another dance hall, a pickleball court, a pool hall and other buildings for games and events. All this is beside a prison with 16 to 18,000 inmates. The town of Florence mostly houses employees of the prison.

Members of the park belong to numerous clubs, such as the golf course, motorcycle, ATV, precious gem, billiards, hiking, poker, and whatever you can imagine. Many residents own their trailers or houses that they return to every winter. It is a community of friends, most believing nothing could be better than this life. Most are older citizens, and the membership changes each year.

Events are planned at the clubhouse by different groups, like the amazing dinners provided by the Canadians and by the Americans, who try to outdo each other. Coffee groups met every morning. There was a dance every weekend with live music and food. I really wondered about the clubhouse manager, Johny, whose writing was nice like a woman's, until I discovered that Johny was a woman.

We went on a few tours from there, to a PGA event in Phoenix, the Superstition Mountains, and others. Small towns in the area had their own attractions, particularly pubs and country dancing. A private dancehall and bar with live music, close to the complex, had bull-riding competitions during intermission. Mesa and Apache Junction towns are close to Florence. Big markets had wonderful fresh fruits and vegetables, and one gigantic market sold everything else.

An explosion of relationships seemed to happen. Everyone was there for the same purpose, retired and wanting to enjoy their life. It was there that I met Sadie, one of three ladies from Minnesota. We became friends, and we would be in touch later.

The drive home through Utah meant much anticipated stops at some of the parks there. They are magnificent, worth visiting again. At one, it was snowing so hard, visibility was about 20 feet, so I had to turn back.

After four full months in the sun, sand, dances and golf greens, I had a scenic trip home to Kelowna. It was action-packed and enjoyable, glad that I was able to spend the time there.

Minnesota

May and October 2014

I would be visiting my friend Sadie in Cottage Grove, an area just outside of St Paul, Minnesota, for a month, twice in 2014. She came to visit me in Canada first.

Sadie's visit to Canada started with a flight to Seattle, where we met at the airport. We drove to Port Angeles for a ferry to Victoria, and spent a few days on the Island before going inland to Kelowna. After a couple of weeks of good times, Sadie returned to Minnesota. I would be returning to Minnesota in nine days to see her again.

My first flight to the MSP airport in Minnesota in May was from Kelowna to Seattle to MSP (Minneapolis-St Paul).

Sadie lives in an average suburban home, with a big well-manicured back yard, filled with flowers, trees, and lots of grass. A fairy garden is a part of the patio. This was and still is her passion.

A favourite restaurant and bar nearby had Mexican cuisine. I was surprised at the low prices at a big grocery store. The big river running through the area is the Mississippi, already wide and fast flowing. We were at the beginning of the river, where you can walk across. It begins as a trickle out of Lake Itasca in Northern Minnesota, and is very big by the time it reaches St Paul.

The Mall of America is situated nearby, owned by the same Canadians, the Ghermezian family, who own West Edmonton Mall. It attracts 40 million visitors a year. It was the biggest mall in the US, until the American Dream mall in New Jersey just opened in 2020, also owned by the same family. They aren't as big as the malls in Dubai.

The Minnesota Twins were playing, and we were fortunate enough to get tickets to a game. The new football stadium in downtown Minneapolis was under construction at that time, just a big hole in the ground, that was six years ago.

Sadie's friend loved to go to casinos. I don't think she gambled that much or with big money, but she loved the atmosphere, so much that she kept getting free rooms for the night. She gave us one in a casino in the north side of the state, where there happened to be an iron ore mine, near the village of Tower. The ore was very high grade, needed for materials used in the Second

World War. Production was stopped around 1962 because it was inefficient and not cost effective.

They had tours of the operation down more than 2,300 feet. We went down in a big elevator to where the mining was done. Mules were taken down to spend three or four months in the hole. They turned off all sources of lighting, leaving a total darkness, an unusual experience.

On the return to her home, we stopped in the little port city of Duluth, population of about 80,000. We watched an entire bridge span being lifted to allow a ship to go through. I had never seen a bridge like that.

We went to many events and activities, like a beerfest with her brother and his wife, church musical gatherings, and dances every Thursday evening at a VFW, the American version of our Royal Canadian Legion. One of the popular bands that played in the area was called "Johnny No Cash."

October, 2014

My return to Minnesota this time was in the fall. I wanted to see the foliage as the leaves change colour, and it was fantastic. The colours were beautiful on the trees and shrubs, with the reds, oranges, yellows, purples, and all shades in between. I will never get tired of seeing the leaves change colour.

We drove past Chicago, into Buffalo, and on to the Catskills. On the return we went a bit south through the farmland, where we saw flocks of wild turkeys. Apparently, they are in southern BC but I have not seen them.

On the way we visited Niagara Falls on the Canadian side. We stayed a night in Buffalo, where we saw the passion Americans have for the NFL, as the Bills were playing that evening and fans gathered at the sports bars.

Another trip was to Racine Wisconsin, south of Milwaukee, north of Chicago. Johnson Wax company headquarters are there in a Frank Lloyd Wright building. A museum exploring the development of the wax products, with the original lab and offices, was worth visiting. One of the Johnsons discovered that oil from the carnauba palm from Brazil could be developed into a polish, which was the beginning of the mega-company.

On that same trip, we visited with a friend we knew from Florence, Arizona. She had just found a new man and wedding bells were in the air.

One thing I noticed is the variety of small "Mom & Pop" restaurants all through the United States. They are usually ethnic, making high quality food from a limited menu.

I so much enjoyed the visits to Minnesota, and Sadie coming to Canada to visit. We had nice gatherings with her brother and his wife, her daughter, son-in-law and their family, as well as her friends and acquaintances. Unfortunately, long distance relationships are difficult, especially from another country.

Alaska Cruise

Aug 2019

Like most or all cruises, the agenda is: Eat, Drink, Sleep, repeat if necessary. I gained 16 pounds in 15 days. My fault, but none the less… The food was definitely outstanding. The scenery is exceptional. The service and attention to detail was much appreciated. It was my second cruise, the first 19 years before. If I never go on another cruise, no problem.

After a short flight on a seaplane to the harbour in Vancouver, we went through customs and boarded the cruise ship enroute to Alaska.

The most exciting thing to happen on the trip was getting off of the ship. In every stop, multiple shops were welcoming with huge discounts on a large variety of gems, most only available at their store. You miss this chance, it's gone. The most exciting happenings on the ship would be the gem shows.

We met a few really nice people. We talked to a nice young couple from the Chicago area. She was a teacher, he was a manager at an investment firm.

He asked, "Where are you from?"

I said, "Vancouver Island."

He said, "So, you're from Vancouver. I've heard of that place."

I said, "Yes, that's where you got on the ship. And we are not from Vancouver, we are from Vancouver Island."

He asked, "Where is that?"

I explained where.

He thought for a moment, and asked, "Are there stores there?"

I replied, "No, they put food on rafts in Vancouver, push it out, and sometimes we get it, sometimes we don't."

He asked, "So, do you have electricity?"

I said, "No. But we should get it soon. But it is difficult to install power poles in the sea with the wires high enough for the ships to get under"

He thought for a moment and said, "Oh!"

We left. They were very nice people.

Another group had bought Mukluk boots and feather down jackets, with mitts and woolen caps to deal with the snow and cold in the Alaskan August.

The scenery was great, and the whales and seals played in the waters, just like we can see from our balcony on the lost Isle of Vancouver.

Canary Islands - Tenerife

SEPTEMBER 06 FOR A COUPLE OF MONTHS

We flew from Canada to Amsterdam, staying the night at a B & B type place with a room in the attic for an arm and a leg. We had trouble getting there, as taxi drivers did not recognize the address. It took hours. The next day I lost my camera at the airport, so bought another one in Tenerife.

There are no little yellow birds in the Canary Islands. The name is from the Latin *canis,* meaning dogs (canine??) which the Romans found many of when they arrived hundreds of years ago. It's the same in the Virgin Islands, no canaries there either.

Tenerife is an island in the Canaries, belonging to Spain, and speaking Spanish. Well, not really. So much of the island is foreign owned, with the north end being German, and the south end being English. The Spanish inhabitants need to speak Spanish and either German or English, depending on where their shop is or where they work. It is a long way from land, but the dust storms coming off of the North African desert make you keep your windows closed. They do make beautiful sunsets. They have more cars per resident in Tenerife than anywhere else. One of the features that I enjoyed the most was the big pools by the sea, with barriers that keep the water calm. They are giant saltwater swimming pools.

As I was staying in the German section of the island, I got to enjoy the German cuisine, which of course is delicious. I was with a German friend whose brother and sister-in-law are the nicest people you could imagine. I would be with them again in Germany years later.

We had a shared car rental, so every second day we ventured out to different parts of the island. There was a lot to see and do, and lots of good German beer and food.

The island is quite hilly, with roads that squirm in tight turns. At one turn, we had to all get out of the vehicle and push it around a tight corner on a steep road. The countryside has banana plantations, vegetable gardens, and barren rocky hills. Rabbits are plentiful, and are on restaurant menus.

The zoo had a rare white tiger and penguins, the aquarium had many species of tropical fish, the Loro Parque had many rare birds, and the arboretum had a great variety of plants and trees. One particular tree only grows there, a strange one, big with needles only on top. Poinsettias grow everywhere in the wild.

They had a daily show with dolphins and orcas, who had the staff trained to feed them lots of fish as a reward for swimming around. It was a great show, jumping in sync, pushing kids around the pool in a little raft, and popping out of the water onto the ledge to talk to the crowd.

We flew back via Amsterdam and on to Las Vegas. My friend flew home to Alberta, while I went to Mexico.

Mexico

DECEMBER 2006 - JANUARY 2007

After a few days of glitz in Las Vegas, I arrived in Mexico City. I checked into a moderate, clean, inexpensive hotel arranged from a kiosk in the airport terminal. It was a convenient location near the *zocalo*, the main town square.

Breakfast was included. I found out that real Mexican cuisine is not what they feed the tourists. It took me three days to become accustomed to the very different flavors. Of course, I was the only non-Mexican staying there.

Having heard about Frida Kahlo and Diego Rivera, it was a must to see the museum. It was the home of Frida and Diego. Her paintings were indicative of her painful and chronic illnesses, a bad vehicle accident, and Diego's infidelity. She is known for her unibrow and small mustache, which Diego encouraged her to keep.

Diego Rivera was well known internationally for his renaissance frescoes, having commissions in Europe and the US. His large-scale murals are amazing. His depiction of the growth of the Ford Motor Company in Detroit is well known. His disagreement with the Rockefeller family had his mural destroyed, over an insertion of Lenin and a Communist theme. I spent a whole day at a public building in Mexico City, where his murals of the Mexican Revolution covered the walls of several floors. They had been funded by the government.

A day at the Museum of Modern Art was a very memorable event. The curator was a very attractive lady who spent the day with me, explaining each painting and the artist. She was delighted to have the opportunity to practice her control of the English language, while I could advance my knowledge of Spanish, in the dialect of the Mexicans. Besides, she was such a pleasure to be with. We said goodbye and I headed to the hotel. Looking at the pictures now, I really wonder why I let her get away.

The Metropolitan Cathedral is a most beautiful church. Another is the Basilica of Guadalupe, dedicated to Our Lady of Guadalupe who is said to have appeared to Saint Juan Diego. This church is the second most visited holy place in the world, so they say. It contains the cloak of Saint Juan Diego, which has an image of Our Lady of Guadalupe on it. That relic attracts millions of tourists and pilgrims every year. The lineup to see it and be close to it was never-ending.

A wedding was going on as I rested in a pew. As usual, the bride looked stunning and the groom looked stunned. The small group following showed signs of happiness and concern. I left.

I toured the pyramids, one of which is the biggest in the world, just 30 miles out of Mexico City. It was built 1000 years before the Aztecs, 2000 years ago, perhaps by the Mayans. I toured with a hippie from Penticton, who wore one of those knitted head covers. He claimed his head was cold. Really, in that heat?? Anyway, his camera wasn't working, so I sent him my pics later. He was a good guy, and the pyramids were well worth visiting.

I took a bus from Mexico City south to Oaxaca. The city was deserted. The situation was the result of an incident in the town square, where a foreign reporter interfered with a peaceful teachers' demonstration while the police stood by in case of problems, normal procedure. The reporter approached the police in a menacing manner, so they shot him. Of course the US government condemned it, and listed Oaxaca as a dangerous place to be for tourists, and Canada had to follow suit.

It was totally destructive to the tourist industry in Oaxaca. I was the only one looking for a place to stay, to eat, and things to do. I hired a taxi to take me around. He had been working long days with not one fare in a couple of weeks. It was heart-breaking, these people have families. He drove me around for a couple of days and I paid him very well, still quite inexpensive for me. He was a great guy, good to be with, even learning a little English.

He took me to the alleged 'largest tree in the world.' It was a Cypress, beside a cathedral. It wasn't the biggest cathedral, but it was dwarfed by the tree. One has to pack a lunch just to walk around it. It weighs 650 tons, more than 2,000 years old, and 140 feet high. It is quite remarkable, a popular tourist attraction.

After a pleasant few days in Oaxaca, I went south to a beautiful little fishing village on the Pacific side, Puerto Escondido. It means the hidden port, and is tucked in a quiet bay with no waves, perfect waters to swim in, with a beautiful beach. Half of the beach was tied up with fishing boats, the livelihood of most people in the village. The other half of the beach was left to the tourists, who provide a livelihood for the rest of the town. I spent a quiet Mexican Christmas there. The locals are Catholic and very family oriented.

I found a nice hostel owned and successfully operated by a wild and crazy Canadian woman. She took me all around the area, to some unique places. She owned a couple of classy condos with a swimming pool that she had rented out for the weekend to two couples for US$2500. We drove to a development where someone had bought seven lots to ensure that some farmer wouldn't be running goats next to his house. This sounds stupid, but he built on the seventh lot. When he moved into his new house and looked out the window, goats were everywhere. And, he had bought and built on native reserve land.

Problems are not unusual for native reserve land. One occurrence in that area was at a resort with a restaurant, stores, and homes. A Mexican resident claimed that his great-grandfather had that property taken from him. Records showed no record of sale, so the resort and others had to pack up and move on. I heard of this happening in other foreign countries as well, where an expat has absolutely no option but to lose everything and forget it. I would not buy in a foreign country. Most times it turns out well, but the other times …

I had a lot of fun with this crazy woman, but it was time to get closer to the beach. An inexpensive hotel room right on the sand was my new home for a couple of weeks. It looked down on a great little bar, the fishing boats, and the beach from my window. The beach was very active with friendly people, and many restaurants. It was interesting to see the boats come in with their catch, and selling it to buyers right off the boat. The boats would come roaring up to the beach, while a helper would throw a couple of skinny poles under the boat just as it came out of the water. I never did understand the process of waiting, but it seemed to work.

One of the special days was spent watching pelicans dive for fish that are stunned by the waves crashing onto the shore. The birds rarely missed a catch, and never lost a stored fish from their pouch. Nearby the turtle eggs were hatching, and the little guys had scrambled to the safety of the sea during the night.

Sunday was special on the beach. The local people came after going to church, in the same clothes, swimming in two feet of water (still same clothes), and having a wonderful family time. Unusual, they did not know how to swim. An expat complained to me at the little bar, that it was really nice here, but those *&#$@* Mexicans show up on Sundays and spoil everything for the tourists. I reminded him which country he was in and who belongs there, and that perhaps he should go home where he was appreciated. He left mad, and I felt good, especially when the bartenders wouldn't allow me to pay for a drink the rest of the day.

A lot of interesting people lived their days on the beach. One in particular was a Vancouver man, about 35, who came every day and walked the beach with his big backpack on. He carried his laptop with him always. He lived with his mommy, and worked as a sweeper on construction sites, cleaning up after the tradesmen. His mommy paid for his vacation. He ferociously protected his territory, using construction trash-talk. It was entertaining to be around him.

A bbq restaurant up the hill was a popular gathering spot for expats. It was run by a chef from Atlanta. One lady said they come there every year because it is the best place ever for a Super Bowl Party. The food was great.

A restaurant where I had breakfast every day had a cute shy lady working in the kitchen. The other girls there convinced her to come out and sit with me. Unfortunately, a complete disconnect due to the language barrier made it uncomfortable for her, and she returned to her work.

I would return to Escondido in a couple of months, after a Panama visit. I left for a short vacation to the lower east coast, and on to Mexico City for a flight to Panama City.

RETURN TO MEXICO - PUERTO ESCONDIDO

March & April, 2007

I returned from Panama in early March to Puerto Escondido, back to the beautiful beach and the hotel I had before. I particularly enjoyed swimming in the calm sea with very little waves. A whole new set of people were there, including some nice ladies from Vancouver. They seemed to know a lot of people, having spent much time in the area. The town was active with local celebrations, like a parade of kids. It may have been an Easter parade.

Mexico - Cancun & Monterrey

December 2008 - January 2009

CANCUN

Escaping the Canadian cold in early December, I flew to a resort in Cancun on the Caribbean side of Mexico. It was an all-inclusive with good food and watered-down booze, in a loud and friendly atmosphere. The water was warm, but the waves dangerous with undercurrent. The beach had been eroded by storms and a hurricane, but was being rebuilt.

I went on a day tour to Chichen Itza, where the pyramids and temples were sacred to the Maya. They had a sports field where they played some game of kicking a rock. The 'most valuable player' would be named and executed as his prize. The Cenote Calavera, a sinkhole with water was an interesting place. I snorkeled for a couple of hours at Isla de Mujeres (the Island of Women). I had a drink at the bar where Tom Cruise made the movie 'Cocktail'. I met some nice people there, but basically a mundane trip.

The second part of the trip was so much better.

MONTERREY

I was in Monterrey because I was supposed to meet someone in southern Texas, and Monterrey was the closest airport to get there. The plan was cancelled, but I was already scheduled there from Cancun. I usually find adventure, and this turned out to be one of the best places ever.

We landed in Monterrey. I asked another arrival if he knew of a decent place to stay. He made a phone call to his people, then turned his attention to me. He asked if I would like a ride to a hotel. He took me to a nice place, and waited until I checked it out. It was good, so I let him know I was okay and thanked him. He asked what my plans were for Christmas Eve. Of course I had no plans. He asked if I wanted to join his family for their celebration. Of course I said yes.

Hector explained that he had been in Canada and was treated very well, so was repaying the hospitality. That was the start of an amazing unforgettable week with him and his family, one that I will never forget.

A Greek restaurant near the hotel was the centre of a few days at this hotel. Nothing much happened, but was relaxing and quiet.

On Christmas Eve, I was picked up and taken to Hector's cousin's home, a long drive away. The quiet part was about to change.

All year is family time in Mexico, but Christmas is all about family in a special celebration. About 40 members of the family were there, from small children to the elderly, and everyone participated. Copious amounts of food and drink were on a big table, never allowed to run out. Singing filled the air as everyone danced in the street. Fireworks at midnight were everywhere, lighting up the sky as far as one could see. Everyone watched and cheered as the little ones hit the piñata with a stick until it broke, as candy and small presents fell out.

I was never left alone and was included in each activity. My buddy took in a bit too much tequila and fell asleep sitting up on the couch. Of course this was an opportunity for merriment. They placed a red mop head on his hair, a woman's purse on his arm, and a teddy bear in his other arm. After a little nap, he awoke and returned to dancing and drinking his tequila.

Around three or four in the morning, I was driven back to the hotel. It was a wonderful memorable time.

On Boxing Day I moved to a hotel downtown, closer to the action. Now I was a bit closer to my new friends. We went to a Mexican buffet. There were no tacos or other tourist food, just delicious real Mexican cuisine. I went sight-seeing with the whole family to Horsetail Falls. They took me everywhere. My buddy asked if I would like to go to a ranch in the mountains, where another cousin was having a bbq. There was beer, stories, laughter, and several kinds of meat. The home was beautiful, with a swimming pool, warm and welcoming.

Hector and his family went away on a holiday trip. I was alone at the hotel, until the next morning.

I ran into a young Mexican fella in the lobby, who had arrived from Houston where he was teaching school. His story was an unfamiliar one. He had been connected with a lady in Monterrey, communicating by phone and email. They had never seen each other, and he had driven down to meet her.

He was a shy guy and was terrified with the thought that she may not like him. He asked me to come along on their initial meeting. I insisted no, but he insisted more. They met in a nearby park. It was good that I was there, to distract both of them, as she was just as nervous as he was. I excused myself after about half a minute, while they just looked at each other and grinned. I ran into them an hour later; everything was better than fine.

The next day she invited me to her parents' home, with her new boyfriend. The idea was for him to meet her parents. He couldn't face it alone, so insisted that I be there, while she insisted also. The meal was great, the conversation lively. He was well accepted and she was happy about it.

They invited me to their New Year's Eve party at her cousin's apartment. It was the usual, dancing, singing with a karaoke machine, drinking, and terrific food. They were making some kind of soup, brewing for hours, the taste of which was unknown to me, but the most delicious ever. I've never had anything like it since.

The next days were spent with the three of us sightseeing. My buddy had to return to his teaching job in Houston. It was time for me to leave also. He drove back to Texas, and was kind enough to have me ride with him across the border. We stayed in Laredo, just north of the Rio Grande, in Texas. The next morning he drove back to his home in Houston. I caught a flight from Laredo airport to Dallas, Vancouver, and home to Kelowna.

Six months later, I received an email from them. The attachment was a wedding invitation.

Mexico - Playa Del Carmen

Dec 2009 for 8 days

A destination wedding in Mexico for Lana's daughter had whole families congregated in Playa Del Carmen. The hotel was excellent, on the beach, and the food great.

On arrival, the groom's mother set her purse on the counter at the check-in, only to find it gone a moment later. She had changed her Canadian money for US currency so that she could get Mexican money with it. I don't understand why people can't use an ATM for local cash money and a Visa for expenses. I believe she had more than US$2,000 cash in her purse.

It seems inevitable for something to happen at an event like this. The wedding was delayed for a couple of hours. The wedding gown needed to be pressed after being packed for the flight. It was nicely pressed, but they had shrunk it considerably. The bride couldn't get into it, not even close. They found a seamstress to alter it to fit, but that took time. Better late than never they say, and all went smoothly with a very nice ceremony and very pleasant reception after. The bride and her husband were moving to Australia where he was working.

We returned to Kelowna just in time for Christmas.

Mexico - Barra de Navidad

December 2010 to February 2011

I was invited to join a friend, Camila, in Barra. She had a nice condo. The area is full of expats, lots of live music, good beer and food. We ate out a lot, with many good restaurants, including a really nice Christmas dinner. We played bridge with some group a couple of times, where we had to list the top 10 conventions that I would be using. I only knew one, which they scoffed at. They were very annoyed when I had the top score one week. Knowing lots of conventions probably does not mean you know how to play cards.

We were in a local bar in Barra, frequented by many expats. I learned that people, and not just a few, drink all day, eat, drink until time to go home. They sleep, go back for a liquid breakfast, and have a do-over of the previous day. I have seen this virtually in every tourist place I have been. Anyway, everyone was watching the news, when they showed a video of a cop kicking a man in the head while he was down on the floor. Apparently, he had shot off a round with his shotgun to scare off some birds from an orchard crop. I was familiar with this, as it happened in Canada, in Kelowna.

A Mexican fella asked, "In what country did this happen??" When he was told "In Canada," his reply was that he sure as hell would not want to be travelling in a country that is that dangerous.

We decided to do some travelling, so we took a bus to Mexico City, with a stop in Guadalajara. Camila had met a lady from Mexico City, who met us upon arrival there. She was an interesting lady, a lawyer with her own practice. She showed us around the city riding the subway. We stayed at her home, which was built into a solid rock hill. It was hot outside, but cool as the dickens where we were sleeping. She was a most gracious host, along with her professional daughter who spoke English well. But with one mistake, she told me I was "unique," but put the accent on the first syllable. I explained in Spanish that I was not a eunuch. We all had a good laugh.

We carried on to the city of silver, Taxco. The markets there are filled with nearly pure silver ornaments, at very reasonable prices. From there, we went to the coast, staying at several nice places along the beach before arriving back in Barra. Camila returned to her condo, while I went to a small town just out of Barra. I can't recall the name.

The beach was good, the water calm, and great for swimming. I found a room in a place similar to a big hostel. Most of the residents were there for the winter, and they all knew each other, good people. One of the residents had a sense of humour based on sarcasm. I almost met my match. He was a soybean farmer from the mid-west US. We got to be buddies.

I met another American fella couple of houses down. He asked if I wanted to go for a beer, at a bar nearby. He was about 80, but very able to put away many beer. He kept saying, "Want another??" And so we had more. When I got the bill, it was for 18 beer, just my portion, his the same. I thought that can't be right, but the bill was only $20 with the tip, so who cares.

Days later, I ran into the same dude. "Want to go for a beer?" he says. His wife did not drink, and didn't like it when he did. This time, I told the waiter to leave the caps from the beer bottles with me each time. I figured I tricked him, he won't be over-charging me this time. When I asked for the bill, the waiter said "I don't know, count your bottle caps". There were 21.

I believe the bottles are smaller, the beer a bit lighter, and easy to take in that heat, and other excuses. None the less, shame on me for doubting him. He got a nice tip.

I was there for a week before heading home to Canada.

Mexico, from Panama

February to April 2012

I arrived in Acapulco in late February. While there, 12 people were decapitated and their heads found scattered at a grocery store parking lot a couple of blocks from my hotel. I was not concerned, I had nothing to do with drugs and was a threat to no one. What did scare me, was watching a guy in the sky being pulled by a boat. When the boat came into shore, he was still high up, and headed toward the buildings, missing by not much. The boat pulled away, dragging him away from disaster. He obviously wasn't instructed well enough, or didn't catch on. And they were charging tourists a fortune to nearly kill themselves.

From Acapulco, I went north to several smaller beach communities, around the Zihuatanejo area to Manzanillo. Every place was very nice, I would recommend every one. Then on to Puerto Vallarta.

I was not too impressed with the flood of tourists in Puerto Vallarta, so made my way to Mexico City for a flight home to Kelowna. The bus I was riding in had great air conditioning, so good that it was set on high, leaving ice on the windows. Everyone was freezing, but no one said a word. I was very cold, can't imagine how the warm-blooded Mexicans took it.

Mexico

November 2019 - February 2020

MEXICO CITY

After a week at my timeshare in Las Vegas, I spent another great week in Mexico City, always a joy. Unfortunately, it is not prudent to be taking pictures in some places and situations. However, I do have some good memories. What I like best is being with the local people, with near zero tourists around.

At the *zocalo*, some young ladies dressed as clowns, were entertaining children and adults with their antics and stories. They moved through the crowds charming everyone, causing merriment and laughter. Then they saw me, an easy alien target. They were fun and very respectful.

My hotel was very near the *zocalo*, an immense square in the city centre. It was being set up for a speech from the President of the country. I would estimate the crowd to be in excess of 200,000 people. He addressed the nation, wife by his side, as the throngs of people quietly listened. It was so overwhelming and crowded that I left the scene, returning to my hotel room to watch on TV.

The town square, or *zocalo* as they call it in Mexico, is gigantic, with many very large buildings, decorated to the hilt for Christmas. They love to go all-out for any celebration, and Christmas is one of the biggest.

The streets are normally crowded in the downtown area, but much more on that day. Hundreds of stores were very busy selling Christmas stuff, tree ornaments, fake trees, and decorations for inside and outside the home. I wonder what they sell when the Christmas rush is over.

A museum nearby had displays of the history of the city, and what the city is comprised of in terms of parks, residential, monuments, water sources, the history and future of the aquafer under the city. The aquafer has been drawn down for decades and continues to be, causing building instability and greater problems for the future.

Traffic was horrendous, and almost cost me. I crossed while looking for something familiar, and got caught in the middle of the street with traffic from both directions buzzing by. I don't think they care if people want to stand in the traffic. I made it though, and never did that again.

About 10 blocks away was a market that sold everything, the usual, fun to shop there. Turning a corner, one couldn't help but notice something different. Police were everywhere, and so were the ladies of the night, there in the daytime. Not a one approached me, or even glanced at me. What's going on? So I politely walked by a lady and said hello. She politely engaged in a light conversation. Looking around, there was a policeman right there. We said our goodbyes and I moved on. I don't know what their cells are like and don't want to find out.

After a week or so, I got a flight to Cancun.

CANCUN

My attraction to Cancun was about a kind of timeshare I had purchased there and had never used. I got a room at a hotel near the airport. I could see the hotel from the terminal, so I went to a taxi kiosk for a trip to the hotel. The price was to the extreme, so I went to the second kiosk with the same result, the third and fourth the same price. The fifth one was a bus. Guess what, same price. I couldn't walk there, as it was around the runway, so I sucked it up and took a taxi. When I asked him about the prices, he told me the same person owns all five companies. When I mentioned the need for a cab to get around town, he took me to the hotel for about a quarter of the price, and he became my go-to cab driver for the time I was in Cancun.

I was able to work out a stay of a week with the timeshare company at their resort, if I agreed to be shown another resort they were building. The resort was nice, the beach was good and not too crowded, but the water was dangerous to swim in because of the undercurrents and large waves. I'm too old to deal with that. There was a little bar, holding about ten people. I met quite a few people there, all kinds, drunks, light drinkers, loudmouths, and quite a few really nice people. Obviously, I spent a little time there.

I met a couple of delightful ladies there. We spent time together, meals, trips, and of course the odd drink. They are from different parts of the US, but met some time ago and have become happy travelers together. I just found out, one of them is inflicted with the nasty Covid virus.

We went downtown one day to shop and look around. Someone had been killed there that day in a drug-related shooting.

They have a Mexican style Disneyland park, with shows and performances by Mexican entertainers that I would highly recommend. A show at a grand stadium depicted life before, during and after the invasion of the Spaniards.

They have a great zoo of exotic animals. The black jaguars caught my attention, housed in a natural depression. There was a great array of exotic birds, many turtles, and other unusual species. An extensive canal system is set up for snorkeling.

The timeshare was going to cost me more money, which I was not going to do. The whole thing was a money grab, and not my finest hour when I purchased it. I wonder how many thousands of people get sucked into these things every year. I never did like Cancun, and now have no reason to return. There are too many tourists, the water is unsuitable to swim on one side, with a lagoon full of alligators on the other side. Time to leave. I would fly to Puerto Vallarta, with a change of planes in Mexico City.

BUCERIAS

On the flight from Cancun, I sat beside a young lady who had the longest fingernails I've ever seen. Each one was a different colour. I asked her about them in Spanish, she asked if I spoke English. That says it all.

She had just received her law degree from university, and was travelling with her family to Mexico City for Christmas. She and her mother were planning to start a business with nails. Her family approved of her following her dream of such a business, and using her education as a backup. Her parents saw me conversing with her, and waited to meet me after we got off the plane. What a nice family they were.

There was an eight hour layover in Mexico City airport. It was uncomfortable, crowded, and lacked services. A new airport is being built. I couldn't help but notice, there were refuse bins labeled for regular garbage and for recycle. When the maintenance person came to empty them, they were both dumped into the same bag.

While in Cancun, I got an email from friends who had just spent a long time in India, and were finishing their holiday near Puerto Vallarta. They said it was a good place to be, and there was a suite available in the building. As I had no plans for after Cancun, I agreed to rent the place. I had the pleasure of sharing Christmas dinner with them.

I was taxied to the address where my friends had reserved a condo for me. The price was reasonable, but what I didn't realize was that the place was isolated from all of humanity. I needed a cab or a long walk to get to a bus to go to a restaurant or pub. I had agreed to take it for a month, so was stuck with it. The woman who was looking after the rental was a bit psychotic, which didn't add to the joy of being there. I had trouble transferring payment because her bank in Canada, a credit union, refused to accept it. She was blaming me and my bank. The light and fan in the TV area had a remote control. Several controllers have the same frequency, which allowed her to play like a child with the fan and light. That was told to me later by her boyfriend.

The nearest little town by bus was Bucerias. It has a great market, about 10 blocks or more long, three blocks wide. There is a variety of restaurants, with some excellent seafood menus, and quite a few on the beach. Bars on the beach have outdoor service on the sand.

A pub owned by a Canadian from Calgary was where I would go most often in Bucerias. Most people were friendly, mostly expats. While having a conversation with a fella from Portland, Oregon, we discovered that we lived beside each other, on the same floor of the same building I was in. We started cabbing it until he purchased a car of his own.

Greg had given up everything in the US, including his house which he gave to his girlfriend, moving to the Puerto Vallarta area to live permanently. He is still there; we talk occasionally.

After a month in the suite, I moved to a hotel in downtown Bucerias. It was full of perennials from Canada and the US, who would be there in the same room reserved a year in advance. The owner was kind and accommodating when my daughter came to visit for a few days. She just missed a sold-out drag show which they had each week. It was quite entertaining.

That was the time of the news of the coronavirus being bandied about. Of course, the Corona beer humour was big. It didn't seem to bother anyone much at the time, a lot of people eating and drinking too much every day. It got to be too much, too many drunks, not much else to do apparently.

A vacant block of land between my hotel window and the sea suddenly was invaded by an exhibition with big rides, slides, loud music, and everything involved in a show like that. It lasted for 10 days, two weekends, then vanished as fast as it came. For the most part, no one was there. How could it survive? I mean, no one.

I learned about this gigantic tree, known as the parota tree. It is one of the best hardwood trees for furniture. It also spans across property and needs to be cut down in order to build homes. It is protected now, and a government permit is required to touch it, even if it is dead. That's a good thing, beautiful tree.

An inviting little coffee-house with a line of clothing had a grand opening. I was invited to attend, where I met the young couple who had developed the very unusual line of lingerie on display there. It was like the old hippy-style places used to be.

With the threat of the coronavirus closing in, I could see what was coming. A seat was available on a flight direct from Puerto Vallarta to Vancouver. It would arrive in time for me to catch a seaplane back to home on Vancouver Island. I was happy about that, because a late flight meant overnight in Vancouver as the seaplane doesn't fly at night. Hotel prices were running around $250 at that time.

Unfortunately, a delay got me into Vancouver late. Fortunately, one hotel had a rate of $110, with a free credit card with $75 on it that could be applied to the room right away. So the room cost $35.

Travel would become much more difficult soon after that, because of the virus. It was the right decision to return when I did.

Life is good sometimes, isn't it?!?

Panama

JANUARY & FEBRUARY, 2007

I arrived in Panama City airport around three a.m., met by my friend Nataly. I met Nataly in Argentina in 2004. I stayed a couple of months at her beautiful home in Panama City. She showed me around the country of Panama. It was the dry season, so the sun shone and the temperature stayed at 91.6 degrees daytime and 91.2 at night. Nataly speaks perfect English and I knew enough Spanish to communicate wherever I went. Some of the neighbours came over for a "Canadian-style" bbq. It's always enjoyable to go to the markets for fresh everything, fruit, veggies, meat, and costing so little. I love the yuca and plantains.

Nataly's home was gated, as most homes are. The house was terraced, open, designed and built by her. With the moderate temperature, and no bugs, glass was unnecessary in the windows. The yard had fruit trees, banana, papaya, mango and some others.

Through Central and South America, many businesses have a television in their windows and inside the stores. If you like the show that is on, that restaurant is chosen. So, I noticed a crowd gathered outside a women's clothing store, a group of men watching a weather report. That's odd, the weather never changes. Then I saw the weather girl. I walked into a sports bar; everybody was glued to the TVs watching a bullfight.

Part of Panama City is an amazing jungle, as wild as any with animals and big tree growth. The lake that carries the Canal boat traffic is on one side, the ocean on the other. A preserved site has the remains of the original town when the Spanish arrived.

I spent days watching the ships enter and exit the Panama Canal at the Miraflores Locks in Panama City. There is a long history to the building of the locks, from the French failing, to the Americans succeeding but with malaria problems, to the takeover of the operations by the Panamanian people. They make a lot of money from it. It can cost a ship a million dollars to go around the tip of South America in rough seas, so it saves half at the canal plus days of time.

The revenue is used by the government to subsidize housing, transportation, health care, etc. for the local people. They still complain, however, thinking it should be free. Non-residents, foreigners, who are retirement age got benefits also, as the government at that time was trying to attract retirees to live there. They have since changed their policies, but it is still cheap for expat seniors.

The stories about the American invasion were sad. They spoke of sneaking out at night to get food, medicine, milk for the baby, while helicopters with search lights patrolled the city during the lock-down, shooting on sight, for nearly six weeks. They knew it was false information at the time, and that they couldn't lose face by backing out once the invasion started. None the less, Panama remains one of the few places in the world that likes and appreciates the American people, not necessarily the government, but they do appreciate the people. There had always been a good relationship with the people building the canal.

My friend Nataly is an amazing woman. Her husband passed long ago of a heart attack, leaving her to raise two children, now both independent and successful. She owned and managed some apartments, as well as three houses that she rented out. Her land in the interior had teak trees planted to be harvested in the future. She planned a city block building for retail business in Colon, by Gutan Locks on the Caribbean side of the Canal. She took over the construction management when the architect failed to do a good job. Dealing with the red tape of government ministries is difficult anytime in Panama, but more so for a woman.

COLON (GUTAN LOCKS)

We took a trip from Panama City to Colon, stopping at her teak plantation on the way. There were many acres of new-growth trees, to be ready for harvest in 20 years.

We stopped at a native settlement, a small village with a common area to work together and make meals. There was a large sloth in a tree nearby, not afraid. A baby sloth was hanging on to a young girl's arm, her pet.

This little port city of Colon on the Caribbean deserves a separate chapter. Nataly needed a permit for the business centre she was building. It took some time to get approved. I'm guessing it involved paying more than just the administrative fee. It was difficult to keep workers, who would disappear for a week or two after payday. Some of the retail space was already spoken for, a large chain store and a couple of offices. This woman had more patience than anyone I know. The government red tape was really something.

We stopped at a beach near town. I did my usual sunbathing while they laughed at me. "You whiteys go in the sun to get dark, we sit in the shade so we don't get darker."

We parked, looking at a dozen or so apartment buildings. They looked unpainted and really run down. It was explained to me that once someone is in an apartment, or house for that matter, they are protected by the government against eviction for non-payment of rental fees. As a result, when rent is not collected, the owner stops doing any maintenance. The renter trashes the place. There were quite a few abandoned houses with the same story. No rent is paid, can't kick them out, so the property is given up and no taxes are paid. It doesn't make sense.

While we were parked at the apartment buildings, about 20 police units surrounded us, with truckloads of armed personnel. They rushed into several buildings obviously doing a raid on druggies, of which there are lots. We got the heck out of there.

We went for a ride to the other end of Panama, to David in Chiriquí. Nataly has a beach lot near the ocean just out of Panama City, where we stopped for a swim. The water was calm and warm. We stopped at her uncle's farm near Santiago, where I was able to pick my first cashews from a bush.

In David, we stayed at Nataly's neighbours' sister's home. She lived with her mother, daughter, brother, and cousin, in the family home. Her name is

Toria, and will be a part of my life later. We spent a few days there, and then returned to Nataly's home in Panama City.

We had dined at some good restaurants, went to the horse races, and generally had a good time. The end of the holiday for me was coming, as I had some business to attend to in Canada, taxes to file, property and a home to look after.

Buses are really inexpensive and comfortable most of the time. I rode the bus north, not in a hurry, eventually arriving in Mexico City for a flight home. The scenic bus trip to Mexico was to San Jose in Costa Rica, then to San Salvador where I spent the night. I stopped in Puerto Escondido for a while, then on to Mexico City.

We had stopped for the night in San Salvador, in El Salvador. After dinner with some people from the bus ride, a young fella and I went looking for a cheap hostel for the short night. He didn't want to spend five dollars, so we found rooms for three. It was worth every penny, if you like dirt and roaches, cobwebs and bare electrical wires in the shower. It didn't smell too bad. The next morning we were back on the bus to Mexico.

It was an amazing visit to Panama. Nataly came to visit in Canada for a few weeks, and it was nice to see her again.

BACK IN PANAMA, 2012

After a week in Florida visiting a friend, I caught the redeye flight to Panama City, where my friend Nataly met me at the airport. She had two bright young boys from David, friends of Toria. The boys followed me around and asked a myriad of questions, while I struggled with my Spanglish. After a pleasant few days, I carried on to David with the boys. Toria had driven to Panama City to get us.

Nataly wanted me to stay to live with her long-term, but I had to go home. She was not as patient as I thought, like choose, stay or go. I explained that I had no choice but to return to Canada. From that time forward she scrambled to get me hooked up with any of the many single ladies that she knew. So, Toria came to visit her sister in Panama City, and had me return to David with her. We stopped in Penonome for a couple of days to tour the area with her brother.

It was all so crazy, but there I was in David with Toria and her ten-year-old daughter. I set about learning more Spanish, as no one there spoke English.

Toria was on vacation from her job at the university. We visited a lot of people, picked beans, and did many other things. The culture is so different. The family is everything. She was her mother's caretaker, who rules all. Her daughter was involved in a lot of activities, especially traditional dancing. The neighbours were friendly.

Her daughter, Angel, was growing quickly, and in high school now. All of Toria's sisters came for a visit, keeping me very busy, while their mother delighted in making fun of my Spanish or lack thereof, all in good humour.

A "thrift" store had new pants and golf shirts for $5 or less. The shirts were from unsold stock in the US. An American asked me if I liked a golf course in New Jersey. I had never been there. He looked puzzled, asking me where I got the golf shirt with the course's name on it.

Time to head for home. In a couple of weeks I returned to Puerto Vallarta in Mexico, then home. I enjoyed the hospitality in David, but I could not and would not stay, as tempting as it was.

BACK TO PANAMA, 2018

Having sold my car and most of my furniture, I moved out of the condo I was renting. All my property, including a condo had been sold. All my assets were liquid. Since I was spending a large portion of each year out of the country, it was and still is the way to go. My new home was a Costco shopping cart (they are larger).

I moved my remaining possessions, mostly kitchen stuff and an expensive bed, into storage. My intention was to move to Panama on a long-term basis. I had been invited to live at my friend Nataly's home. I arrived in early December of 2018.

She had a new home, as she had given her previous home to her son and his wife, while building a duplex for her daughter and her husband, and for herself. It was almost completed, very nice.

I enjoyed the markets there, with fresh vegetables and fruits unknown to me. One very delicious fruit was eaten to cure constipation, so I found out. Seafood is always available, as is meat of all kinds.

We made a trip to Colon. Nataly needed to check out a problem with a business in her business block. They had not paid their rent for over a year, and had let the place get run down, not allowing her to get in there.

Government protection would not allow her to evict the tenant. It was set up as a pizza place.

I entered alone as a customer and ordered a coffee. They struggled to make a cup, and I was the only client. They had a little kid delivering pizza boxes, obviously empty by their weight and the way they were carried. Well, not empty, they would be moving drugs in the boxes. Nataly came in and talked to the manager, but he just smiled at her. I still don't believe it. The rest of the block was rented and the businesses doing well.

It's hard to believe, much less to explain, some of the corruption in the government agencies. It seems that one of the ministers who had access to the tax base and the personal information of home owners, was searching out old retired people and sending them tax notices for thousands of dollars. They didn't understand, did not have the money to pay the taxes, and couldn't reach the ministry to complain. Someone would repossess the property and sell it. The original owners would get notice to move out, because someone else would be moving their furniture in the next day. In the short time I was there, Nataly helped out two families to prevent the loss of their homes.

We attended a brass musical performance the first night there. Being the Christmas season, we drove around town where the parks were decorated, some very elaborate. We went to a restaurant down a back alley, and had the best fish meal ever. I went with the whole family to a Chinese restaurant for Dim Sum. We all met at her daughter's home next door for Christmas Eve dinner and gift opening. Most spoke English, but not all, so we mainly spoke Spanish.

It soon became obvious that I couldn't stay, it was best to move on and let her get on with her busy life. Nataly was totally preoccupied with her businesses, and her kids' pregnancies. No time was left for social activities, or travel, or me. It would have been a life for me that was removed from everything that I wish to do, except the climate and fresh food.

I understand. She was setting up her kids for the future, and normally they would have been doing a good part of the work. But, with two pregnancies, they were not much help.

I found a nice hotel downtown, where I stayed for a few days. Once again, my David friend Toria was in town. I met with her, her daughter who was now in university, and her sisters from Panama City. We had a nice lunch and spent the next day touring the downtown area. Refugees from Venezuela were everywhere, fleeing from the conditions in their country. A set of bleachers for an audience of 100,000 people was being built, for a visit from the Pope. There was an expectation of more than a million people to flood into the city for the Pope's visit. He was coming soon, time to leave!

Large groups of religious people, pilgrims, called 'peregrinos' in Spanish, arrived in the country. They were looked after for food and bed by local groups, attending sermons and activities for days on end. The rush to Panama by the peregrinos, from all over the world, happens every year. And this year, exacerbated by the Pope's visit.

TO DAVID AND BOQUETE

Toria gave me a ride to David, to stay at her brother's house. I had spent time with her brother, Henry, on another visit, when he was a salesman for the brewery in Penonome that produced the most popular beer in the country. Since that time, Colombians had taken over.

Many Colombians were flooding the country, buying companies like the brewery. They would lay off the employees and provide jobs for other Colombians.

Her brother switched to selling medical equipment, and moved to David. He lived in a nice home in a quiet neighbourhood. I had to take a cab to get to a couple of big malls. Toria was at work, and looking after her mother in the evenings. We went to the mountains north of David, where it was much cooler. The next day I took a bus back there to find a place to spend the rest of the time I would be in Panama.

I found a comfortable place there in Boquete, where I stayed for a couple of months. The town of about 20,000 residents includes about 3,000 expats, mostly from the US and Canada. Situated fairly high in the hills, the ambient temperature is much lower than the intense heat in the rest of the country. Some of the finest coffee beans in the world are grown there. A beautiful 18-hole golf course was empty, with a nice empty restaurant. A friend and I rented a golf cart and rode around the course.

Bars owned by expats kept a lot of people on the bottle, and was where I hung out. They were the gathering spots for a lot of us, a place to socialize. Drinks are really cheap, not a burden on a lot of people who had little money. Quite a few of them would go home and get into the hard stuff, and then have a toke to help them sleep. Most of them smoked weed. They would be back for opening the next day. What a life!!

I wondered why it was going to cost me so much for health insurance, while all these people of lesser financial means were living there permanently. I discovered they don't have insurance, hoping that nothing will happen. In Panama, minor medical conditions are inexpensive, like broken bones, doctor visits due to illness, and prescriptions. If you have a heart attack or stroke, you're doomed, die physically or financially.

Some people were hiding from the law in their home country. One fella from Europe had an expired passport and no means of renewal. He was a wanted felon in Europe. When travelling from Boquete to David, a check-stops requires a passport check. The country is really sticky about the six month stay limit without registering. It requires leaving the country for a day every six months, stamped in the passport. This guy would get out of the vehicle prior to the check-stop and skirt it about half a mile out and return after to get picked up on the other side. It is a dangerous way to live, as jail is the penalty.

The owner of the bar I frequented liked to have a shot of coke on occasion. He had a bad one, insulting his wonderful wife beyond anything that any human being should be subjected to, then attacked us for not helping her. I changed bars for a couple of weeks. When I went back to see how the boys were doing, he asked why I wasn't there, and if he had done something wrong. He was sorry he asked, but humbly apologized and brought me a beer. There is no excuse on earth for this behaviour.

The music scene was very active, with most bars having live entertainment most nights of the week. Some very talented musicians had moved there, older but still very good. One of my buddies was the lead guitarist with a well-known and popular Canadian group before arthritis set in, although he was still good for one tune, and a pleasure to be around.

There were some positive reasons for staying there, like live theatre, good music, a newcomer's club, good people, lots of activities, and great weather all year round. If you have the resources you can buy into the exclusive neighbourhoods. They were good.

HEADING HOME

There were many legitimate reasons to not stay in Panama. Firstly, my friend Nataly had changed, being more engrossed in her work than ever. She was building up an empire for her son and daughter to take over, but both families were pregnant and unable to help her. She was very busy, unable to take the time to travel or be involved in social activities. There would not be much of a life for me.

Personally, I realized that most or all of the activities I have become accustomed to would not be available. I would have to buy a car, or be totally dependent on Nataly to do anything. The traffic situation in Panama City is absolutely horrible. The final spike was the cost of health insurance. A few years earlier the government encouraged expats to retire there, and made available very good and inexpensive health plans. The new government changed all that, so it was necessary to go to an international agency. My medical history is clean, but due to my age, the cost would be very prohibitive. It was still tempting; Panama is a beautiful country with beautiful people.

My friend in David, Toria, was retiring from her job at the university. Her idea was for me to build a house for us in David. This was not to my liking, along with possible expenses for her daughter's education in university. Along with the constant heat and lack of activities, it would not be wise. We could have lived in Boquete, but I found there to be a lack of acceptance of Panamanian women in the expat community, and that would cut out a lot of life there. I found out early when I was at an event with a lovely woman, when a white trash woman asked me which street corner gutter I picked her up. Actually, my friend was 10 times classier, but that is the attitude.

I returned home to the island in Canada after three months in Panama. It was a great trip, as always, but good to be home and thinking about another trip. In fact, a month later I was in South Korea.

Cuba

A 40 DAY VISIT, DECEMBER 07 & JANUARY 08

I wanted to visit Cuba before a ban by the US government may be lifted on Americans going there. I booked a 14 day all-inclusive resort in Veradero, because it was less expensive than a return flight to Havana. My interest was not to hang around with tourists at a resort doing watered-down drinks and stuffing with food. So I used the resort as a resting place, and a base for touring the Island. Americans were there, arriving through Canada or Mexico, and returning home the same way. Of course, the Cubans want all the tourism they can get, so they help by not stamping passports.

Cuba was interesting to visit for the scenery, history and landmarks, the forests and tropical swamps with alligators. More interesting were the people and their customs, the conditions of living under the strict rules of communism.

The story of Che Guevara and Fidel Castro leading a successful revolution was much celebrated. Everywhere you go, you will find statues and pictures of their heroes, Che and Fidel. The museum about the Bay of Pigs invasion by the US aptly documents how the situation was handled. They had a piece of the spy plane on display that they shot down, and the invasion plans they found on the plane.

After two weeks at the resort, I purposely missed the return flight home. Instead I was on a bus to Havana, and had no intentions of going home at that time.

I spent the first day or two at a hotel in the capital. One of the guests was a lady from Hong Kong who would spend one day in Havana, then off to some island for a day, then somewhere else. I don't know how that could be rewarding.

Then I met a lady walking down the street, friendly and interesting. She was single with a six-year-old daughter, a younger sister, and an uncle. She found a legal private home for me to stay, but I spent a lot of time with them, in their apartment or touring around the city. I could have stayed in their home, except it was illegal and punishable for anyone to put up a tourist unless their home is registered and licensed. The little sister was about 10 days from being of legal age, so I could not be seen in public alone with her. The consequence would be jail for me.

Being in Havana was an adventure. It was a pleasant time there, the old cars in immaculate shape, the little coffee bars, the generally happy demeanor of the people, the old railroad. I attended an opera in their beautiful Opera House, with talented artists performing. I had a pleasant conversation with five of Mother Theresa's nuns, noticeable by the light blue habits they wore. We went swimming just out of town, at a nice beach.

There was no motivation to maintain the buildings in Cuba, particularly in Havana. No maintenance was being done, and as a result they were falling apart. One area showed watermarks on the buildings where the wild sea flooded whenever there was a big storm, which was often. The buildings were marked two blocks in from the shore.

My new friends in Havana taught me a lot about life there. They are basically happy. Education, including university, and medical and dental services are all free and available to everyone. As part of the high school curriculum, students spend time at a vegetable farm learning how to provide for themselves. Everyone gets a paycheck, regardless of their work, and food was readily available as far as I could ascertain. Music is very important, so many people play instruments and sing. The only people complaining were foreigners who thought it was total poverty because they weren't living up to North American standards. The only problem is, doctors work as waiters because they earn more with the tips. It is worth noting that the level of medical training, at that time funded by Venezuela, was advanced enough for doctors around the world to go to Cuba to learn procedures.

There are not enough resources to waste on cremations on the island, so they have a different ritual. After being buried for two years, they have a celebration where they dig up the remains, and collect the bones to be put in a box. The box is placed in a plot with the rest of the family, thus saving much space at gravesites.

A must visit was to a cemetery in Havana, where the scene is much the same as anywhere in Latin America. The mausoleums for entire families are well maintained, big and beautiful, some like small churches, and big statues.

There are two currencies in Cuba, the local Peso, and the tourist money. To make a purchase, such as bus fare, would be two or three times more for a tourist. A high-roller Cuban guy was pulling out a roll of bills that barely fit in his fist, flashing it in front of everyone, buying everything he could. I couldn't help but laugh, and he had a big grin on his face.

My friends lived in an apartment with access to the rooftop, where one could relax in the sun, or hang out their laundry. I spent Christmas day there, having the usual Cuban Christmas dinner. As I remember it was some kind of pork in a broth, very tasty. I bought a colouring book and crayons for the little girl for a present. They were readily available at the store, but she didn't have them. The little girl was looked after by everyone, not necessarily by the mother. The uncle sat in his chair drinking rum and listening to music being played at such a level that it moved me to the rooftop, especially when he started singing with it.

Everywhere you looked from the rooftop, there was a satellite dish, allowing them to watch American TV programs. Of course this was bringing discontent to the people, who thought that all life in America was like what they saw on TV.

After about three weeks in Havana, I returned to Veradero for a flight back to Canada. It took a week to get a seat, which cost more than the original resort for two weeks plus flights. It was worth it.

India

A STOP IN SINGAPORE, SIX MONTHS IN 2008

Singapore

A local travel agent in Kelowna booked a flight and a hotel for me because I would be arriving late in the evening. She booked a room at a hotel in the redlight district, which she thought was very funny when I asked her about it later.

It was good, lots to see, easy access to downtown and the port.

The area had the sex trade signs common to Viet Nam and Thailand. The women happened to be Vietnamese, posed in a glass enclosure for the pleasure of men to peruse and choose as they may see fit. It is disgusting, but that's life.

I ran into a young fella, Mahid, staying at the hotel I was in. We decided to tour together to see the sights of Singapore. He was a good guy, early twenties, and a Muslim from Turkey. It was almost embarrassing to hear him in a restaurant, asking in a loud voice if the fork had ever touched pork. We spent a few days together and got along well. He invited me to come to visit him and his family in Turkey someday, and I'm glad he did.

Singapore has great architecture, like the famous Raffles Hotel. It has one of the largest ports in the world, good restaurants, nice beach, and malls. It seemed that the local people were used to foreigners for business, rather than as tourists.

On to India.

India

Immediately upon entering the terminal at the airport in New Delhi, the feeling of closeness overcame me. I would soon get over it, as that's the way it was and the way it would be for the next six months. The first thing that happened was an ATM failing to deliver Indian currency cash. The next ATM worked. Fortunately it was only10, 000 rupees, or CDN$200.

After a good night's sleep, I went for breakfast, and was again overwhelmed by the denseness of humanity. It was so different culturally that I didn't feel confident to go out sightseeing on my own. I found a tour agency that provided me with a car and sort-of English-speaking driver. He would be guiding me on a tour of Rajasthan. He told me, "We are driving slowly car," which meant that the car didn't have much power. That was fine, as it is difficult to get up a lot of speed when you share the road with elephants, camels, cows, and trucks with a balloon of hay ten times the size of the truck. In fact, I did have the opportunity to ride on a camel and an elephant along the road. The locals really enjoyed having me do that. We were moving the same speed as the cars.

Transportation in India was something to behold. Old buses, trucks, would be jam-packed with people, some hanging out the back and sides, or crowded on top. Buses had produce piled high on top. Trucks with a balloon type of container would be as wide as the whole road, making the vehicle invisible.

Men and women with their shops in the street would have their workbench on the sidewalk. They would squat, not sit, and work at their craft such as shoe repair, or watch repair at ground level.

Along the road, a man at a desk was on his cell phone, with advertising for his businesses. They included: safaris by camel, horse riding, taxi, money changer, travel tickets by airplane or bus, and a few other things. He had the most inclusive business that I have ever seen, and he was a one-man-show.

The streets in the towns along the way were cluttered with marketplace businesses selling everything you can imagine. Monkeys are tame from spending so much time around people. On occasion a wild pig would come wandering through looking for food scraps on the floor. But cows did roam freely. You would be very blessed if you could lure one into your home, and they say, a sacred event if it left a cow pie on the floor. So the story goes.

The same company that produced Kingfisher beer and owned Kingfisher Airlines was in the process of making a car costing about $2,000 for financially disadvantaged people. Kingfisher beer still has the biggest share of the beer business in India. The owner is one immensely rich Indian man. The disparity between the very rich and the very poor is obvious, but how many are at a level in between is obscure. Everyone seems to be happy with their lot in life. The type of dress separates the very poor.

I'm sure there were hungry people in India, but I can honestly say that I never saw one person in distress from starvation. If you have seen the movie *Slumdog Millionaire*, you would remember the 'slums' it was shot in, showing despicable conditions. I spent an afternoon walking through this very same 'slum' in Mumbai where the film was made. Certainly it is not where we would like to hang our hat. What was there was a lot of people, crowded like everywhere in India, skinny like everywhere in India (because of the vegan diet), but strong and happy.

Incidentally, I found the Indian people to be the kindest, most sincere, and most enjoyable people to be with, anywhere in the world. They were not the top caste people, and almost no one was wearing a turban. I felt completely safe at all times everywhere I went. As an example, I got on a train, into my car area with six beds. An Indian fella had just put his dinner on a plate. When he saw me he divided his meal onto another plate and handed it to me. These acts of kindness were common.

India is the most diverse nation in the world, in every aspect of living. Despite the attempt to eradicate untouchability by doing away with the 'Caste System,' it is still dominant in the social system. The levels of social acceptability, education, wealth, are clearly divided. The problem as I see it stems from the fact that the top caste is the wealthiest and has the most political power to make change, and that is obviously not to their benefit.

Religion in India is about 80 percent Hindu and 14 percent Islam, with a fusion of many others. Their 'Gods' that they consider to be important number in the thousands (some say millions) to includes animals, such as the monkey, tiger, elephant, cobra, even the rat, but especially the cow. The Bishnoi religion is purposed to protect trees and animals. For centuries, grand temples have been built and the people use them as a purpose for living. They are magnificent, beyond description with endless meticulous artwork and sculpturing.

The availability of education is very much dependent on the caste level. An English newspaper had an article stating that the system for a certain group or level was being upgraded for schooling to being granted to 24 percent from 17 percent of the students over 14 years of age. English has been the language of instruction in most schools. English is spoken by most people, a result of British rule.

Apparently, the "Begging Mafia" controls who begs and who doesn't. It's not hard to figure, if you don't pay, you don't beg. The Mafia chief was said to live in Hong Kong.

One afternoon in Delhi a lady was begging for money. She looked so pathetic, I really thought if I don't give her something, she'll be dead by midnight. I learned a long time ago to not give to beggars, but she really looked bad. A phone was ringing, to which she reached into her sari and produced a cell phone. She cheerily said "Hello," with a big smile on her face. She finished the call, put the phone away and grinned at me. She put on such a convincing performance, I gave her something for the show.

An Indian wedding party was moving on the street. With all the pomp and ceremony, the parents on both sides seemed to be having all the fun as they led the couple around. The bride and groom both looked miserable, just wanting this thing to be over. All the ladies in the parade looked amazing in their colourful saris and jewelry. Indians love their jewelry, especially gold. During the wedding season in India, the price of gold in the world increases. Not that they are superstitious, but wedding dates can be unlucky, like July is bad. There are unlucky wedding colours, such as yellow, red, gray, and others. But gold will always be lucky.

Throughout this chapter on India, I find myself thinking in superlatives to describe people, places, and events in my experiences. It is well earned.

RAJASTHAN

The tour was based on the Golden Triangle, from Delhi to Jaipur to Agra and back to Delhi. I left with my driver to explore Rajasthan. It was the perfect decision, although a bit costly but worth it. The first stop was for lunch, where a young boy in a costume danced for me, expecting payment for his services. That's how he made a living. Each mile along the way had some new amazing never-imagined sights of people, temples, animals, shops. I don't have the words to express the sights and the emotions that I felt. Every personal contact with the people was with pleasantly unexpected kindness and sincerity.

The temples and other buildings of a religious nature were beautiful, only describable with photos. The hordes of people who flock to these temples are very fervent.

The homes can vary significantly between rich and poor. At one location, a group of people lived in loose straw and tarps, or under a wagon. They have been living that way for 1,000 years. Turning around, there were two big hills, little pyramid-shaped mountains, with a mansion on top of each. They were owned by one man, who kept his wife on one hill, and his mistress on the other.

We checked into a hotel in Jaipur, the Pink City. The next morning my driver took me around to see some of the temples. He dropped me off at the large temple with a lake up against the steps. The lake was considered sacred for cleansing the body, and maybe the soul People came every day to bathe. After an hour or so, I returned to the car and driver. There he was, gone! The SOB assumed that I wanted to wander around for the day, so he left. I made the mistake of not having a hotel business card, and was unable to remember the name. I was lost.

We had been driving in circles, so backtracking was impossible. Jaipur is a big place. Soon all hotels looked the same, and I would have to ask at the desk if I was registered there.

I walked into a temple, a man asked if he could be of assistance. On hearing of my situation, he burst into action to help me. I described what I could remember, and one particular thing stood out for him. He took me to three or four hotels until we finally hit the one my bags were in. I thanked him, and he said he would return. Turns out he was a High Priest, and insisted on giving me a blessing.

He should have given my driver a blessing for what I was going to say to him in the morning.

The blessing was with words, prayers, beads, in exchange for a very small fee to help his mission. He wanted my contact information at home. I found out why much later when he sent a hand-written letter requesting that I sponsor him and his family and send money for them to come to Canada.

One of the extraordinary buildings was the Hawa Mahal. It is grand and ornate, intended for royalty, built with small honeycomb windows so that the public can't see in. There are many other temples, including one built in the middle of a lake, and a fort on top of a hill.

Young women were very friendly but only in groups, safety in numbers, I think. The young men were inquisitive about a lot of things.

The road to Agra from Jaipur was a mishmash of slow-moving cars, trucks, elephants, camels, tractors, cows, bicycles, motorbikes, and people walking. The cows had the right of way. If they stopped, everything stopped. We passed a production process with a high stack for making blocks for buildings. Several places had cows, the produce being cow-pies formed into discs to be used as fuel for cooking. Grain harvesting was under way.

Agra is the home of the Taj Mahal, the next stop. The marble is white, bright, and beautiful. The intricate windows are built of a single thin layer of marble, with an exact pattern of holes. The whole place is amazing. The popular white building is only a part of the palace. Reddish-brown buildings surround the Taj, and as usual are amazing structures.

Memories of Agra are of giant traffic jams. That's not unusual, but there it was important to lean on the horn forever, even when it's obvious no movement was possible. And to make it worse, they had advanced decibel horns to make you crazy, and deaf.

The city of Varanasi is on the banks of the Ganges River, where they perform cremations and associated ceremonies. When a person dies, the family gathers on the banks, lighting on fire a huge pile of wood with the cadaver inside. They would remain for sometimes two days for the coals to cool, then gather the remaining bones to place in the river. Paper bowls with flower petals and a lit candle were set afloat.

The Ganges is one of the 'sacred rivers' where everyone bathes to cleanse their body and soul. The river is revered. It was thought that the water might be filled with bad bacteria, but no one gets sick. Giant fish in the river are said to grow large from eating the unburnt remains going into the water.

Every evening after dark, hundreds of people gather in a light ceremony, with multiple priests giving sermons. The people in attendance set many floating bowls into the water. I was on a boat watching the rituals. Pictures were prohibited, but I couldn't resist.

There is another city nearby where they place the dead on the peak of a nearby mountain, where the vultures would come to feed. It stopped being an effective process, as the birds had trouble hatching their eggs due to pollutants. There weren't enough birds.

We stopped at Sarnath on the way back to Delhi. It is the birthplace of Buddhism. Sites were being dug up, with ancient ruins nearly 2000 years old. They say the Lord Buddha preached his first sermon there.

Upon return to Delhi from the Rajasthan tour, I met up with my friend from Japan, whom I had met in northern Thailand. She was suffering from a shoulder injury she got in Viet Nam, when a guy on a motorbike rode past and ripped the purse from her arm. We would be travelling together on and off throughout India. She was married, and while it would be a sign of weakness in Japan for her husband to allow her to work, she had nothing better to do than travel. If she worked it would mean that he was unable to financially support his family, a big shame for a Japanese husband.

We toured around Delhi, saw some historical and beautiful sights. One I recall, was a church that was built for the poor. So to pay for it, they had to charge people each time they attended, a fee that very few could afford. The result, there were a lot of tourists there, but no Indian people. The government grounds were impressive.

I met a friend of my Japanese friend, a young Indian fella, who looked exactly like Mr. Bean and played the part perfectly. They are big into movies there, with Bollywood producing more movies than Hollywood. We went to a movie theatre to see one. It was in English, with a subtitle in Hindu. I didn't think it was that good, but the Indian audience seemed to like it. I walked by a Bollywood production, and unknowingly came a little too close. I was quickly escorted away, with authority by a couple of henchmen. They wouldn't tell me why but I saw a sign.

TO CENTRAL INDIA

The incredible train system in India is how most people travel. I went to the Delhi train station, got a ticket to go south, and got on the train. But not so simple. There are many tracks that fan trains to different regions of the country. I asked how to get to the car I was in. He snapped and a kid came, looked at the ticket, took my bag, and led me up a stairway to a gangway that crossed 100 tracks. He led me down to a platform, to a car on a train that had my name on a sheet attached to the car. He took me inside to my section, which was a division of the car with six beds, three bunks on each side. I'm not sure how I got off at the right stop.

The plan was to go to the central part of the country, away from tourist areas, where a lot of temples are. I bought a train ticket in the Delhi train station, bound for somewhere around Nagpur. I stayed in several places, moving from one place to another by bus or train. I lived in the area for more than two months. In that time, I stayed in the best hotels, ate at the best restaurants, rickshaws to temples, chai tea every morning, drank copious amounts of beer, and travelled. I could not spend $10 a day. There was not a tourist to be seen for 1,000 miles. I lost 35 pounds from the fantastic vegan food, so delicious, and felt really strong.

Three dollars a night was the most I paid for hotel rooms. Some restaurants let me into their kitchens to help prepare food. I got used to the heat, and would order food hot, not tourist hot but Indian hot. They would gather around my table to watch, as they didn't believe I could handle it. Beer was good, about 20 cents a litre. I would return to India tomorrow, just for the amazing food.

There seemed to be thousands of temples, and I could not get enough of them. The intricate patterns, the sculptures, murals, the multi-headed gods, the colours were all amazing. Every one of them was an adventure.

One bad thing that happened—someone cut the bottom out of my pants pocket and got my wallet as I got onto a train. One sad thing, I was downloading pictures from the camera memory stick to CD when the power went out, deleting 1,000 pics, mostly of the temples, from the stick and the CD, everything gone.

KERALA

The southern tip of India has nice beaches. That would be my next stop, a train ride to the state of Kerala. The lady next door at the motel asked where I was from. I said Canada. She said British Columbia? I said yes. She said Kelowna? I said yes. She said Lower Mission? I said yes. She was a stonesthrow neighbour of mine back home, and somehow she recognized me. I gave up on the idea that I can hide.

I saw construction workers carrying pieces of slate, 10 high on their heads. They were throwing pails of cement in a relay, up several stories. They never missed. The floors of each level were being held up with sticks, as I saw in Africa and Thailand. It must work as no buildings were tumbling down.

I met a young lady from Japan who had come to find an Indian boy to spend a couple of weeks with. I later learned this is very common. Ladies would come from all over the world to spend time with young Indian men, then leave knowing there would be no ties or after-effects. It is so that if an Indian woman is not a virgin on the wedding day, she is unfit for any man, and is shunned and undesirable forever. So we have a big supply of frustrated horny young men, waiting for their parents to pick out a bride for them. The word on the street was a caution for tourists, "If you sleep with one, be prepared to take her home with you, there is no escape."

I remember a pizza from a Pizza Hut franchise in Kerala, with Indian food on it. It is one of the best pizzas I have ever had, only rivaled by a pizza that I had in Panama City at a Domino's franchise.

Kochi was the next stop, up the west coast, a fishing city of about 600,000 population. All sorts of mechanisms for netting fish were set up along the shore. The restaurants were all about seafood. Markets were lined with sellers of spices. It is one of the finest natural harbours in the world and was the centre of the world spice trade for many centuries. The Portuguese spice trader Vasco da Gama lived and died in Kochi.

BANGALORE

On to Bangalore, the Silicon Valley of India, a city of about five million. It was the most progressive and developed city, blessed with a great climate, a modern metro system, and great pubs, restaurants and shopping. IT companies had flocked to Bangalore where the tech talent was being concentrated. Night-life seemed to be everywhere, the biggest attraction was turning on the lights of the parliament buildings, and where thousands would gather to see what was spectacular.

The city grew so fast, it has since become what they call a "dead city." It is unplanned so no sewer system or road planning was done to keep up with the growth. Corrupt politicians and greedy real estate people have been blamed. The result now is that water resources are being depleted, greenery is gone, and slums developing. Too bad, I really liked Bangalore, where my Japanese friend joined me again. We were strictly friends, but she was an interesting companion, as she had spent a lot of time in the country.

We headed north along the coast stopping at several small towns and cities, considerably less developed than Bangalore. Monkeys were everywhere and the odd litter of pigs would be rummaging the streets. The colourful transportation vehicles, be it trucks or tractors, were painted up like their temples, with fresh flowers and wreaths on them.

I helped a team of about 30 fishermen on the beach pull in a gigantic net from the sea. While some were holding the net on one end, the rest of us tugged from the other side. A lot of fish were pulled in, of which they offered one big one to me. Now what would I do with a fish? They were happy and kind, and appreciated my help.

My Japanese friend went her way again, while I continued north to who knows where. Anyway, I stayed there for a few days. I hired a rickshaw taxi driver to show me around. The vehicle was a three-wheel motorbike. We became friends, and he still emails me.

He wanted to take me to a park. I said okay, and an hour later we were there. I hadn't figured out his agenda. The park was nice, with rivers and jungle-like trees, animals everywhere. Then I realized that it was his home. He took me to his mother's house, small, plain, and no furniture. She insisted on cooking me a meal of shrimp, for which I paid generously. Then he drove me around to meet the neighbours and friends in the village. They were all really happy to talk to me, as my driver stood proudly by. He was showing off to his friends. That made him very happy. One neighbour was milking a cow. She had a PHD and was teaching at a university, but lived simply in a moderate home and had a cow with a calf in a pen attached to the house. It was all very interesting, but I missed the bus and had to stay another night, no problem.

On the way to Goa, I stopped at a beach where I ran into some people from Norway. One amazing lady was an artist by accident. She had done several paintings, and unknowingly broke protocol by taking them to a gallery to be looked at. No one does that, they wait then make appointments. The head of the gallery gave in and looked at them. He put them in the next showing and they all sold. When she decided to go to India on a holiday, she did a painting and sold it, which covered all of her vacation expenses.

There was a fair in the area. If you can imagine, a Ferris wheel was being turned by young fellas running up poles built out the sides of the seats. They would run onto the bottom pole, and jump to the next pole to keep the wheel turning. Their weight would bring the pole down and the thing turned. Hard to explain, but it was weird and unsafe. Where was my camera?!?

I met some Aussies there. One was a chef who just got hired to work on a private yacht. They asked him what dishes he cooked, he told them, "Whatever is in the frig," and they hired him on the spot. I would later travel with them from Goa to Mumbai.

GOA

The state of Goa was Portuguese controlled until the Indian army moved in and took over. There was no opposition, so it was done. Goa is famous for the hippies being there, free love and lots of cheap opium in the hippy days. When I was there, it was a favourite vacation area.

I found a nice little room on stilts for little money, at an area called Palolem, on the beach. Nearby were lots of restaurants with dances and entertainment. I met some nice ladies from England that I hung around with. I am still in touch with one of them. Lila divided her time between Goa, Melbourne Australia, and Brighton, England. Her daughter lived there in Goa with a baby son. I spent a couple of weeks there on the beach. As the end of the season was coming, the water warmed up to have bugs that give me the 'itch.'

I was having breakfast one morning, when I saw a cop hitting a woman with a stick. She was carrying a baby, and had a youngster on her hand. I thought it was a joke of some kind, not a believable action. Later I was told that she was being beaten and driven off the beach because she was begging, and hadn't paid her begging fees to the cop. It's fortunate that I didn't know the truth, or I would likely still be in an Indian jail.

There was another happening where a 14-year-old tourist from England was in a shack on the beach with some local boys, when she OD'd on their drugs. They took her away and hid the body. Everyone knew who did it, but it took days for the police to investigate. Meanwhile the shack was removed, the body was found and an autopsy done, saying she died of natural causes. When the parents demanded the body go to England for a proper autopsy, they found that all of her organs had been removed, so there was no way of finding the truth. There is no question of corruption in the government, the police and anyone with authority.

Soon it would be monsoon season. This meant that all of the accommodations, including the one I was in, would be dismantled and removed from the area, as the flooding would take it to sea.

So I caught a train to Mumbai, oddly enough with my buddies from Australia.

MUMBAI

The extreme heat in Mumbai didn't get to me. In fact, I stayed at a hostel without air conditioning. As long as I had an overhead fan, I was comfortable, acclimatized. The one thing I liked was the bathroom cleansing, with water spray. Toilet tissue is not to be found there. I really appreciate having a bidet.

There was an accident on a bridge where a motorcycle went down. Ambulances arrived on both sides of the bridge. While they argued for a long time about which side of the bridge he was on and whose area he was in, the guy died. It was in the newspaper.

There was a big kafuffle down the street at some big fancy hotel, where diplomats were being shot. It was an international incident and created quite a commotion.

Mumbai is an interesting city, the financial capital of India. Many nice parks and museums are where my time was spent. I went to Kamala Nehru Park, a big zoo. I walked a part of the Mumbai slums.

My time was done in India. It was the end of my visa and I had to leave. I caught a flight from Mumbai to Delhi, and Delhi to Seoul, and home to Vancouver. It was a long amazing time in such a diverse and friendly country, an experience I will never forget.

Turkey

A TWO MONTH QUICK TRIP 2012

The young fella that I met in Singapore, Mahid, had invited me to visit him in his country, and was the inspiration for me to go to Turkey. The time there was loaded with kindness, respect, history, and baklava with tea and Turkish delights. The population is 98 percent plus Muslim, so there are many mosques. There is a big tourist industry in parts of the country, particularly in beautiful Istanbul, and some resort areas on the beachfront.

Fortunately, I have some notes from my time in Turkey, making it a lot easier to write about. Reading about it and seeing the photos makes me realize even more what a friendly and kind people live there.

The culture of course is strange from what I am used to. Life is the same in so many ways, like the way they dress, go to work, swim, play cards, and drink beer and Ouzo. They are gracious as hosts, friendly and accommodating.

Their food is similar to Greek cuisine, but they have their own also. It is very rich, very sweet, and you eat often. I felt stuffed like a turkey. Tea or coffee is served at least every hour. Turkish pizza is very thin, with tomato paste and ground meat, made crispy. With spinach and shredded carrot salad, it cost $1.50. Besides the donair, the Turks claim they invented the shish-kabob. They have a drink in Turkey and the Balkans called Ayran, made with yogurt, water, and spices. It is very refreshing and stays with you.

Turks are very close to their families and look after each other. They amazed me with their sense of family and community and dedication to help one another when in need, not just for them, they did it for me.

The men talk to each other, and to women, like they are mad as hell. The women give it right back. Then things go back to normal.

I thought the men all had wives 15 years younger, but not true. Women are two or three years younger and look after themselves 12 years better than the men do.

All taxis are driven by Turks, and there are no 7-11s. Everyone eats at least six slices of white bread with every meal. They love to play cards, in coffee shops every table is used. They deal and play their hands counter-clockwise, opposite to how we play. Horses race clockwise, the opposite of races in North America.

While in Turkey, I saw very few women clothed to only show the eyes. A few of the older women dress in traditional Islamic clothing, and a few of the middle-aged women wear scarves. You would never know from the young people where you are. They love the water and it's hard to swim in burkas.

They call it the new freedom. There were stories about Iranian women changing to cover themselves as their plane lands in Tehran.

I had received several emails with negative comments about the Muslim people. Some were serious, some meant as jokes, but all pathetically ignorant of reality. The true character of nearly all Muslim people is kindness and understanding. It is true that there are some radicals, just enough to match the radicals opposed to them. I found the people of Turkey to be a close match to the people of India, as being the best people to be with.

Some Turk Muslims follow the faith reverently, pray five times a day, no alcohol, etc. But many do not. They have a drink, dance, and listen to modern music, divorce. But they still have the family values, respect for elders, support one another. I did not see a Turk with too much to drink, or even a sign of it. I did not see any stonings.

I was told by a Turk engineering student that Turks are kind to strangers and their own families, but not so tolerant of other factions or the government. They are very strong in their beliefs, to the point of being radical. The radicals are feared because they will turn on you if you don't believe in their cause.

The great majority of the Turkish people are peace loving, and are as concerned as we are about the radical movements within their own people, and how the total Muslim population is viewed so negatively by western countries.

I met a young couple from Holland who had just graduated with psychology degrees, with little chance of getting jobs. They were hitch-hiking and camping in people's yards (with permission). Their plan was to go through Turkey, then Iran, eventually to Australia. They were apartment-swapping and being very successful at it. And I thought I was adventurous.

ISTANBUL TO ISKENDERUN

İ spent three days in Istanbul seeing the sights, the famous Blue Temple (famous because it is blue, inside and out), Sofia, the Sultans castles, but mostly fighting traffic. The city is in Europe on one side of the water, and in Asia on the other side. It is an interesting city, especially the market which it is deservedly famous for.

The city of Iskenderun is a two hour flight from Istanbul, near the Syrian border on the Mediterranean coast. Population is about two million, with many villages in the hills nearby, with about 30,000 people. My friend's family was living in their summer homes on the sea. They also have three winter homes.

Their business is a transportation company, with six locations in Turkey. They had 150 tractor-trailer units with 40, 64, and 80 wheels, articulating 180 degrees by remote control, designed to move extreme loads from the ports to inland destinations. Some trailers were worth more than $five million. The father ran the business, while the two sons worked there. One son looked after another location, while the other son, my friend, ran around the world supposedly learning about the trucking business elsewhere. I learned so much watching his father interact with his employees. They spoke to each other with total respect, and the rewards were obvious. Everyone was happy, working together, helping each other. He got me into his office to spend some time together, but all we could do was share that candy, Turkish Delights, and smile at each other. I really admired the man.

With great fortune, I arrived in Iskenderun on the first day after Ramadan. Ramadan is four weeks of fasting (no eating during the day), no alcohol, and no sex. İt ends with three days of celebration, when family members get together. My goodness, what a lot of cousins.

When four weeks are over, all heck breaks loose. (Hell can't break loose, they don't know what it is. I suspect they find out what Hell is about a week or two after they get the 40 virgins).

The first day is offering of sweets. Everywhere you go you get strange little chocolates. They have a million sweet desserts. We went to a classy restaurant on a mountain in the village of Belen, where we had the greatest lamb for dinner. My friend's father and I drank a bottle of Ouzo, after a couple of beer each. The kids are not allowed to drink alcohol. He slept on the way home, then we went for a swim in the warm waters of the Mediterranean. The beach in front of their home was one of the few on the Mediterranean that was sandy, and not covered in small rocks.

The whole family treated me like royalty, eating often, drinking tea, great deserts, swimming, playing cards, meeting the cousins and uncles, some speaking a bit of English. All were very pleasant, inquisitive, and very respectful. They found a Canadian flag which they pinned to a palm tree in front of the home. A couple of the women expressed their concern to me that all Westerners think they are terrorists. Normally the women stay to themselves, but they each felt comfortable enough to talk to me about that. One of them had the cutest little baby that Mahid adored.

The war in Syria was ramping up at this time, bringing an estimated 100,000 refugees to camps across the border from Aleppo into Turkey.

Mahid and I went to his late grandfather's home. They had offered the home to some refugees from Syria. Eighteen were living there. It was sad to see people so frightened. Their houses in Syria were bombed in the night. None died, but a couple of the kids had scars on their faces from being thrown from their beds. The kids had not been able to sleep more than a few minutes at a time since then, afraid of another bomb exploding on them. The families had converted their cash that they had into dollars, and fled across the border with the children.

We visited the refugees from Syria in the camps along the border. In one place where they were without water, a local electrical company donated labour, and another a new water pump. Everyone helped each other. A father told us with tears in his eyes that some foreigner in town told him that he was a terrorist. All he ever wanted was to protect his kids.

AFTER ISKENDERUN

I left the hospitality of Mahid's family. I wrote a letter of appreciation to the father, but received no reply. An American journalist had been pushing the theory that Allah was a pedophile, and I thought that was why there was no reply. I found out years later that his wife had died shortly after I left. I had not met her, as she was on the journey to Mecca, which they all make once in their lives.

I was beginning to understand the culture, but had a lot to learn. At a resort town just down the beach, I went into a store to look for a shirt. None fit, but when I went to leave, the lady called me back and gave me a container of food from the fridge, roasted fish with rice and beans. I said no but she insisted, then I tried to pay her, but could not. It was delicious.

The bus to Meris was an adventure, to say the least. Things don't always go well, but this was ridiculous. We got to Adano and changed buses. The driver got into a fight with police for blowing his horn at a car that was stopped in the bus lane. Two cops and the driver were shouting and waving their arms, buses behind were honking. The passengers voted that he should shut up and drive and all verbally expressed that. So we parked and someone else started in on him. Not smart. We all grabbed our bags and got on another bus.

This bus was full. At one point, the door opened and one got on and two fell out. Thought I was in India again. We all voted on the situation again (seems very democratic) and everyone confirmed the results again to the driver. He didn't seem to care much.

Then the bus had a low tire, so everyone grabbed their bags and changed buses again. All except me, as someone had taken my bag and left his. While fixing the tire, a group of tea drinkers got word of the problem. We dug into the bag that he left and found an army ID. One man who spoke a little English called his mother for advice, while everyone else waved their arms and offered suggestions, while I had tea.

We proceeded to the bus station where the army guy was standing with my bag. We exchanged bags while about 30 bus drivers were grinning, insisting that I have tea with them before leaving. After tea, there was a lot of handshaking. I've never seen so much joy over a found bag.

Mahid's brother, who ran their business office in Meris, had waited for me at the bus station. He gave up as I was so late from the bus issues. We met the next day, touring the area and doing some neat things. One surprise was that he had a lamb slaughtered in my honour as a favoured visitor to his family's country. How many of you can say that?? The meat was cut up and delivered to the homes of his employees. A treasured part of the lamb was a massive deposit of fat that was distinctive to that particular breed.

He took me to his office where several employees were gathered. A funny thing happened there. An employee got a call from a woman in Spain, Marcia, who wanted to meet him. She said she was wealthy and so gave him 35,000 Euros. He put some in the bank, and bought a new car. Then he found out that she was going to jail for stealing 100,000 Euros from her ex-husband.

When they asked her for the money back, she said that she gave it all to a man in Turkey. Now he was afraid they will come after him. When I came into the office, intros were made. I told him. "Marcia es me esposa" which is Spanish for Marcia is my wife. He knew it was Spanish, and got scared. I explained to my friend in English what I had said, he translated to Turkish, and everyone in the place roared with laughter. Lucky Marcia will have 65,000 Euros waiting when she gets out of jail.

I asked the taxi driver to take me to a hotel not too far from the bus terminal, not expensive, with a restaurant nearby. Thirty-five minutes later, and 25 miles away, I'm at this hotel, 300 bucks a night. Seems they only understand what they want to. So he took me to another hotel, 50 bucks a night, beautiful place, had everything. I was looking out the window in my second floor room, while a wedding was about to take place right on front of me in a large courtyard. The bride and groom just arrived in a horse and buggy.

At least one wedding party a day was happening in the courtyard, with the music playing and guests dancing. The first night featured a crazy blonde, lots of dancing. Surprising how many blondes there, natural of course. Another custom is dying the roots black. Fireworks go with weddings.

I went out to dine and another wedding dress sat at the next table, with groom and best man. She looked miserable and ate with her elbows on the table. I wanted to warn him, but noticed that his tie was in the salad dressing, so I decided to mind my own business. That evening, as I viewed the ceremonies from my room, there they were. He had changed ties. They were sitting by themselves at a reception table for the marrying couple, while the rest of the guests were singing, dancing, drinking, but never paying any attention to the bride and groom. Only a little boy hung around them. I felt very sorry for them being totally ignored, and they didn't get up to join in the dancing and no one asked them to.

I watched some other weddings. Only one bridal dress was not bright red. They have some rituals of dancing and toasting the couple, while some brides are more outgoing, they all seemed to be having a good time.

Finally I ran into a bad Turk. They tried a scam that I'd seen before. I walked into a bar, they brought me a beer. Waiter then tells me he has girls that will give me sex, and has them come to sit with me. I said NO. He brought some coloured water to them, and I knew what he was up to. I moved to a different table. He brought more drinks to the hookers. I was informed that I have to pay for their drinks, 14 lira each drink. I got up to leave, and three guys blocked my way. He gave me the bill for my drink, which was for 100 lira, plus 14x4 for the girls' drinks, for a total of 156 lira. That would be about $80 CDN.

I put five lira on the table and left. What could they do?? Nothing. At no time was I in any danger what-so-ever. They try to intimidate, but it didn't go well for them this time. Two lira is about one dollar. Normal price for a beer is seven to nine lira.

These people were not true Turks, they were Russian, or maybe gypsies from Bulgaria. Russians are slowly taking over the beaches in Turkey. I found the same thing in Goa and Sweden, where the Russians are moving in.

A second unfortunate extortion attempt happened at a stop while travelling by bus. I used the bathroom, then gave the lady one lira. In a wild act of greed, she informed me that the price was four lira. I said no, but a member of the Mafia Latrina, aka crapper cops, came over to inform me that she was right. I countered by pointing to a sign saying WC 1 lira. I paid my lira and walked away, avoiding an international incident.

Whenever you are near a tourist area, these things will happen. Some tourists will be unfamiliar with the currency and will be taken advantage of.

I went for a haircut. The young barber did a good job, then offered this special treatment that he said everyone gets there. With me not knowing what was happening, he put this sticky stuff in my ears and up my nose. He later yanked it from my nose, pulling my eyeballs with it. Then he did the same to each ear. The pain was severe.

ALANYA TO CAPPADOCIA

The city of Alanya has about 35 miles of all-inclusive resorts on a nice beach, packed with tourists. I had a difficult time finding a place to stay. It is full of Germans and Brits, nothing new.

I went on a tour by bus to Cappadocia, with good company and of course bad driving. In Turkey, the centre dotted line on roads is a tool for motorists to align the centre of their vehicle when in motion, from both directions.

Drivers are a crazy bunch, and ours was leader of the pack. He passed a bus on a solid line blind curve while a taxi was passing all of us, when an oncoming car appeared. We all lived and the driver laughed. Ten minutes later an overturned minibus like ours was in the ditch with dead people. On the way home had traffic stopped for an hour with a body on the middle of the road. The British women on the trip were very vocal. Being in total control of their husbands, they thought they could handle the Turk driver as well. He never did conform to British standards.

Scenery in Cappadocia was spectacular. The "Fairy Chimneys" were strange looking, some with homes inside them. There were dug out of the hillsides, or inside those funny-looking domes. A 4.5 square kilometre city underground, called Derinkuyu, had several levels of homes, animal shelters and food storage. Several hot air balloons were taking people to see the site from above. The guide was personable and knowledgeable. All fourteen of us on the tour had fun.

We went to a traditional Turkish seven-dance performance, with snacks and lots of booze on the table. One of the Brit ladies got caught trying to take a bottle of vodka from the table. The security guy indicated to me that he was pretty smart catching her, but he didn't know that she already had bottles of raki and wine in her purse.

People on the tour included a couple, both doctors from Iraq, who were working at the university hospital in Saskatoon. She was in one of the classes that my brother-in-law, a professor, was teaching. A lady from Moscow gave me her email address, insisting that when I get to Russia I should stay with her and her husband. I emailed her, and said, "Hello Irena," but my spellchecker changed it to, "Hello Urinary." Fortunately, she had given me a wrong email address. I am more careful now.

A British couple recounted when their son and five of his friends were there on a visit to Turkey. Reservations at a B & B had been made for them. The kids went to the wrong address and announced themselves, and said they would be there for a week. An elderly lady made them lunch, and showed them where they would be sleeping. She made meals for them and did their laundry for three days, when the kids discovered they weren't in the right home. So they moved. She refused to be paid for those three days. Sounds like a typical terrorist to me.

Our guide asked what my plans were. He spent the next hour telling me where best to go, what routes to take, best way to travel. Then he called hotels and booked me for the next week at their tour prices, about half the normal. I've never been so organized.

ANTALYA, TO PAMUKKALE

Next day was to Antalya, further up the coast. Antalya has more than a mile of big resorts along its stony beaches. They were all filled, with tight security to not allow anyone to enter without being a registered guest. At most of them, I was unable to even enquire. I was lucky to find a place to stay.

I found a pension where no one spoke English. I ordered from the menu pictures, and got eggplant instead of a steak. At breakfast, I arrived five minutes before they opened. We watched each other for five minutes, then he smiled and waved me in.

It was an adventure finding the bus station to Denizli. Like the Latinos, they are always wanting to help you, even if they have to fake it rather than say they don't have a clue. I finally took a taxi there, near where the pension was.

It was a gorgeous drive to Pamukkale, less than four hours. We travelled from the sea into the mountains, pine trees then deciduous, into scrub land, then corn, veggies, and olives with irrigation. Villages along the way each had three or four spires, each belonging to a mosque. A valley appears, filled with a very large city, Denizli. Funny thing, 15 minutes before the bus station, we stopped for a half hour for lunch.

From Denizli, a mini-bus went to the village of Pamukkale and the limestone pools. The ancient Romans used the pools as a spa and resort. The word Pamukkale means 'cotton castle'. Mineral-rich warm water fills the pools, leaving deposits of calcium where the run-off is, down to the next several levels.

The pools were a small part of the area. The ruins of a first century AD Roman city were in great condition, including a 15,000 seat amphitheatre. A museum has early brass-age findings in it. A lot of tourists were there.

On a mini-tour to a museum, our guide showed us a statue that was found, the God of fertility. It was tiny, about three inches high, with a two inch thingy, and a little grin on his face. Priceless. So, this American says in a loud voice, "In Texas we call that a medium," and broke out in uproarious laughter. Several groups had to wait for him to stop laughing, while he stared at each one in the group, seeking approval. None was forthcoming, but that didn't bother him. He seemed satisfied that his wife giggled.

The next morning I was on a bus to Selcuk.

EPHESUS THE ANCIENT ROMAN RUINS

Selcuk is a small town near the Ruins of Ephesus, south of the Turkish capital of Ankara, and east of the city of Izmir.

I stayed in a hotel in Selcuk for a week or so, visiting many amazing sites in the area. The famous ancient Roman city of Ephesus is well preserved, well presented, and visited by many cruise ships. The city used to be by a deep river going into the ocean, but has since filled in with silt over the centuries. The city of Ephesus was abandoned when the silt buildup prevented ships from entering the harbour, resulting in the stopping of trade.

I was admiring the remains of an aqueduct by the hotel in Selcuk when a parade passed by. A young boy, about nine years old, dressed in a beautiful white robe, was riding a horse, with a big smile on his face. About 40 people all dressed up were drinking and dancing to the drumming.

I enquired about the big party. I was told, "Today he becomes a man, so his family is celebrating. He is being circumcised today."

"Why is he so happy?" I asked.

"Well, two reasons. First of all, he has to make a wish before he gets off the horse, and he usually gets what he wants, like a bicycle or laptop. Second reason, he hasn't been clipped yet."

More parades would come to the streets with young boys all dressed up real fancy. Some were on horses, others in carriages, some looked happy, others seemed to know what was happening. It must have been the season.

THE WONDERS OF EPHESUS

The tour of Ephesus was nothing short of a marvel. It was full of amazing history and ancient ruins. The archeological digging has unearthed a magical city called Ephesus. It was the number two city in the Roman Empire and represented another continent being conquered, shortly into the AD. It had been buried by a big earthquake and discovered very recently. A museum has artifacts dating back to 5,000 BC.

They had the second largest library in the world; only archives in Egypt had more documents. A large hospital with the snake symbol was dug up, with many small operating tools, including syringes. The rich had large homes, many slaves. There were hundreds of merchants with shops along the main street. It was a port, so ships came to trade their goods. They had a Love House with proper signage, showing a broken heart and a money sign in their advertising. Apparently, the wives did not like their husbands going there. So, the men dug a secret tunnel from the library to the love house. See where this is going???

The amphitheatre had 25,000 seats, known to be about 10 percent of the population. Tablets show that they had daily rituals with Gladiators vs Lions, with many people dying. I didn't see the scoreboard.

In the earlier days in Ephesus, when the population was 30,000, half of the people died. Some brilliant person discovered it to be malaria from the mosquitoes, so saved the rest of the city. Someone forgot to pass that info along to the people in Panama.

The ruins had an open biffy with many holes and a stream of running water to carry it away. The seats were made of marble, so would be very cold. That's where the slaves and servants came in. They would sit on the seats until warm enough for their masters to sit. It is written.

I'm not sure how the tour guides survive the stupid questions from tourists. I wrote down some that I actually heard asked. I also made notes of my thoughts of how they should have been answered.

Can they grow strawberries here? In Washington we have strawberries.

No. The FBI controls who can grow strawberries. Turkey is not on the "approved" list.

After they get everything dug, will there be anything left?

No and yes. They will dig until all that old stuff is removed. Then they will build a McDonald's

What did they use for toilet paper?

Not sure. Was that before Eaton's?? If so, stone tablets written by infidels would be used.

Did the women do all the shopping in those days?

Yes. All the men were busy at the library.

BVM

The Blessed Virgin Mary lived there! Have you never wondered, "Gee? What could have happened to Mary? She had her day with the birth of Christ and 33 years later when her son died, but where did she go from there??"

Well, she had a chapel near Ephesus, and I was in it. There were no burning bushes, but several thousand people each day went there, by the cruise ship load (seven of them that day) to see this, and Ephesus.

Saint John was there in Ephesus also. I asked the guide, where was Joseph?? His answer, Mary and Joseph fled to Egypt. The word is, Mary returned to Jerusalem to have the baby, but Joseph stayed in Egypt. Think maybe Joseph thought he might not be the father? So who was by the manger?

The writings they found say that when Jesus died he asked his most trusted apostle, John, to look after his mother. (Joseph was a no-show). It says that John moved her into his home.

Anyway, Jesus died at age 33. That made BVM about 50 to 55 years old. From Jerusalem she hiked to Ephesus with John the Evangelist, which took about three years. They built her chapel, and she preached in the people's homes, and died of natural causes in her sixties.

Saint John meanwhile, preached Christianity in public. He was making enemies, so the police took him off to jail for his own safety. They say John was the only one of the 12 Apostles to die a natural death.

I visited the ruins of a massive basilica near Ephesus, built in honor of St John in seventh century AD. It was huge, one of the biggest cathedrals in the world. It was destroyed in the fourteenth century by a massive earthquake. The tomb of St John lies under the central dome.

One mystery remains. So who was the man at the manger? It is written that Joseph tied his ass to a tree and walked all the way to Bethlehem, but that's a stretch. They say he remained in Egypt, while Mary returned to Bethlehem. I'm not sure how much hay is being spread here, but there isn't a real strong Christian representation there, about one percent, and 98 percent Muslim. So, the info may be slightly skewed.

BTW, Mary is mentioned four times in the Koran, the only woman to be mentioned.

At my Selcuk hotel, a conversation started with a 21-year-old Japanese girl named Yukiyo. She was travelling with her mother. Japanese husbands are tied to their work and wives are not allowed to, as it is a sign that he cannot support his family, so the mothers travel. It is convenient to go with the daughters, who speak English.

We chatted, her English very good, while her mother did not understand. Time came for them to walk to the bus station. Yuki's mother had bought so many souvenirs, she couldn't move her suitcase. So I dragged her luggage for three blocks and waited with them a few minutes until the bus was ready to leave. Yukiyo was a very chatty girl, with a sparkling personally.

She reached into her suitcase and brought out a little Japanese fan and gave it to me. She said, "I have been carrying this around in my travels for two years and have been looking for someone nice enough to give it to. Finally I found someone. I would like to give it to you." I believe it's called "ego-boost."

I got an email from her later. She had dinner with the president and some other executives of a trading company she would work for when she finishes her schooling. She is proficient in English and Spanish, and would be working with clients in Central and South America. Very nice young lady.

My waiter at the hotel became my friend. I ate there mostly, as little choice available with the tourists being from cruise ships. He nearly choked me with a big bear hug when I was leaving.

It was moving day. I flew from Izmir to Istanbul, and on to Sofia in Bulgaria. Total lack of info on transportation north of Istanbul left the only option to fly. The main train station in Istanbul burned down six months prior, still showing trains departing.

The Balkans

2012

It was the start of a very different cultural experience. The people have been put through hell and back many times, and it shows. They have been relieved of the modernization of the Western world, slowly recovering especially with the youth.

The children at age six knew more about politics than the average North American adult. It is essential to everyone there to know what to avoid, who to trust, and how to respond to different situations. They may not play or be happy the same way that we do.

The Balkans, Serbia in particular, for thousands of years have been in the path of some aggressor. Every time one goes by they take a swipe and kill a few thousand people. One town near Belgrade has been destroyed and reconstructed 29 times in its history.

No one eats breakfast in the Balkans. In fact, there are 20 coffee houses at least (serving only coffee) for every bakery that serves sandwiches, and 20 bakeries to every restaurant. I need breakfast, so it was a bit of a problem for me.

In Belgrade I found this big hotel near my hostel. Hotels can include breakfast with the price of the room. They had a big buffet going, looked great, so joined in with about 100 others. After eating, I could find no one to pay, so returned to my room.

Next morning, I thought that I should get this straightened out so I went back. I had breakfast again, picked up cutlery (carried in pocket), ate, and searched for someone to pay. But no, they were saying, it goes with the room. So again I left without paying. On the way to the hostel I felt something in my pocket. Guess what—not only did I not pay for two days, I stole the silverware. My compliments on the quality, the knife cuts tomatoes and bread. Breakfast would likely have cost about three dollars.

Bulgaria

The plane landed in Sofia, Bulgaria. I spent the next three days in an inexpensive hostel.

The post-Commie world is always an interesting place to be. The buildings are mostly six stories, with narrow long rooms, offices or living quarters. They are painted with pastel Commie colours where the plaster has not fallen off. Their clothing generally fits that pattern as well.

The men generally dress just fine, casual and clean. But, scatterings of odd combinations appear, such as a nice dark suit with a bright yellow roadrunner tie and red running shoes. Shoes are always polished (North America is the only place in the world where shoes do not get polished). There are lots of "be-afraid-of-me," tough guys dressed in black, with a diamond stud earring. The men still carried the look of distrust and talked in a tone of superiority. Perhaps another generation is needed.

The women however, were another story. Long pointed shoes, with a variety of strange combos. Imagine this: plaid rubber boots, bright blue spandex pants, with a lovely blouse of pink and white with yellow frills, and an orange sweater.

The older people have obviously had a hard life, rode hard and put away wet. The middle generation is scarred but moving forward. Then the youth don't seem to get it that life is tough and they shouldn't be happy!! They must drive the older people crazy with their laughter and enthusiasm, modern clothes, and appropriate makeup.

Makeup. That's another thing with the 40 plus crowd. No one sneaked behind the curtain and showed them how to use it, but the youth knew. And hair had been transformed from a crow's nest, to a neat clean and simple hairdo with the youth.

Otherwise, nice people as always. Everyone smokes, it stinks wherever you go, including restaurants, same as in Turkey.

Serbia

I moved on to Nis, central Serbia (pronounced Neesh). It was raining, so I had to drink beer, 60 dinar a bottle (1$ = 100 dinar). My hostel had marks on the wall from one of the cluster bombs going off in that street.

The only concentration camp from WW2 that is in original condition is located just out of the town of Nis. It is known as the Crveni Krst concentration camp, or the Nis concentration camp. Sixteen thousand Serbs, Jews, and Muslims were put to death there, twice that many were taken to Norway as labourers. Pens that held prisoners had barbed wire nailed to the floor in a pattern that forced the prisoners to sleep on it. The encampment has been made into a museum, with many actual photos of activities in the camp.

A "skull tower" was erected in 1809, with more than 900 Serbian skulls embedded in cement to teach them a lesson. It was an ugly reminder for the people to toe the line or suffer the consequences.

In 1999 the United Nations dropped three cluster bombs there, trying to take out the airport. They missed and instead hit the downtown area and the hospital, killing 24 and injuring dozens.

I made a mistake at the ATM, worried about asking for too many zeros. I read it wrong and got $20 worth of dinar. I had to do it again. I got all this from my memoirs.

It was a short bus ride to the Serbian capital Belgrade, known as the European party town, with many open-air bars along the Danube River. Belgrade is one of the stops of river cruises on the Danube. Lots of buildings were down or damaged from bombings. There were many parks and flowers in the downtown area.

I talked to an American Embassy worker, his first time out of the US. I asked if he felt safe there in Belgrade. He said he felt a lot safer there than he did at home in Detroit.

I missed an Il Divo concert in Belgrade as I didn't know soon enough. That would have been good.

I met a Canadian from Ottawa who had a masters in sociology and politics from London. He was a contractor to the UN and had been working in about 15 of the worst war-torn countries. He was so interesting to talk to. He seemed to have a bit of PTSD. He spoke in detail of some of the atrocities he had been in the middle of, the worst being the fight between the Hutus and the Tutsis in Rwanda. He spoke of several others. I listened to the experiences he was going through, very emotional for him. He expressed how much he appreciated having me listen, saying that he hasn't had anyone that would listen to him. I had to; I was speechless. It was definitely a memory moment for me. For him, he would be going back in, as he knew no other life.

He said that Canadians have a habit of expressing their opinions when they don't have the knowledge or experience to make judgment. Let's reflect on that, we are not perfect? Listen more, talk less??

It matches with my theory that you don't learn by talking, you learn by listening.

Bosnia-Herzegovina

When they talk about pretty scenery, they don't mention Bosnia. They talk about Slovenia, Montenegro, and Croatia. I would place Bosnia well up there with the rest.

When we crossed the border into Bosnia we were in the mountains, like a little Switzerland. There were forests, lakes, rivers, a little town on every flat space, and houses built up the hillsides. The houses seemed much newer, in better condition, and no poor areas that I saw.

Then we came to Sarajevo. What a delightful surprise. It has been called the cultural centre of Europe. Imagine how that would annoy a few cities. But it was amazing. In Old Town Sarajevo many buildings showed the scars of being under siege for four years. One apartment block had about 100 bullet marks around one window on an upper floor. Perhaps a sniper??

Sarajevo had hosted the Winter Olympics in 1984. Then someone bombed it for four years. Milosevic created conflict between the Croats, Serbs, and the Muslim Bosniaks. The Bosnian war started in 1992 and ended in 1995.

On to Mostar, about three hours by bus through hills, tunnels, following the Neretva River from Sarajevo. The countryside was rugged mountains with orchards and vineyards.

I had a tasty dinner in a unique orchard setting in Mostar, in the company of some local people. It overlooks the famous Old Town Bridge, or Stari Most, which stood for more than 400 years until destroyed in 1993 during the war. It was rebuilt in 2004 and became a UNESCO Heritage Site in 2005.

I recall thinking how happy I was to be there, and how fortunate I was to have followed my instincts to be in the Balkans.

Some of the people I met or travelled with in the Balkans include: Armando - Vancouver, Lars - pilot from Denver, Pete - government worker from Brussels, Jeff – Dutch freelance journalist, and Al – fraud investigator in LA

The next day I took the bus to Dubrovnik, in Croatia.

Croatia

The beaches in Croatia are about 70 percent naturist beaches (nudist that is). I'd been considering devoting my life to restoring some sensibility to this bad behaviour. Then I thought "Nawww, 12 hours a day for a month is enough."

Croatia is all about tourism. Italians, Germans, Austrians, everyone flocks there for a relatively cheap vacation, the wonderful beaches, the beautiful islands.

In reality, the beach two blocks from where I lived in Kelowna is nicer than any I have seen since leaving home. The islands are nice, but rocky with scrub brush, beaches stony, nothing near the islands off of Vancouver Island. No place like home, I guess. The weather was nice though, one day of rain, and hot sun with 30 degrees the other days.

It was nearing the end of tourist season and several months were approaching without an income for a lot of people in Croatia. They seemed tired and irritable, trying to drag the last kuna out of anyone who had some. In nine months, on July 1, 2013, Croatia would become a full member of the EU. The people were feeling the impending crunch of higher prices but the same income. Many were going to be hard pressed to make a living. Unemployment was at 20 percent and would jump up when the tourist season was over.

Their president had stated that about 120 families will get richer from belonging to the EU, and he doesn't care about the rest of the people. That's the word on the street. No wonder the people were nervous.

Croatia was twice as expensive as Bosnia, but still less than other parts of Europe. Passengers from several cruise ships were flooding the downtown area with tourists. Services were lacking. It is popular because it is on the ocean, and easily accessible from the rest of Europe, particularly Austria and Italy. My guess was that many of these people have never seen real sand on a beach before.

One beach is in town, another is a 15 minute bus ride (gravel beach). The "fabulous" one in town was at a hotel, with no public access. So I went to the hotel. Looking down some 50 metres, one could see the water splashing on vertical rock, except for one area of relief about 20 metres long, where a cement ledge had been placed extending into the water. This was accessible by a set of cement steps from the hotel.

So, I thought, what the hey, checked out the hotel, looked very average, can't be expensive. A single was 266 euros per night, but they were booked up for the next three weeks. Fortunately, it was well into the off-season.

Not being particularly impressed with Dubrovnik, I thought maybe catch a ferry to Split, see the islands along the way. No ferries were running, as this was the off-season. So I caught a bus. It is 209 kilometres and it took four and a half hours for the first half, then an hour on a beautiful freeway for the last 100 kilometres into Split.

Things are different there—more people, crowded, lots of restaurants, good entertainment in the square, lots to do. They even have a beach, only a 30 minute walk from the square. It has real sand, about 100 metres long, 10 metres wide, and rated at capacity of 3,500 people.

I had a decent place to stay, an apartment near the main square. The plan was to stay for a week or so and take a catamaran to some islands (day trips).

From Split I went to Hvar, an island hyped up to be the most beautiful place. It was very ordinary. Seven dollars for the ferry, $35 for the taxi to town (each way). So I asked, "What's in town?" They said, "Nothing." So I returned to Split and saved $70.

Split is a nice city. The people were just trying to make their way through life. It was very tough for them with the wars and the politics.

My favourite restaurant was a block from where I was staying. They served very good food with friendly service and a varied menu, but were not that busy. I returned often. After a couple of meals, the lady server brought me a dessert, on the house. The next dinner she brought me a beer, on the house. I thought she was hitting on me. Then she called a man over and introduced him as her husband. They were a beautiful couple, like many of the people there.

One day I was relaxing on a bench at the train station. An older man cleared his throat with a disgusting hork and spit. A three-year-old boy with long blonde hair was sitting with his grandmother. The boy decided to imitate the old man, about a dozen times, while his grandmother patiently tried to get him to stop. Very funny.

A Croat woman was carrying a bag of groceries and had a child in hand. When some items tumbled out of the bag I approached to help. She started yelling at me angrily, so I left. Two blocks away, I could still hear her swearing at me. I definitely could visualize a war with hammers and axes.

A lot of houses were empty in Croatia and in Serbia. The explanation was that Serbs used to live there in Croatia, and Croats used to live in Serbia and Bosnia.

I enjoyed the city of Split and the people in it. From there I was on my way to Zagreb by train, continuing on to Budapest in Hungary, my next destination.

Hungary

2012

The beautiful city of Budapest would be my new home for three weeks. Unlike Prague which was not disturbed by WW2, Budapest had been hit hard by the Germans and then by the Russians. It was left with scars but was beautifully rebuilt. Museums of the wars display the history and events. The architecture is beautiful, the buildings are old and mostly magnificent. The parliament buildings are something to behold, a beautiful sight from the other side of the Danube.

The Danube River divides the city of Budapest, with Buda on the west side and Pest on the east side. The two cities combined to become Budapest. The river is a highway for cruise ships. You will always find several docked for a day or two for city tours.

The people appeared to be pretty happy, hard-working, well dressed, with a social structure unlike North America, in that they value family more than we do. The Hungarian language, like the Finnish, is unrelated to any other in the world. There was no use trying to learn a few words, enough people spoke English.

The cuisine was different, but delicious, with many peculiar combinations. I always looked forward to mealtime. According to my notes, I had "minty lime soup with orange capuche cheese."

I felt a chill in the air, decided to have some soup to warm up. To my surprise, the soup was thick, delicious, and cold as ice. Speaking of odd things: where I ate breakfast, every table had a little stainless steel garbage can, about six inches high, on the table. Very cute. One of my dinner restaurants, quite classy, brought a little stand to the table, with six notches in it. Each notch can be fit with the tip of a big spoon with a curly handle. The spoons, one for each patron, will have some goody on it as an appetizer. I had never seen it before, cool.

I had dinner with a couple of Austrians and a couple from Nova Scotia. Imagine this: A Swiss guy moved to Nova Scotia and now arranges dental work in Budapest, including flight and hotel, saving thousands of dollars for dental patients. The NS people met the Austrians at the dental office.

From my hotel in Pest, I was able to walk up a hill to a fort and park, a historic place called Gellert Hill. It was a quiet peaceful place to relax for an evening, looking down at the sights of the city all lit up.

Short leather skirts were worn. They could have been made from a few mouse hides, they were so small. The women seemed to like their fake furs, on coats, purses, shoes, dresses. Men not so much, just their fur hats.

I got another haircut. This time I made them promise to not use a pasty stick to pull my brains out through the ears, like the last time in Turkey. I got a nice cut for eight bucks.

The main topics there, and around Europe at that time, were Malala, the girl from Pakistan, and Amanda Todd, the Canadian who committed suicide from cyber bullying.

ARRIVAL

It was the only tragedy of the entire trip. I caught a cab and got fleeced for about $40 extra. Apparently, they can change the rate of charging with a screwdriver on their metres. I wondered why it was spinning so fast. He had my luggage in the trunk until I paid. I was just happy to get to a place to stay. Major aggression with prejudice and malice was my first thought, but not so smart in a foreign country.

The cabbie took me to the Hotel Gold on the Pest side, east of the Danube River. The Pest side is newer, on flatter land. The Buda side is downtown, older architecture, and has much more shopping, restaurants, events and activities. I stayed at that hotel for a week, then moved to another nearby for a few days, until I was able to find a place to stay in downtown Buda until leaving the city.

I was lucky to get a room in a hotel just across the river in Buda. The whole city had been fully booked, even one hotel at $4,000 per night.

GETTING AROUND TOWN

I spent two days on a hop-on hop-off bus, all over the city. Graduation meant a week pass for bus/tram/subway. Next day I was on the bus, the tram, and on two of the three subway lines. It seemed easy, until the mix-up started. I took the bus across the Elizabeth Bridge and got off, then onto the tram running along the river, to a huge multi-level indoor market.

The market had everything you could imagine. One floor had kiosks selling meat and vegetables, fantastic, fresh. Another floor had jewelry, chocolates, and miscellaneous things. The upper floor had many restaurants serving amazing dishes. I ate there several times. Love local markets.

I left there, then returned because I was lost, found the tram, took the bus to a Metro station, and started the adventure in earnest. The first ride was easy. Then came the Central Station where the three lines meet. I wanted to go on the red line, but ended up on the yellow line platform. I had come in on the blue line. Suddenly no one speaks English.

Finally someone was available to ask. "Where am I"?

"Well, you are at zszgyùºõñïg, of course. Can't you read?"

I smiled and said, "I knew that." Then I retreated to a dark corner and waited for someone, the odd glance at my watch, and a look of disgust because they were late. I kept thinking of that old song about the guy who couldn't get off the train because he didn't have a nickel, so he rode it forever.

I left the station, found some nice kid who knew all about trains. Next thing I was riding all over the city.

I made a stop at the Parliament buildings to get some pics, and maybe a tour. I had my toes past a chain at the grounds, and some freaky post-communist throwback security cop started hollering at me. He might have scared me, but I'd seen it before. That's how the Russians talk to people if they have some authority. I guessed that a tour was out of the question. He made a comment about some "stupid turisto" or something like that.

I went for a tram ride out to see the island on the Danube River. Just before the bridge the tram stopped. I'm thinking next stop was mine, middle of the bridge. They tricked me, the tram reversed and went the other way. Wondering why so many people got off, I pretended that's what I had planned.

The tram took me back to the big indoor market. It's one pm on a Saturday and the shops are closing for the weekend. By three p.m., every shop in the city was closed, only hotels, bars, and restaurants remained open.

Saturday night, and I'm out for dinner downtown. I felt like a grub, everyone was dressed up—we're talking suits and dresses, young, old, middle, everyone dressed up, except us tourists. When was the last time you saw a 20-year-old wearing a suit to take his girl out for dinner? Of course she wore a nice dress with a corsage.

I was having a beer at an outdoor restaurant. The table down from me had three ladies in their 80s drinking wine, laughing and giggling, dresses and fun-furs, having a wonderful time of it. As they left, remaining wine was put into a plastic cup and capped to take away. They left still giggling, but returned moments later, as one had forgotten her cane.

Restaurants were full of couples, no kids. Saturday night is for adults. Four crazy Finn ladies crashed my table (place was full), claimed they were giving their husbands a holiday by going away. I believed it.

Sunday was family day, kids everywhere, playing, eating, running around, and just having fun with their parents.

I don't understand it. Am I missing something??? Saturday is the best day for a business to make money. They should be open till midnight, and the same for Sunday. That way their employees could work all weekend. And for shoppers too, the best time to look for bargains.
Or:

Perhaps there's a lesson to be learned here.

Now I'm finally in the "old town" where all the action is. I found some great streets very close by, no vehicles, just walking. Restaurants were still serving outdoors everywhere. The night was pretty cool, and indoor tables available, but the hardy folk here prefer to dress for outside. Besides, they must be outside to smoke. A lot of women were smoking, men not so much.

I toured the Opera House, Camila was playing, but was sold out. I got a ticket for The Barber of Seville. Fifteen dollars got me a box seat, front, first level up, looking down on the orchestra pit. The performance was in Hungarian, and yet it was so enjoyable to listen to the singing, and the music was great.

How did I get to the Opera House? It's one thing to just wander the city, but now I have a destination. Catch the bus to Ferencik Metro 3 station blue line subway to Deak Ter central Station, and switch to Deak Metro 1 yellow line to the Opera station.

The plan was on track, until the Deak Metro 1 yellow line. Police were refusing entry to the platform. A glance inside had a body wrapped up, obviously deceased. Police told everyone, "*Busz, otobusz.*"

I said "*ratsz*" and left the station. Now how do I take a '*busz*' there?! I've been on this run before on the Metro, but not a lot of landmarks pop up as I lurch forward from the big wormhole. And, funny how no one speaks English at these times. Some nice kid then told me it was a short walk to the Opera House. I arrived in plenty of time.

The opera performance was marvelous, as was the orchestra. After 17 minutes of taking bows, they were still coming out for more, so I left. I think if you stop applauding they will stop bowing. Anyway, it was great.

Budapest has been famous for its hot springs and healing waters, since the days of the Roman Empire. I thought I should try to heal something, whatever is not perfect. So I spent $25 to go to one of their special hot mineral pools.

The place was hard to find, with signs only in Hungarian. I made it in, and was given a special watch with a chip so they can track you. I arrived at my locker and changed. The guy says, "don't worry, I have the only key," and walks away. I had to chase after him to tell him it won't help if he doesn't lock it.

One pool was at 38 degrees C, one at 36, and the main pool at four degrees. It was a glorified swimming pool without slides, diving board, and lanes. Doesn't matter, it was cold enough to make ice cubes shiver. I was getting used to it, when some lifeguard, whose lineage tracks directly to Attila, chased half a dozen of us out of the pool for not wearing a hair cover. He reminded me of Joe Peshi in that gangster movie. I had to track down the guy with the key to my locker, get money, and buy a hair cover.

All this and it didn't heal a thing. I still needed glasses and couldn't play the piano.

Some of the amazing places I was fortunate enough to visit were the very spacious Peace Park, a beautiful cathedral, Fisherman's Bastion, Buda Castle, and the Citadella. There were many other places of note, but the names have escaped me.

The Bastion and the Castle were magnificent buildings. From the bell tower in the Cathedral, I was able to see most of Budapest.

The Citadella was close to the Hotel Gold where I was staying, a walk up a steep hill, to a park and a fort. The fort was built in the 1851, the walls taken down in 1900. It was invaded by the Soviets and used to shell Budapest in the Hungarian Revolution of 1956. From the hill, you can see the river and its bridges, and the buildings on both banks, including the Parliament Buildings. It was a most impressive sight when all lit up at night.

The time had come for me to go home. I could have spent a lot more time in Hungary.

It was an adventure visiting in six countries—the cultures, food, dress, but most of all the kind people who live there, and those I met along the way.

Every place I have been, I look at as a possible home where I could spend my remaining years. There has never been a thought about not returning to Canada, the best place in the world.

China

A TWO WEEK TOUR 2014

We left on a plane out of Vancouver. From the moment we stepped on the plane until stepping off the plane returning two weeks later, never once was there a need to think, make a decision, or choose an activity. Not only did I not have to, I was not able to, as everything was arranged.

We were assigned seats on the plane, which restaurant to eat in, which table and which chair and who to sit beside at mealtime. We were given entertainment to attend. We were assigned seats on a bus to go to a park. We were given the freedom to roam any part of the park before returning to the bus two hours and 15 minutes later. Hotel rooms were arranged, and the wakeup call would advise what time and what table and what seats we would be having breakfast at.

I understand this is ideal for a lot of people, everything is safe and never get lost. That's nice. But I felt like a prisoner. I wanted to go on this kind of tour to see if this would be an acceptable way to travel when I become unable to think for myself and am in danger of wandering and getting lost. I hope that it will be a long time from now.

We stayed over for one night in Vancouver on returning. I saw more Chinese people in Richmond than I did in China, where I mostly saw Canadian tourists.

Aside from that, we saw a lot of awesome scenery, architecture, boats, dams, and bridges, and many busy people. Beautiful ornate lobbies, with lots of marble, were the norm in the 'better-class' hotels. The streets were crowded with scooters and bicycles, many buses, and a lot of new cars, particularly in Shanghai.

The Beijing Palace complex is ancient and takes in an immense area. It was closed to the public until the last few decades. The City of Beijing was covered in smog, so many people normally would be wearing masks. Due to the predominant westerlies, the Chinese pollution blows over to Korea and Japan, not just a minor problem for them. Most of this pollution is the result of everyone cooking with coal.

The Olympic Games had been held in Beijing in 2008. We toured by the buildings left from the Games, including the "Bird's Nest."

We went on a river cruise. How we arrived where the cruise began is a mystery. Which river is another mystery, although it could have been the Yangtze. We went through some gorges with very steep and high banks, with ancient buildings on whatever flat spot afforded the possibility of not sliding into the water. The food and entertainment on board the ship was excellent, and the service great. The scenery along the river was unbelievable.

We went through the locks at the Three Gorges Dam, on the Yangtze River. The dam is immense, by far the largest hydroelectric dam in electricity production in the world. The stop at the site had a guided tour of the dam construction and the locks.

We stopped somewhere in South China and visited the Jingzhou Museum, which displays a well-preserved mummy from Tomb No 168. It is referred to as being found "lacquered," as many other artifacts were. The mummy dates back to 167 BC.

No, we did not get to see the Terracotta Warriors.

The terrain is such that roads would make travel very slow and difficult, if not impossible. Much of China's industries rely on supplies delivered by boat on the rivers. The boats were delivering goods such as gravel to a construction site, or foodstuffs to a city. Many roads required bridges over the broad rivers.

I believe we flew to Shanghai from a big airport where we got off of the boat. Shanghai appeared to be more modern and wealthier than Beijing and the other big city we were at. There are more than 17,000 residential buildings of greater than 10 stories in Shanghai. When new blocks were built, construction would be on 10 or more high-rises at a time.

The bullet train ran between the airport and the station downtown. There was a wait at the airport, so several of us took the opportunity to go for a ride, with a guide of course. It was capable of up to 500 km/h, but only went 300 to save on fuel and the low ridership at that time of day. It was 10 or 20 cars long, so when we passed the train running the opposite way, I expected to see something pass by quickly. However, the passing speed would be 600 km/h, which was such a flash, it was hardly noticeable.

We were herded onto the plane for a long trip back to Vancouver.

Germany

A TWO MONTH ADVENTURE 2018

The adventures in Germany were outstanding, with amazing places, history, architecture, food, and scenery. It was an excellent journey, fast-paced with nonstop activities. This was made possible by the generous and gracious hospitality of my friend's brother and his wife, where we stayed when not travelling.

Breakfast in Fritz and Runi's home was something to wake up for. It was a feast of eggs, spreads, fish, veggies, fruit, juice, sausage, and anything else German. I finally had some horse meat, barbequed. Restaurants were high-class throughout the land, serving that delicious German cuisine. Desserts were to die for, lots of chocolate, berries, nuts, and, of course, ice cream.

The autobahn was racy, with all speeds acceptable. We were doing 150 km/h, when a car passed us so fast I wondered why we were parked. It all goes well until there is an accident, when all traffic comes to a halt very quickly and delays are lengthy. Detours are good, as all roads seem to go in circles, so any road takes you there. All in all, it appeared to be quite safe. Maybe drivers pay better attention at break-neck speeds.

Travelling the country, my friend and I were in a camper pulled by a new Kia. Her brother Fritz and his wife Runi led the way in their motorhome. Each night we would be in a campground. Other day trips, the four of us went in his car.

Their home is in Norderstedt, which is a suburb of Hamburg. From there we did day trips to the North Sea area, the port in Hamburg, and other attractions within reach of home in a day or two, and to Berlin for a few days. When camping, we followed the Rhine to Austria. Most days it was a new adventure at a different destination.

NOTES

Only tourists wear sunglasses or short pants.

Government buildings in Germany are called 'Rathaus.' We have the same, but called Ottawa.

A tradition for couples being wed is to have a monogrammed lock hung from the safety fencing on bridges.

Dr. Oedker of frozen pizza fame, lives in Hamburg.

The entire country has canals running everywhere. With all the canals and rivers, Hamburg has more bridges than Venice or Amsterdam.

Germans like German food. Many times I saw a restaurant that is Asian, Mediterranean, Thai or Arab, having zero patrons. The German restaurant across the street will have a lineup waiting for a table. Also, every second store is an ice cream shop, and a lineup at every one.

A unique 10 story round apartment building on the Elbe River has suites that were selling for six to eight million.

My friend's brother Fritz lives in a big house on a big lot. If fact, it was large enough to build another house behind, out of sight with the front facing the street, like being across the back alley. The reason for the big lots was for the requirement to grow vegetables, in their case potatoes, for the soldiers in the WW2 war effort.

Most buildings were of brick construction, except further south where materials to make cement were more readily available. Most roofs have a 60 degree slope, but not to keep the snow off. They have always been steep.

Gutan tag, or *moin-moin* as they say in Saxony (old Germany). They speak 'low' German. Further south, *moin* is good morning, and the double *moin* is for the afternoon.

When the nuclear power plant accident happened in Chernobyl, the German government immediately shut down their nuclear plants, and stopped construction on another. They since have supplemented the supply with massive fields of wind turbines, and big fields with rows of solar panels.

The land near the North Sea has a steady wind from the ocean, making it ideal for turbines. The road to Berlin was strewn with fields of solar panels.

The Germans are a happy people, seems everything is a joke to them. The young are particularly gracious, kind, knowledgeable, most speak several languages. It is a beautiful country.

There was never once a case of unkindness or disrespect to me. I enjoyed the time there immensely.

I lied. On the way over, long plane ride, I was up walking. I sat on the stewardess' chair for a moment, when the Lufthansa Stewardess, Adolpha, addressed me.

Adolpha: Do you haff permission to zit on zat zeat??

Me: Could you give me permission?

Adolpha: You do not haff permission to zit on zat zeat. You must remove yourzelf immediately. You vill return to your zeat at vonce!!

Me: Vill I go to za concentration camp now, or vill I haff time to zay goodbye to za children?

Okay I didn't say the last line, but I wanted to. The rest is a quote.

LUNEBURG

The Sharnebeck twin ship lift was built in 1974, near Luneburg, south of Hamburg. The first day trip was to that site, where ships are lifted or lowered on an elevator from or to a canal leading out to sea. The two canals have a height difference of 125 feet. The trough is about 350 feet long, so can lift a large barge. It is an engineering marvel, the biggest of its type in the world at that time.

The town has a historical background. The Sande market square where we had a coffee had a sand base before the cobbles, hence the name. A group of young ladies approached me there. It was a bridal group, doing a ritual of drawing a heart on a man's face with lipstick. After a big commotion, they gave me a little bottle of Apple Schnapps.

PORT OF HAMBURG

The tunnel under the Elbe River was built in 1911. Four elevators take cars, bikes, and people from street level, down about 80 feet to the tunnel. Two 20 feet diameter tubes nearly half a kilometre long run to the other side, to the same operation of lifts.

The Opera House in Hamburg, nicknamed Elphi, has a brick exterior for the first seven floors, but the interior is another story. It is appropriately adorned and has the longest escalator in Europe, running the full seven floors. The showcase above has distinct architecture and a warm and pleasant theatre inside for performances. It is one of the largest concert halls in the world.

A small lake near Norderstedt was set up for water skiing, but not with boats. A wireline ran around the edges of the little lake, pulling skiers through a course of ramps and slaloms. It is an amazing idea that I would never have imagined. It was fun to watch them wipe out off the start.

Wunderland is a world of miniature trains, planes and autos. It comes complete with an airport, towns, mountains, volcano, and models of places in the world. Everything is moving, as it would in real life. Planes take off and land, fuel trucks go to service the planes. Trains are running, the autobahn traffic is going. At one display, they are paving on one side, with bi-directional traffic in a jam on the other side, while the paving packers are moving. On a closer look, one packer is being pulled by an elephant. Wunderland filled up two huge floors and was being expanded. I spent two half-days enjoying the surprises.

The carnival grounds by the Port were in full gear. From the high wheel, you can see a monstrous cement building, which was a WW2 bunker, a bomb shelter built during the war.

ISLAND OF NEUWERK

At low tide, the Island of Neuwerk, 10 kilometres off Cuxhaven, is connected to the mainland by a sandbar at low tide. Rides on horse-drawn wagons go to and from the Island, but rain and wind kept us on a boat. It is in the North Sea, and can be very chilly with rough waters.

The Island has a 700-year-old lighthouse, used as a hotel. It had a great view from the top, but no elevator. We stayed in a motel. It was surrounded by eight foot high reeds, the kind they use to make thatched roofs which are becoming popular again. A lot of heavy horses roamed the pastures.

BERLIN

The road from Hamburg to Berlin seemed strange. The first third seemed normal, with lots of forest, beautiful homes and farms. Then it seemed less maintained, trees gone, all farmland. Reason was, the Soviet Union took over that part of Germany after the war. Land was put into agricultural use. The farmers got nothing to keep up their properties, and it still shows. A Russian trappi car was displayed up high on a tower, with a stork nest on top. The trappi car was built out of pressed cardboard during the war, as all metals were needed for the war effort.

The one destination I looked forward to the most, was definitely Berlin. I had a lot of expectations, and in some ways I was disappointed. Perhaps it was just the parts of the city that we visited. Now this was my point of view only. Others were telling me how wonderful they found the city to be, and they were very happy there. The people were nice, helpful, and many spoke English, as they did everywhere in the country.

There is so much history, every building and every space has a name and a violent past. It was amazing to be at such places as the Berlin Wall, Checkpoint Charlie, and the Jewish memorial.

I found Berlin to be messy with strewn garbage, hate wall paintings, buildings rebuilt but not maintained, subways dirty with squealing escalators and loud subway car wheels, with low tech info in the cars. Nothing seemed modern or having an appearance of being cared about or maintained. I found out later that the subway condition was because we were in what was East Berlin.

The Jewish Memorial is unique, with different size rectangular slabs of marble, to symbolize the tragedy of the holocaust. It had to be a difficult task to arrive at a suitable format for public display.

We had lunch at a bbq outdoor restaurant at a giant park inside the city. The park was used to run, hike, meet in groups, and generally enjoy nature. In one area, thousands of LGT people were camped. I couldn't help but think about what will be the eventual outcome with the growth of the Muslim populace, whose religion calls to eliminate homosexuals, of whom there are about 400,000 in Berlin.

LUBECK

The city of Lubeck, the name meaning 'the beautiful', was a real gem. Everything about it seemed to be pristine, historical, old but clean and well preserved. An artificial waterway runs through town, a canal that connects the rivers Elbe and Trave, connecting the North Sea to the Baltic Sea.

It is the birthplace of Marzipan, healthy and delicious. It is not poisonous, as some sources suggest. Remember how cranberries were said to cause cancer? Turns out, you would have to eat 200 pounds per day for 30 years. Anyway, the original Café Niederegger where the marzipan was born, served delicious infused treats with pure marzipan. It was developed due to the need for healthy food to replace flour during the famine in the 15th century.

The Holsten Gateway into town is 550 years old. One of the towers is leaning, putting stress on the connecting brickwork. It is one of many UNESCO World Heritage Sites in Germany. Five story ancient buildings overlooking the canal, beside the Gateway, have been converted into apartments. The top floors have cranes used to move cargo from barges in the canal centuries ago.

The Rathaus (City Hall) has been in continuous service (longest in Europe) since the year 1230. It was sinking and being reinforced. The original marble floors and woodwork is worth seeing, along with the artwork on the walls, and the old furnace. Our Haus of Rats is in Victoria.

St Mary's Church, a big cathedral, was destroyed in the war and rebuilt. View from the belfry looked over the whole city. The two big spires indicate that the church was named in honour of a female. One spire means it is named after a man, true for most Catholic churches.

BUSUM

This fishing town is in a bay on the North Sea, where the lighthouse is the main attraction, along with a museum. I went out on a shrimp boat, a tour that cooked the catch and we snacked on it. The guide was showing the mostly kids crowd the different forms of sea life.

We had a nice dinner of curry wurst, a dish as popular as schnitzel. We stayed in a hotel there, and went to an amazing beach the next day.

ST PETER-ORDING

A beach on the North Sea coast runs for 20 kilometres and is pure sand inland for a kilometre, then sand dunes with tufts of grass. It is at St Peter-Orden. Being on the stormy North Sea, violent waves have built up the sand far inland, and have required that buildings be built on stilts to avoid flooding from the storm waves. The water is a bit cool, but the sand is great. A sulphur spring nearby is a spa for multitudes of tourists.

There are hundreds of bikes everywhere you look, and a big parking lot for vehicles. Wooden chairs for two or three with sides and a canopy are for rent. The bathrooms are at a stilted building connected to a catwalk and a set of stairs to get there. Setup was the same for a big restaurant.

It was midweek in the off-season when we visited there, but it was still very busy. There is a large nudist colony nearby. I visited, and found lots of heavy breathing, snorting and grunting. No real action, just old people getting up from their chairs.

Not far away, the River Eide has flood control for North Sea storms. Four massive gates control the water passage, while the fifth opens for ships to go through. Before the controls were installed, the crops and homes for miles along the river were being wiped out by the frequent floods.

THE RIVER RHINE

The Rhine River was the starting point for some serious camping. Many floating hotels, or river cruise boats, along with commercial ships use the waterway. It is a deep river with hilly banks. There had been a period of drought resulting in low water level, causing the cruise boats to have to cancel some trips resulting in moving their clients by bus.

Castles are numerous on the hills along the river. Vineyards and wineries grow on the banks. Towns are numerous, supporting heavy tourism.

COLOGNE

We camped on the shore of the Rhine, watching the ships go by. The weather was sunny and warm. It was time to switch to 'moin' for the good morning greeting. We rode bicycles into town to see the sights of Cologne, by interesting architecture, to the Cologne Cathedral. We passed some buildings shaped like an upside-down capital L, supported by a column in the middle. They look like they should fall over.

The Cathedral is one of the world's biggest churches, started in the year 1248. I can't imagine anyone thinking such an edifice would be necessary. It goes well beyond astounding or amazing. The height of the ceiling makes it difficult to imagine how it was built. The spires outside are many and ornamental. The church was damaged in WW2, and is still under repair. I have always admired the big churches, but this one topped them all.

A big castle can be reached by taking a cable car up a hill, way up. The steps inside were made to allow horses to climb. An abundance of wine-making equipment had a big wine storage capacity. I discovered that the wine was not a high alcohol content beverage, but was needed to replace water which was often causing illness and death. The wooden storage vessels were immense.

BRAUBACH

We camped again on the river shore, by a nice little town about 1300 years old, with a little castle on the hill. Houses in this area are made with rock and cement, plaster covered. The roofing is thin pieces of slate instead of the red ceramic on the brick houses to the north part of Germany.

We went to an event a half hour south of Braubach that was attended by about 100,000 people. It was a celebration of the river, with a parade of boats, castles lit up, the town lit up with red lights. It was a spectacle, ending with a full half hour of non-stop fireworks.

The parade had about 50 commercial boats and some cruise boats, all of them lit up. It was quite a sight.

The evening was topped off with dinner. I had *brauenschnitzel mit kartofelen*. That would be fried potatoes with bacon, schnitzel with a fried egg on it. As always, very good.

The Marksburg Castle in Braubach had a good view of the town and the river. The castle had the usual amazing artifacts, and very large wine storage. A display of torture equipment was scary. Beds for women always had a canopy but I can't remember why. They displayed a chastity belt device for women, one that would cut it off upon retraction if you were silly enough to fight the system.

HAMELN

The Pied Piper story from the year 1284 is home to the city of Hameln. Short version is that a rat-catcher was hired to rid the town of rats during an infestation. He played his flute to attract the attention of the rats. They followed the music out to river where the rats all drowned. The mayor reneged on payment for the services and accused him of extortion. The Rattenfanger returned for revenge.

While the parents were at church, the children were left at home. When the rat-catcher played, the children heard the flute and following him to a cave. They were never to be seen again. So it is said. All kinds of theories have been suggested concerning the disappearance of the kids.

The residence of the flute player is marked, as is the route of the rats out of town, marked with brass plaques in the cobblestone streets.

Just outside of Hameln is a big old castle with a moat. The same family that built it still owns it and lives there. Rooms are rented out as apartments. There are three small rooms that hang out over the moat, which turned out to be biffies, if you can imagine.

KOBLENZ

A slow boat trip took us to Koblenz, a city of more than 100,000. Most of the city was destroyed in WW2. The Mosel River joins with the Rhine there, the routes of much shipping. As an important trade centre, the busy waters made Koblenz a target during the war. A giant monument to himself, Kaiser Wilhelm 1st had it built in his honor at the joining of the two rivers.

A big important brewery (they all are) stands on the shore there, making their Pilsner beer, Koblenzer.

HEIDELBERG

This city was not damaged in the war and is the most beautiful city that I saw in Germany. It is a university city, bustling with young people and many tourists.

The mountain railway runs to the Heidelberg Castle. The Castle was built around the year 1200. It was in disrepair at parts of the exterior. It had been damaged by lightning fires, an explosion in the powder room, and by centuries of turmoil and wars. Inside, it was well taken care of. The view from the castle looks on a most beautiful little city with the Neckar River running through it, with the arched Old Bridge of 1788 connecting the old town to the newer town.

Healthy water was transported daily to the castle in a horse-drawn water wagon. It was still not good for drinking, so wine became the beverage of choice once again. The wine storage had one barrel that holds 220,000 liters, or 58,000 little US gallons of wine, plus several smaller casks. Built in 1750, it is the largest wine barrel in the world, and has a dance floor built on top of it.

We drove through several villages to the start of the big hills in the municipality of Schwangau in Bavaria. The Bavarian countryside was very green, even though it was said to be in a bad drought condition. The farm buildings looked picture-perfect, with the fields of grass and cattle, with forests in the background.

SCHWANGAU

Near the Austrian border, a beautiful little town called Schwangau rests in a valley of flat land with steep mountains behind. We stayed at a campsite near a little lake. There were cows, with bells, in the middle of town. Many small towns have a barn with cows. Why?? No one knows.

Nearby is a slightly bigger town called Fussen. They have a unique thermal pool centre. It has eight big pools with advanced technology, hot and not so much, with different concentrations of salt, some inside some out, with jets and gadgets. One had a current circulating the water around an island. Another had a salt concentration of 25 percent. People tried to walk on it. The cost was an arm and your first born, but it was worth it.

A Catholic church in Fussen had a beautiful granite pillar altar, a set of organ pipes that displayed faces, and a pagan statue with clawed feet, wings, and the head of an animal with a serpent's tongue. Next to the altar??

A mile-long cable car goes to the top of a hill. In the winter, it is a ski hill. Snow caps on the mountains are permanent. The famous castle Neuschwanstein Schloss was riddled with tourists. The only way to see the inside was with a tour. It was not worth the price to tour inside, but the outside was great to see. The castle was the hideaway of the Mad King Ludwig, about 150 years ago. There are many castles in Germany, so many visible along the Rhine.

Another long cable car ride had a nice restaurant and other attractions about 1,000 metres up in altitude. Of particular interest was the beautiful view to the valley where we were camped, and the spot for paragliders to take off. The hot air currents were right that day, so it was good for flights.

This was the beginning of the Austrian Alps, very high and very steep.

RUHPOLDING

We camped in the little village of Ruhpolding, Bavaria, not too far from Munich. The houses and buildings were adorned with flowers and murals, very nice.

Despite the gracious presence of Fritz and Runi in their motorhome, my friend got to be way too much. I left the journey and caught a bus to Austria. It had been a fabulous trip to that point.

Austria

A short ride through some breathtaking mountain roads stopped in Salzburg, Austria. Salzburg is renowned for its architecture, 27 churches, and is a UNESCO World Heritage Site. It is also the birthplace of composer Wolfgang Amadeus Mozart. No doubt it is one of Europe's most beautiful cities, with the lakes and mountains of the Alps. Everything in Salzburg is a reference to the movie *Sound of Music*.

I had seen enough churches and castles.

I love the train rides. In less than three hours I was in Vienna. I found Vienna to be rather expensive. My desire to see things was diminished.

I stayed in a hostel that was more than 700 years old, with magnificent architecture, and it seemed quite ordinary to me. The adventure had been compromised by familiarity. As wonderful as Vienna is said to be, I wasn't seeing it. To get to the nearest on/off tour bus, it would have cost me about $150 for taxi to/from and the tour ticket. I was burnt out, for the first time in all my travels. I needed some rest. Unfortunately, I missed the amazing sights of Vienna, it would have to be another time.

It was another great train ride, opportunity to relax and reflect, off to Frankfurt.

FRANKFURT

My return flight was from Hamburg to Frankfurt and on to Vancouver. My idea was to skip the first leg and go directly from Frankfurt. I discovered I couldn't do that. If I'm not on the flight at Hamburg, that ticket would be scrapped and another ticket must be paid for in full, no refund on the original ticket. So the decision was to be in Frankfurt for a few days, then to Hamburg.

It was really nice to be alone for a change, free to do as I wished. It was liberating!

I got out of the train station in my shorts and golf shirt to find everyone else dressed in winter clothing. I thought it was overkill, maybe raining a bit. Some guy cat-called me. So then I had long pants on for the first time in Germany.

It was a nice clean train station, but outside was a kind of rough area. After a block of exploring, I was in the erotica zone. There were lots of sex shops, selling toys among other things. I was grabbed many times to come in to the bars, and there were many. They get you to have a beer, girls sit with you, you have to buy them a drink, it's usually juice, and then they charge you something like $25 each drink, while a big security guy blocks the door. Not going to happen, had seen it before.

I got a room in a hostel on that street, a block away from the train station. From the window, I could see Arab halal shops selling their kebobs and falafel sandwiches, some oriental cafes, and Dr. Muller which has pole dancing and private lap dancing. Down the street I could see The Sex Inn, Hotel Angel, and bars where companions would be available. I walked around the streets and found them to be safe enough, so long as you don't go into the bars. There were some rough-looking dodgy characters around. The restaurants were very good.

After three days of R & R, I was on a train to Hamburg.

HAMBURG

I got a hotel room near the airport, where I found an excellent Italian-German restaurant with a great breakfast and a dinner buffet with a great variety of dishes, including seafood cooked with a German flair. With lots to do in the area to keep me busy and interested, I stayed about five days, relaxing and enjoying the delicious German cuisine for as long as I could.

I had gone to the airport, an easy walking distance from my hotel, to get familiar with the terminal. I had changed my ticket to a day earlier than originally planned. The hotel next door where I had been feasting most days had a shuttle to the airport, so I asked if I could catch a ride. They recognized me from the restaurant, and happily allowed me to go, as the shuttle was not full. That was better than walking while dragging a bag.

I boarded the flight from Hamburg to Frankfurt where I changed planes, and flew direct to Vancouver. I still can't believe the inflexibility, especially as I had to change planes in Frankfurt.

It had been a fabulous trip, thanks to my friend and her brother and his wife. It was a lot to do in such a short time, busy every day. I hold no grudge with my friend, and have much gratitude to Fritz and Runi for their hospitality and friendship and a wonderful vacation in their beautiful country.

HOME AGAIN

There was a lot to ponder upon return.

What would the country be like if there had been no wars?

From the wars, an explosion of technology and innovation, engineering and design. Bridges and buildings and churches were replaced or repaired, renewed urban planning, the effects of the Soviet takeover of Eastern Germany.

If beer is cheaper than coffee or water, anyone with fiscal responsibility should make the proper choice, yes??

South Korea

APRIL - JUNE 2019

Korea has a distinct culture that I enjoyed immensely. The people are generally happy, very respectful. The level of success in business, technology, and the arts is due to their advanced education system and the attitudes about it. Their delicious cuisine made me look forward to every meal. I discovered that their medical system is modern and inexpensive. They care about their children, seniors, and visitors like me. Cash is unnecessary, credit cards are used for everything, no matter what the cost.

I arrived in mid-April, the season for cherry blossoms and other spring flowers. I stayed at a hotel in an area not too far from the airport, until I could get used to the time change, currency, climate, food and figure out what I was going to do.

The air was polluted, blown over by the prevailing winds from China. On occasion the wind would shift and be from the south. The air would become absolutely clear.

My hotel was in Incheon, in the town of Jung-gu. A park covered in cherry blooms with hiking trails was the view from my window. At night the trees were accented by different coloured lights.

The main floor had a huge dining area for a fabulous buffet breakfast, my first encounter with Korean cuisine. Dozens of different courses were available, including different types of kimchi, meats, veggies, eggs, seafood, and breakfast cereals. Being the only whitey in the place, I noticed that I was given special consideration for seating and specialty dishes. Obviously the trip to Korea was going to be very pleasant.

Heartburn has been with me all my life, but from the time I started eating kimchi in Korea until the return home, I never needed one Tum.

Incheon is on the sea, and is a port for fishing. Seafood of every sort imaginable was being processed and on display in a few stores. The restaurants had mostly seafood menus, fantastic. I decided to move on after three days.

SEOUL, THE BIG CITY

I caught a cab to the city centre on the north side of the Han River. I didn't realize just how big Seoul was until the taxi ride went on for more than an hour. The city never quit, only changing between residential to industrial, less money to more money, with good highways and streets with many lanes. The population of Seoul is about 10 million people.

Korea was one of the poorest countries in the world. They experienced rapid economic growth since the Korean War to become one of the wealthiest. A credit for this growth would be their education system, and we know that the secret to success is education.

The Western education system of reading, writing, and arithmetic starts in preschool. Korean preschool and the next three years or so are used to teach the kids to have respect. They start learning the arts, music, painting, performing, and those things that give them confidence. They learn life skills, like communicating, table manners, values, dressing. They start to learn English. They know how to treat their elders, parents and seniors, how to speak to them and how to listen. They learn about life, then arithmetic. Can you imagine a year of a class in 'morals??

The hordes of very good musicians, singers, and dancers in Korea are the result of promoting the arts in early schooling, and support from the parents.

Troops of 10 or so little kids with little back packs would be seen on the street, led by their teacher, going to an art gallery, or City Hall. Many times they stopped to say, "Hello, how are you." when they saw that I was English-speaking. Then they would giggle while the teacher would be smiling and trying to get them under control.

I signed up for a cooking lesson at a Korean government tourist building. My contact was a delightful young Korean lady who spoke English and had gone to University in Vancouver. The lesson was to learn to make the Korean pancake, not very useful, but the process was most enjoyable. The instructor was a female chef at a high-end restaurant. Most chefs in Korea are women, while men do the bbqing.

A high-school girl was one of the helpers. She told me that in order to graduate from high school, students are required to perform about 150 hours of volunteer work. She complained that they had to work so hard, while American students don't even have to try and they can't fail, but are pushed ahead no matter what. We had a long discussion after the class about how fortunate she was to have the opportunity to learn about life and be held accountable. That seemed to make her very appreciative of the Korean system. Or perhaps she was using her 'respect' skills to make me think that. I don't think so, they are all such nice young people.

Parents spend big money on extra classes for their kids after high school attendance during the day. Some say they go too far with the camps and clubs for developing models. It is costly, but big money if they make it. Korea is big in the fashion industry in clothing and models. It is said that tomorrow's New York fashions are yesterday's Korea fashions. Fashion shows are a big thing in Korea.

The buses have seats in the front half for seniors, spaced better. Young people head to the back. When I got on one time when it was full, a kid got up and pointed to the seat for me to sit.

From the hotel window I could see a shrine, decorated with many bright colours of decorations. It was a holiday celebration for who-knows-what, but it was well-attended and many people were praying. It was a religious site from hundreds of years ago. Also from the window, looking down was a major street with eight lanes each way. Almost all cars were new, most black, white or silver, and orange taxis, and are either Kia, Hyundai, or Toyota.

Speaking of windows, there was one in the bathroom, with curtains outside, very weird. Everything is digital of course, including flushing, bidet, lighting, everything but blinds for the window.

Television in the room had cable that included three channels of billiards, five channels of computer games, two dog channels, five on Korean baseball, four on golf, many on soccer, several food channels, with all having the option to convert to English language. TV movies haze out any tobacco, as well as bare body parts. Smoking is a problem, and cigarette butts were being swept up endlessly. The streets are very clean, as are the buildings and the people.

Very few people are not skinny. Young women wear a large variety of fashion, including some see-through. It should be sheer delight for the men, but they don't seem to notice. The young men downtown look really sharp in their black suits.

I was staying in a high-class hotel, not too expensive for the room, but the restaurant on the top floor was way out of line, $13 for a beer and a very small dinner for $65. The same meal at restaurants on the street would be four dollars for a beer, and around $10 for a meal. Several times I ate at chicken restaurants, great tasting and serving twice what I could eat.

Well, seems there had to be some drama. I had bursitis in the knee, extreme pain, couldn't walk or sleep. After three days of not getting better, I went to hospital emergency. In a couple decades of travel, I have never had a problem before. It's not nice on vacation, but sometimes you just gotta dance to the music that's playing.

Hotel reception was sooo helpful. They got a taxi for me to go to the hospital. I checked in, and was sent to a specialist doctor, the nicest young fella, knowledgeable, spoke of Butchart Gardens in Victoria. He arranged x-rays and did an ultrasound. After discussion, he wrote a prescription, and a nurse gave me two shots in the butt. The nurse rolled me outside and around the block in a wheelchair to the pharmacy, got the meds, got a taxi for me to return to my hotel. All this in JUST LESS THAN ONE HOUR. Upon return, the reception ladies had bought me a big cookie.

Within a couple of hours, the change was amazing. Pain and swelling were down. I had appointments to see the doc again.

The entire cost for this was about $100, including x-rays, ultrasound, shots, prescription pills, and two taxi rides. Subsequent visits cost around eight dollars each visit. The doctor told me how much the Korean people appreciated the help from Canadians in the Korean War. His father and friends had just been to Canada to meet with Canadian veteran friends from the war.

Near the hotel was a variety of small businesses. A small grocery store was packed neatly with goodies, displays of fruit and veggies outside that I thought were pretty expensive. Across the street was a bakery where I had breakfast some mornings. It had coffee and the most amazing breakfast sandwiches, with delicious pastries. And, every place in the world has to have an Irish pub. Up the street was my favourite pizza joint, with outdoor tables and good beer, to go with the great pizza.

Near the hotel was a hair clinic, recommended by the reception girls. I got a shampoo, head massage, and haircut from two lovely ladies for not that much money. I tipped them, but found out later that tipping suggests that they don't have enough money to look after themselves. So it is an insult to tip.

Another business was a cybercafé, but set up with about 50 or more stations. Kids gather to play against each other, which they call 'eSports'

A few blocks away I discovered a huge underground mall. I walked and walked forever, hundreds of stores of all kinds, all upscale. I came to some stairs going down to another two levels of stores.

SOUTH SIDE OF THE HAN RIVER

My knee was healed and I was walking 10,000 steps a day. I moved across the river to the main downtown centre, close to City Hall and the biggest street market in Korea. From the hotel I often got lost. One time I had to catch a taxi back, and he got lost. The street signs are difficult to make sense of. Fortunately, there was usually someone around to help. One older gentleman that spoke some English looked at me and said, "Are you lost? Can I help you?" Fortunately they are a kind people.

I was able to devise new ways of tracking and retreating. I used a Starbucks as a point of reference, and found out there is a Starbucks on every street, and they are all full. It was no problem being lost, as I never saw a dangerous person, or anyone affected by alcohol or drugs.

I arranged a trip out of town through the government tourist agency. It was an all day trip, at a cost of $12, to an ancient village, where they did shows and performances. Young ladies in old wedding costumes were on the street, meeting guys in old costumes.

More interesting was the three and a half hour bus ride to and from Jeonju. Early morning traffic was brutal, except for one lane exclusively for buses. We travelled at break-neck speed while five lanes were in a stall. When finally into the countryside, rugged hills were densely forested, and every flat spot was in rice paddies or greenhouses for vegetables. Homes had rice paddies in their back yard. Isolated clusters of 10 to 30 high-rise apartment buildings, 30 stories high, appeared in the middle of nowhere.

It was a terrific trip. On the return to Seoul the bus stopped at a different location than where we departed, so I took a taxi. Once again he got lost, and drove me around in circles around the hotel. He didn't charge me for all the extra, and apologized.

The on/off bus is always a great way to see the different parts of a city, then return to the interesting parts later. I took it three times, stopping at different museums, City Hall, and other places. The City Hall area was interesting enough that I moved to another hotel a block from it. It was the perfect location for walking,

From the hotel window, the home of the President of Korea was visible at the base of a mountain. Directly below my room was a massive digital billboard. Across the street an all-glass building reflected another building beside my hotel. Looking down, the street of 22 lanes was very active with parades and demonstrations. Beside the street, two basketball courts were set up to have a tournament. At the same time, a gay parade had shut the street down on one side. Busloads of police had set up pylons to separate the event and control traffic on the other side. Other parades would shut down the entire street for many blocks.

Close by was a building named "Internet Addiction Prevention Centre." It was near the "B S Building."

City Hall was a new building, all glass and all curves, quite a magnificent structure on the outside and inside. Groups of students were always on tour. The park outside City Hall is grass with artsy ornaments. On weekends, a stage is set up with live entertainment and an audience of a 1,000 people. Vendors were selling food, ice cream, and drinks. Groups of all focuses would meet there. The parades would be organized and begin there. Demonstrations would always be going on, all totally peaceful.

A couple of streets over, a canal runs in the centre of the street. A festival is held every Saturday and Sunday. Food trucks are set up on each side for street food. Decorated floats were lit up on the water. Thousands of young people gather to socialize. A great blue heron was in the canal seeking dinner. It caught a fish and everyone applauded.

Across the street from City Hall is an ancient royal palace and many buildings. Performers wear the centuries-old costumes to display the old customs and ritual marches.

The subway system ran all directions from that central point, with numerous entrances from the street. I never did get on the trains, which I regret very much. But I did explore the underground at many locations, where there were massive malls, all types of retail stores. I didn't even find these underground places for the first month in Seoul. I found two major museums, history and architecture, and two shopping malls under City Hall, about six blocks long and three blocks wide. When I found my way out, and not at the end of it, I was lost again.

The other side of the street from City Hall, a few blocks away, is the biggest street market in South Korea, the Namdaemun Market. It was founded in the early 1400s, with the South Gate, a major arch structure, the main entrance to the ancient city. Of course I got lost a few more times, it became a game to find my way home.

I spent a few days wandering around the Namdaemun Market. They had unlimited goodies, with reasonable prices. Shoppers packed the streets. They wear mostly black clothing, so if you see a colour, it is usually a tourist. They don't make eye contact. All manner of cuisine is available in little kiosks and big restaurants. It may sound boring to you, but these are not your average markets.

They use the same system as the Latin countries in that a camera store for example will be surrounded by another dozen camera stores, shoe stores all in a group, etc.

I took a bus to the Seoul Tower. I missed the stop and had to return on foot from the next stop. Another bus ran to the top of a hill in city centre, to the Tower. The structure is massive, many displays and points of interest on the lower levels, inside and out.

The observation deck is at the 90 story level, so being on a big hill meant a 360 degree viewing of the city, as far as the smog would allow. Every direction is a view of endless buildings, with forested mountains, rivers, bridges, and parks. Three weeks earlier I had watched a massive display of fireworks coming from the Seoul Tower above the observation deck. I watched from my hotel on the north side of the Han River, likely about 10 kilometres away.

I took a trip to Jeju Island, a popular vacation place off the southern tip of So Korea. The flight was less than $50 return. The airport on the Island handled flights in or out about every five minutes, very busy. My arranged hotel was in the middle of nowhere, so lots of walking and had to learn the bus system. The on/off bus did a tour of the area.

The Island is all lava. The rocks were used to make fences between properties. The sea was not too rough, just enough to make people believe they could surf, fully covered in a wetsuit and up to their waist in water, riding their boards into shore 30 feet away. Several sandy beaches were popular and being used for swimming or just relaxing.

I went into a resort to look around, see what they had. I asked a young fella at the concierge a question, about where I could find some place. He started explaining, then said it was too far to walk, come with me. We got into his personal vehicle and he drove me there, dropped me off and returned to his work.

One of the tourist attractions was a large area of pretty yellow flowers. It turned out to be Canola.

I didn't get to see the other side of the island, as there was too much to see and do where I was, and only there for four days. I took that time to feast in their seafood restaurants.

Back in Seoul, I returned to the same hotel, but got a higher room on the same side overlooking the street. The parades were often and interesting to watch, most with a political overtone. There were a couple of gay parades there, and one big gay parade many blocks away. Police presence was strong at all times, but I never saw an incident, and felt perfectly safe. At one parade I counted seven busloads of young guys and gals in police uniforms, plus numerous police cars.

The big issue was with President Moon, wanting him removed from office because he favoured alignment with China and aid to the North. The parades were favoring protection provided by the USA and opposing the North. The second issue was that they felt the previous president had been falsely accused of corruption and should be released.

 Besides the parades, they set up stages for political speeches with hundreds of chairs, and a major stage with entertainers, music and fire effects. Cranes were used to direct huge speakers to the throngs of people lined up for a couple of blocks.

One Saturday a large gathering of LGBT took over the grounds at City Hall, with flags and signs, while another group of women wedged their way in to set up drumming and signs in opposition to same-sex marriage. A Christian group of men were set up with signs opposing same-sex marriage. Meanwhile, many blocks away, another LGBT parade had a long line of people on motorcycles, floats, walking and dancing. There was a heavy presence of police at all locations, without any sign of an incident.

A 10 story building contained duty-free items, such as watches, handbags, jeans, jewelry, and cosmetics. They were nice to look at, but way out of my wallet's reach. A couple of watches were over $100,000. And I don't even wear a watch!

It was a wonderful visit to South Korea, but far too short. There were things that didn't get done.

Looking Back

I learned a lot from my travels. People are wonderful. Being a global citizen requires the understanding of personalities that are less compatible, with different processes of thinking, and different cultural norms. I believe I have gained an increased empathy for others. From travel, I have true friends around the world. I have learned more about people from my adventures in any one year, than I have in my lifetime at home. One must live it to understand it.

I know that I have not been on the 'real' cutting edge of travel. I still have a fear of being in certain areas of the world, perhaps a heightened awareness of the dangers that lurk, or the scuffle that could erupt on a moment's notice. I have seen others that travel anywhere without fear, but I have much respect for the dangers of the behaviour of callous individuals, and it only takes one, especially as I travel alone. I learned to be vigilant of my surroundings, but some things cannot be controlled. I have been fortunate to have travelled trouble-free for the most part. The places I very much want to visit in the future include Dubai, Italy, St Petersburg, Moscow, Egypt, Iceland, Norway, Ireland, Scotland, England, and a few others.

Surprising to me, was the revelation of how badly people treat each other. The world is full of bullies. On the first trip, I noticed how women were thought of and easily dismissed as not being at the same level of consideration as men are. It seemed to be accepted as normal behaviour. Perhaps I was naïve, but it didn't seem right. From the conditions of my own childhood, I am aware of dominating behaviour. I was vigilant of how everyone, women in particular, are treated all over the world. My belief is that everything revolves around how you make people feel, as in relationships in marriage, raising children, at work—peers, leaders, employee/supervisor, police, government officials. It's hard to understand how people get to think being a bully is okay.

In the end, I have survived the changing phases of my life, as experienced in my adventures. Hopefully I have become a better person for it.

CPSIA information can be obtained
at www.ICGtesting.com
Printed in the USA
BVHW080022060822
643931BV00006B/35

9 781039 127388